The Complete Instant Pot Cookbook For Beginners

600 Everyday Pressure Cooker Recipes
For Affordable Homemade Meals

Matilda Armstrong

CONTENTS

CHICKEN RECIPES 33

SOUPS & STEWS 83

PASTA & SIDE DISHES 93

INTRODUCTION

Thank you for choosing my Instant Pot cookbook. I've put my whole heart into it to make sure it's the only book you will ever need to start your journey with Instant Pot. I have prepared 600 recipes to give you plenty of opportunities to fall in love with this magic device.

These book's chapters are filled with easy yet tasty 600 recipes created to help you turn on your Instant Pot adventure. Designed to show you how to best use your Instant Pot to prepare simple everyday meals, most recipes use widely available ingredients to create incredible meals effortlessly and rich in flavors and textures.

Each recipe contains the number of servings, the cooking time it takes to prepare and cook, and nutritional info per serving. The "serve with" section of most recipes is a suggestion to help you put the meal together, but feel free to improvise.

My small tips for significant results

To start, go through each recipe completely and prepare all the ingredients you need in advance. Measuring tools are a must-have in every kitchen for optimal results in your cooking. A little prep work before goes a long way, like everything else. It will save you time in the long run, I promise. And above all else, have fun!

Author's note: the "Total time" provided at the beginning of each recipe does not include the time the Instant Pot pressure cooker takes to come to temperature or the time it takes for the auto release function.

Instant Pot – what do you need to know

If you're new around the block and haven't yet had fun using Instant Pot, let me quickly introduce you to it. Instant Pot is a multi-functional device that has been conquering the kitchen appliances' stage for a good decade, and it's not slowing down. It has acquired sort of a cultish status among its raving fans, whose number multiplies every year.

What's the secret of Instant Pot's popularity? Well, there isn't just one. With our daily schedules getting busier and busier, we love any piece of technology that saves us time and allows us to spend it in a better way.

So if you're looking to save a few hours a week, you've made the right choice. And if you think that 2 or 3 hours a week aren't that much, then think for just a moment how you would feel if you let yourself go out for a nice dinner once a week. That's four times a month. All I'm implying is that even small improvements made daily compound to something more significant when you look at them from a long-term perspective. In this regard sense, Instant Pot is a huge time-saver.

One of the most significant benefits of using the Instant Pot is that you can set a specific time, and cooking will automatically stop when it's over. That gives you the freedom to do other things in the meantime, not worrying about the safety of your house. You can go to the gym, go shopping or clean your home without checking the pots every ten minutes.

And, if for whatever reason, you cannot eat right after cooking, Instant Pot has got you covered. It will maintain warmth in the cooking chamber for even up to ten hours. Forget losing time rewarming your meals again.

Instant Pot is also pretty hassle-free when it comes to maintenance. As soon as you're done cooking, you just have to clean the inner port, and you're done. So, you can forget having a stack of dirty dishes in your sink.

So, are you excited yet? I would be! And I am sure you'll find plenty of flavorful recipes for you and your family in this book. There's a lot to choose from, even if you're the pickiest person out there. So, go ahead and experiment! Discover your guilty pleasures anew, and don't be afraid to tweak recipes here and there if you find it necessary. After all, eating should be all about celebrating. Let's begin!

BEANS & LEGUMES

Oregano Sausage & Bean Cassoulet

Total time: 55 minutes | **Servings**: 4

Ingredients

2 tbsp olive oil
2 shallots, chopped
1 lb white beans, soaked
1 green bell pepper, chopped
1 tsp dried oregano
1 bay leaf

2 smoked sausages, sliced
1 (14-oz) can diced tomatoes
4 cups vegetable broth
¼ cup white wine vinegar
1 cup water
Salt to taste

Directions

Set your Instant Pot to Sauté, heat olive oil, and cook the sausages for 5 minutes; set aside. Add in bell pepper and shallots and cook for 4 minutes, until tender. Pour in broth, tomatoes, oregano, beans, water, and bay leaf. Return the sausages and stir to combine. Seal the lid, select Pressure Cook on High, and set the time to 30 minutes.

When done, perform natural pressure release for 10 minutes, then a quick pressure release to let out the remaining steam. Remove and discard the bay leaf. Taste and adjust the seasonings; drizzle with the vinegar and serve.

Go Green Navy Bean Soup

Total Time: 40 minutes | **Servings**: 4

Ingredients

3 tbsp olive oil
3 garlic cloves, minced
1 medium yellow onion, diced
1 cup chopped asparagus
1 cup navy beans, soaked
4 cups chicken broth

5 sun-dried tomatoes, chopped
1 bay leaf
Salt to taste
1 cup baby spinach
1 cup baby kale
¼ cup grated Parmesan cheese

Directions

Set your Instant Pot to Sauté, heat oil, and cook garlic, onion, and asparagus until softened, 3 minutes. Add navy beans, broth, tomatoes, bay leaf, and salt. Seal the lid, select Pressure Cook on High, and set the time to 20 minutes.

After cooking, do a quick pressure release. Remove bay leaf and set the pot to Sauté. Add spinach and kale and allow wilting for 5 minutes. Adjust taste with salt. Serve bean soup topped with Parmesan cheese.

Fennel & White Bean Tempeh Chops

Total Time: 35 min | **Servings**: 4

Ingredients

2 tbsp olive oil
2 lb tempeh, chopped
1 large yellow onion, chopped
1 small fennel bulb, chopped
3 carrots, cubed
3 garlic cloves, chopped
1 cinnamon stick

1 bay leaf
1 ½ tsp ground allspice
1 tsp ras el hanout
½ tsp ginger paste
6 large tomatoes, chopped
4 cups vegetable broth
1 (15-oz) can white beans

Directions

Add the oil to the inner pot and select Sauté. Pour in the tempeh and fry until golden brown on all sides. Remove to a plate. Put onion, fennel, carrots, and garlic into the pot and sauté for 6 minutes. Drop in the cinnamon stick, followed by bay leaf, allspice, ras el hanout, and ginger paste. Stir-fry for 2 minutes. Pour in tomatoes and broth and stir.

Seal the lid, select Pressure Cook on High, for 2 minutes. Once it beeps, do a natural release for 15 minutes, and open the lid. Select Sauté. Stir in the tempeh and beans; cook to warm through, 3 minutes. Serve with pita bread.

Bean Soup with Tomato-Avocado Topping

Total Time: 55 minutes | **Servings**: 4

Ingredients

2 tbsp chicken bouillon, crumbled
2 tbsp olive oil
1 yellow onion, chopped
2 garlic cloves, minced
1 cup pinto beans, soaked
1 jalapeño pepper, chopped
2 bay leaves
¼ cup pureed onion

5 cups water
1 tsp pureed green chilies
Salt to taste
2 large tomatoes, chopped
¼ cup chopped cilantro
2 avocados, chopped
3 oz grated mozzarella cheese

Directions

Set your Instant Pot to Sauté, heat olive oil, and stir-fry onion and garlic until softened, 3 minutes. Stir in pinto beans, jalapeño, bay leaves, pureed onion, bouillon, water, green chilies, and salt. Seal the lid, select Pressure Cook on High, and set the time to 30 minutes. When done cooking, do a natural release for 10 minutes, then a quick release.

Discard the bay leaf and press Sauté. Allow bean sauce to thicken. In a small bowl, combine the tomatoes, cilantro, avocado, and mozzarella cheese. Dish beans and top with tomato-avocado mixture. Serve with tortillas.

Crispy Prosciutto & Navy Bean Chowder

Total Time: 45 minutes | **Servings**: 4

Ingredients

6 prosciutto slices, chopped
1 medium carrot, chopped
1 cup chopped white onion
1 Yukon gold potato, cubed
1 tsp mixed dried herbs

1 cup navy beans, soaked
3 cups chicken broth
Salt and black pepper to taste
4 tbsp heavy cream

Directions

Set your Instant Pot to Sauté and cook prosciutto until brown and crispy, 5 minutes. Transfer to a paper towel-lined plate and set aside. Sauté carrots, onion, and potatoes in prosciutto grease until slightly tender, 5 minutes. Stir in mixed herbs, navy beans, broth, salt, and pepper.

Seal the lid, select Pressure Cook on High, and set the time to 25 minutes. When done, done, perform a quick release and unlock the lid. Stir in heavy cream and top with prosciutto. Serve and enjoy!

Corn Chips with Bean-Avocado Sauce

Total Time: 45 min + cooling time | **Servings:** 6

Ingredients

Corn fritters

2 tbsp olive oil + for frying
2 ½ cups canned corn, drained
3 garlic cloves, crushed
2 tbsp ginger powder

2 tbsp chopped parsley
1 fresh red chili, minced
½ cup fresh chopped oregano
Salt and black pepper to taste

Bean-avocado sauce

2 ripe avocados, pitted
2 tomatoes, ripe
½ lemon, juiced
3 garlic cloves, crushed

6 green onions, chopped
1 tsp maple syrup
3 tbsp canned pinto beans
1 celery stick, chopped

Directions

In a food processor, add the corn, 2 tbsp olive oil, garlic, ginger, salt, pepper, parsley, red chili, oregano, and ¼ cup water. Blend the ingredients until evenly combined. Form patties out of the batter and refrigerate for 20 minutes.

Set your Instant Pot to Sauté and heat 3 tbsp of olive oil. Fry the patties until golden brown, 15 minutes. Remove them onto a wire rack to drain the oil. In a blender, add avocados, tomatoes, lemon juice, garlic, green onions, maple syrup, pinto beans, and celery stick. Process the ingredients until smooth. Serve patties with the sauce.

Sesame Seed Soybeans

Total Time: 55 minutes | **Servings:** 4

Ingredients

1 tsp sesame oil
1 cup dried soybeans, soaked
4 cups water
½ cup soy sauce

¼ cup brown sugar
1 tbsp rice vinegar
2 garlic cloves, minced
2 tsp sesame seeds

Directions

Pour soybeans and water into your Instant Pot. Seal the lid, select Pressure Cook on High, and set the time to 20 minutes. After cooking, do a natural pressure release for 10 minutes, then a quick pressure release. Unlock the lid.

Meanwhile, in a bowl, combine soy sauce, sugar, sesame oil, rice vinegar, and garlic; set aside. On the cooker, press Sauté, add soy sauce mixture, stir and cook for 15 minutes. Spoon beans onto a platter and garnish with sesame seeds.

Moroccan-Style Chickpea Curry

Total Time: 30 minutes | **Servings:** 4

Ingredients

2 cups canned chickpeas, drained
2 medium carrots, chopped
1 celery stalk, chopped
4 garlic cloves, minced
1 yellow onion, finely chopped
1 green bell pepper, chopped
1 red bell pepper, chopped
½ cup chopped tomatoes

4 cups vegetable broth
2 tbsp ras el hanout
½ tsp turmeric powder
Salt and black pepper to taste
2 red chilies, minced
2 tbsp chopped parsley
2 tbsp chopped scallions

Directions

In your Instant Pot, combine chickpeas, carrots, celery, garlic, onion, bell peppers, tomatoes, broth, ras el hanout, turmeric, salt, pepper, and red chilies. Seal the lid, select Pressure Cook on High, and set the time to 10 minutes.

After cooking, do a natural pressure release for 10 minutes. Unlock the lid and stir parsley into the curry. Adjust taste with salt and pepper. Spoon curry into bowls and garnish with scallions. Serve chickpea curry with rice.

Brazilian Black Beans with Smoked Bacon

Total Time: 60 minutes | **Servings:** 4

Ingredients

4 dried Guajillo chilies, soaked, liquid reserved
4 oz smoked bacon, cooked and crumbled
¼ cup avocado oil
1 lb dried black beans, soaked
1 yellow onion, chopped
5 cloves garlic
1 ½ tsp ground cumin

½ tsp dried oregano
1 bay leaf
3 cups tomatoes, chopped
5 cups vegetable broth
1 bell pepper, chopped

Directions

Cut the stems of the Guajillo chilies and deseed. Put in a blender along with garlic and onion, and process until finely chopped. Mix all the spices in a bowl. Set your Instant Pot to Sauté and heat avocado oil. Place in the chili mixture and sauté for 5 minutes, stirring frequently. Pour in the spices and cook for 30 seconds until it is well combined.

Pour in the reserved chili liquid, beans, tomatoes, broth, and bell pepper, and stir to combine. Seal the lid, select Bean/Chili on High, and set the cooking time to 30 minutes. When done cooking, do a natural release for 10 minutes, then a quick pressure release. Unlock the lid and discard the bay leaf. Stir in the bacon. Serve immediately.

Sriracha Kidney Bean Dip

Total Time: 45 minutes | **Servings:** 4

Ingredients

1 tbsp coconut oil
1 cup dried kidney beans, soaked overnight and rinsed
1 red onion, finely chopped
4 garlic cloves, minced
Salt and black pepper to taste

2 tbsp tomato paste
1 tbsp curry paste
4 cups vegetable stock
1 tbsp Sriracha sauce
1 lemon, juiced
1 tsp honey

Directions

Set your Instant Pot to Sauté, heat coconut oil, and stir-fry onion and garlic until softened, 3 minutes. Season with salt and pepper. Add tomato and curry pastes and cook for 2 minutes, stirring frequently. Mix in kidney beans, stock, and Sriracha sauce. Seal the lid, select Pressure Cook on High, and set the time to 30 minutes. Do a quick pressure release.

Mix in lemon juice, honey, and using an immersion blender, puree ingredients until very smooth. Spoon bean dip into small ramekins and serve with julienned vegetables.

Split Yellow Lentil-Arugula Pancake

Total Time: 45 minutes | **Servings**: 2

Ingredients

1 cup split yellow lentils, soaked
2 garlic cloves, whole
½ tsp smoked paprika
1 pinch turmeric
¼ tsp coriander powder
¼ tsp cumin powder
3 eggs, cracked into a bowl
2 cups chopped arugula

Directions

Line a cake pan with parchment paper and set aside. In a blender, process lentils, garlic, paprika, turmeric, coriander, cumin, eggs, and ½ cup of water until smooth. Pour mixture into the cake pan and mix in arugula. Cover with foil. Pour 1 cup water into the pot, fit in a trivet, and place the cake pan on top. Seal the lid, select Pressure Cook on High, and set the cooking time to 35 minutes. After cooking, do a quick release. Slice and serve with Greek yogurt.

Beluga Lentil Stir-Fry with Zucchini

Total Time: 15 minutes | **Servings**: 4

Ingredients

2 cups canned beluga lentils, drained
2 tbsp olive oil
2 large zucchinis, chopped
4 garlic cloves, minced
½ tbsp dried oregano
½ tbsp curry powder
Salt and black pepper to taste
¼ cup chopped parsley
½ cup chopped basil
1 small red onion, diced
2 tbsp balsamic vinegar
1 tsp Dijon mustard

Directions

Set your Instant Pot to Sauté, heat the oil, and stir-fry zucchinis until tender. Mix in garlic and cook until fragrant, 30 seconds. Top with oregano, curry, salt, and pepper. Allow flavors to combine, 1 minute, stirring frequently.

Pour in lentils, cook for 3 minutes, and stir in parsley, basil, and onion. Sauté until the onion softens, 5 minutes. Meanwhile, in a bowl, combine vinegar with mustard and pour the mixture onto lentils. Serve and enjoy!

Chili Pork & Pinto Bean Cassoulet

Total Time: 25 minutes | **Servings**: 4

Ingredients

2 tbsp olive oil
1 lb pork roast, cubed
Salt and black pepper to taste
1 cup dried pinto beans, soaked overnight and rinsed
3 cups chicken broth
1 small red onion, chopped
1 cup tomato sauce
2 green chilies, chopped
1 tsp garlic powder
1 tsp chili powder
¼ cup chopped parsley

Directions

Set your Instant Pot to Sauté, heat olive oil, season pork with salt and pepper, and brown it for 4 minutes. Add beans, broth, red onion, tomato sauce, green chilies, garlic powder, and chili. Seal the lid, select Pressure Cook, and set the time to 10 minutes. After cooking, do a quick release. Unlock the lid. Stir in parsley and adjust the taste to serve.

Rosemary Squash & Mushroom Beans

Total Time: 30 minutes | **Servings**: 2

Ingredients

1 lb white button mushrooms, quartered
1 tbsp olive oil
1 medium white onion, diced
½ lb butternut squash, chopped
¼ tsp dried rosemary
1 cup chopped tomatoes
3 cups chicken broth
2 cups baby spinach
1 (15 oz) can navy beans, rinsed
1 lemon, juiced
Salt and black pepper to taste

Directions

Set your Instant Pot to Sauté, heat olive oil, and auté onion, mushroom, and squash until softened, 6 minutes. Sprinkle with salt, pepper, and rosemary and cook further for 1 minute. Stir in tomato and broth. Seal the lid.

Select Pressure Cook on High, and set the time to 3 minutes. After cooking, do a natural pressure release for 10 minutes. Press Sauté, add spinach, navy beans, and allow spinach to wilt, 3 minutes. Top with lemon juice and serve.

Tofu Scramble with Black Beans

Total Time: 30 minutes | **Servings**: 2

Ingredients

1 (14 oz) extra-firm tofu, crumbled
1 tbsp ghee
1 cup canned black beans
2 cups vegetable broth
1 red onion, finely chopped
3 garlic cloves, minced
3 tomatoes, chopped
1 tsp smoked paprika
1 tsp turmeric powder
1 tsp cumin powder
Salt and black pepper to taste

Directions

Pour beans and broth in your Instant Pot. Seal the lid, select Pressure Cook on High, and set the time to 10 minutes. After cooking, do a quick release. Transfer the beans to a medium bowl. Drain excess liquid and wipe the pot clean.

Select Sauté and adjust to medium heat. Melt ghee in the pot and sauté onion, garlic, and tomatoes until softened, 4 minutes. Crumble tofu into pan and cook for 5 minutes. Season with paprika, turmeric, cumin, salt, and black pepper. Cook for 1 minute. Add black beans, stir, and allow heating for 3 minutes. Dish scramble and enjoy!

Gouda Cheese Bean Spread

Total Time: 50 minutes | **Servings**: 4

Ingredients

¼ cup grated Parmesan cheese + extra for topping
1 cup kidney beans, soaked
4 cups chicken broth
¼ cup grated mozzarella
¼ cup grated Gouda cheese

Directions

Pour beans and broth in your Instant Pot. Seal the lid, select Pressure Cook on High, and set to 30 minutes. After, do a natural release for 10 minutes. Stir in cheeses until melted. Spoon over toasts and top with Parmesan cheese. Serve.

Brown Lentils with Goat Cheese & Rice

Total Time: 50 minutes + 2h chilling time | **Servings**: 4

Ingredients

2 tbsp olive oil
1 cup brown rice, uncooked
2 cups vegetable broth
1 cup brown lentils, picked
4 cups water
1 bay leaf
4 green onions, chopped
1 red bell pepper, chopped
1 medium cucumber, chopped
½ cup crumbled goat cheese
2 tbsp red wine vinegar
½ tsp dried thyme
Salt and black pepper to taste
1 lemon, cut into wedges

Directions

Pour broth and brown rice into your Instant Pot. Seal the lid, select Pressure Cook, and set the time to 22 minutes. After cooking, do a quick pressure release. Transfer rice to a salad bowl. Pour lentils, water, and bay leaf in the inner pot. Seal the lid, select Pressure Cook on High, and set the time to 10 minutes. Do a natural release for 10 minutes.

Remove bay leaf, add lentils to rice bowls and combine with green onions, bell pepper, cucumber, half of the goat cheese, olive oil, vinegar, thyme, salt, and pepper. Toss until well-coated and refrigerate for 2 hours. Plate, top with remaining goat cheese, and serve with lemon wedges.

Kale & Cilantro Red Lentil Dhal

Total Time: 35 minutes | **Servings**: 4

Ingredients

1 tbsp ghee
1 tsp mustard seeds
1 tbsp turmeric powder
1 tbsp cumin seeds
½ tsp cayenne powder
1 onion, thinly sliced
3 garlic cloves, minced
1 tbsp grated ginger
1 cup dried red lentils
2 cups chopped tomatoes
3 cups vegetable broth
Salt and black pepper to taste
2 cups chopped kale
2 tbsp chopped cilantro

Directions

Set your Instant Pot to Sauté. Melt ghee and stir-fry mustard seeds, turmeric, cumin seeds, and cayenne powder for 1 minute or until fragrant. Stir in onion, garlic, and ginger. Cook for 2 minutes and mix in lentils, tomatoes, and broth.

Seal the lid, select Pressure Cook on High, and set the time to 10 minutes. Once done, do a natural pressure release for 10 minutes. Unlock the lid, stir in kale and cilantro, and adjust the taste with salt and black pepper. Select Sauté and allow kale to wilt, 3 to 4 minutes. Spoon dhal into bowls and serve with mango chutney and bread.

Leek & Carrot Green Lentil Curry

Total Time: 35 minutes | **Servings**: 4

Ingredients

2 tbsp coconut oil
1 cup dried green lentils, rinsed
1 large carrot, finely chopped
1 leek, chopped
1 medium onion, chopped
2 garlic cloves
2 tsp turmeric powder
1 cup chopped tomatoes
½ cup coconut milk
2 ½ cups vegetable stock
Salt and black pepper to taste
2 tbsp chopped cilantro

Directions

Set your Instant Pot to Sauté, heat coconut oil, and stir-fry carrots, leek, garlic, turmeric, and onion until softened, 5 minutes. Mix in tomatoes; cook for 3 minutes. Pour in coconut milk, stock., and lentils; season with salt and pepper.

Seal the lid, select Pressure Cook on High, and set the time to 10 minutes. After cooking, do a natural pressure release for 10 minutes. Garnish with cilantro and serve.

Avocado & Chickpea Tacos

Total Time: 35 minutes | **Servings**: 3

Ingredients

1 tbsp coconut oil
1 medium red onion, chopped
1 red bell pepper, chopped
1 garlic clove, minced
1 tsp cumin powder
1 cup canned chickpeas, drained
1 cup vegetable broth
Salt and black pepper to taste
3 corn tortillas
1 large avocado, chopped
½ cup shredded red cabbage
3 tbsp chopped cilantro
3 tbsp tomato salsa
½ cup sour cream

Directions

Set your Instant Pot to Sauté. Heat coconut oil and sauté onion and bell pepper until softened, 4 minutes. Add garlic and cumin and cook for 1 minute until fragrant. Mix in chickpeas, heat through for 1 minute with frequent stirring, and pour in broth. Season with salt and pepper. Seal the lid, select Pressure Cook on High, and cook for 8 minutes.

After cooking, do a natural release for 10 minutes. Adjust the taste. Lay tortillas on a flat surface and divide chickpea filling at the center. Top with avocados, cabbage, cilantro, salsa, and sour cream. Wrap, tuck ends, and slice in halves.

Hot Beans with Sweet Potatoes

Total time: 65 minutes | **Servings**: 4

Ingredients

2 tbsp olive oil
8 oz dried kidney beans
3 ½ cups vegetable broth
1 onion, quartered
1 garlic clove, minced
2 tsp chili powder
Salt to taste
¼ tsp cayenne pepper
4 sweet potatoes, scrubbed
½ cup crème fraîche
3 spring onions, chopped

Directions

Set your Instant Pot to Sauté and heat the olive oil. Cook onion and garlic for 3 minutes, until tender. Stir in chili, cayenne, and salt. Mix in beans with 3 cups broth. Seal the lid, select Pressure Cook on High, and set to 15 minutes.

When done, allow a natural release for 10 minutes, and unlock the lid. Add in a tall trivet, and arrange the potatoes on the trivet. Lock the lid again; select Pressure Cook on High, and set the cooking time to 10 minutes. When done, allow a natural release for 8 minutes. Remove the potatoes and let cool for a few minutes. To serve, make a hole in the middle of each potato and stuff with bean mixture; top with crème fraîche and spring onions.

Vegan Chickpea Spread

Total Time: 55 minutes | **Servings:** 4

Ingredients

1 tbsp olive oil
1 cup dried chickpeas, soaked
3 cups water
1 onion, chopped
Salt and black pepper to taste
1 garlic clove

½ lemon, juiced
2 tbsp tahini
¼ tsp ground cumin
A pinch of paprika
2 tbsp parsley, chopped

Directions

Place chickpeas, water, salt, onion, and pepper into the inner pot. Seal the lid, select Pressure Cook, and set the time to 45 minutes on High. When done, do a quick pressure release. Unlock the lid and drain the chickpeas. Set aside.

In a food processor, puree the chickpeas, lemon juice, tahini, olive oil, 2 tbsp water, garlic, and cumin until smooth. Season with salt. Top with paprika and parsley and serve.

Venezuelan Black Beans

Total Time: 70 minutes | **Servings:** 4

Ingredients

2 tsp olive oil
2 cups dry black beans, soaked
1 onion, chopped
1 red bell pepper, chopped
2 garlic cloves, chopped
1 tbsp chili powder

½ tsp Worcestershire sauce
½ tsp ground cumin
Salt and black pepper to taste
6 cups chicken stock
1 lime, juiced

Directions

Set your Instant Pot to Sauté and warm the olive oil. Add in onion, garlic, chili powder, red bell pepper, cumin, Worcestershire sauce, salt, and pepper and cook for 5 minutes until tender. Add in beans and stock and stir.

Seal the lid, select Pressure Cook on High, and cook for 40 minutes. Allow a natural release for 15 minutes. Unlock the lid and mix in the lime juice. Select Sauté and stir until the liquid reduces by half. Adjust seasoning and serve.

Black Beans with Cotija Cheese

Total Time: 35 minutes | **Servings:** 2

Ingredients

1 tsp olive oil
1 large white onion, chopped
1 tsp grated garlic
1 cup dried black beans, soaked
3 cups vegetable broth

1 tsp Mexican seasoning
¼ cup chopped cilantro
Salt to taste
½ cup Cotija cheese, crumbled

Directions

Set your Instant Pot to Sauté, heat olive oil and sauté onion and garlic for 3 minutes. Add beans, broth, Mexican seasoning, and salt. Seal the lid, select Pressure Cook on High, and set to 12 minutes. After cooking, do a natural pressure release for 10 minutes. Unlock the lid. Spoon beans into plates, top with cheese and cilantro, and serve.

Pinto Bean & Beet Hummus

Total Time: 20 minutes | **Servings:** 4

Ingredients

¼ cup olive oil
2 large beets, peeled, chopped
2 cups canned pinto beans

2 cups vegetable stock
1 tsp garlic powder
½ lemon, juiced

Directions

Combine beets, drained pinto beans, vegetable stock, and garlic powder into your Instant Pot. Seal the lid, select Pressure Cook on High, and set the time to 13 minutes.

After cooking, do a quick release and unlock the lid. Transfer mixture to a blender and process until smooth. Add lemon juice and olive oil and blend again to combine. Pour mixture into bowls and serve.

Pinto Beans with Pancetta

Total time: 55 minutes | **Servings:** 6

Ingredients

1 tbsp olive oil
4 oz pancetta, chopped
1 onion, finely chopped
1 garlic clove, minced
1 lb dry pinto beans, soaked

4 cups water
½ tsp ground cumin
Salt and black pepper to taste
3 tbsp parsley, chopped

Directions

Set your Instant Pot to Sauté. Heat oil and cook pancetta, onion, and garlic, for 5 minutes. Stir in beans, water, cumin.

Season with salt and pepper. Seal the lid, select Pressure Cook on High, and set the time to 40 minutes. When done, do a natural pressure release. Top with parsley and serve.

Rice & Bacon Cannellini Beans

Total Time: 35 minutes | **Servings:** 4

Ingredients

2 (15-oz) cans cannellini beans, rinsed and drained
3 bacon slices, chopped
1 cup cooked white rice
½ cup canned tomatoes

1 tbsp ground mustard
1 tsp chili powder
¼ cup chopped mint

Directions

Set your Instant Pot to Sauté and cook the bacon for 6 minutes until crispy. Remove to paper towels to soak up excess fat. Add cannellini beans, 1 cup of water, tomatoes, mustard, and chili powder to the pot. Return the bacon.

Seal the lid, select Pressure Cook mode on High, and set the timer to 8 minutes. When done, perform natural pressure release for 10 minutes, then quickly release. Remove the lid. Stir in the cooked rice and garnish with mint. Serve warm.

EGGS & VEGETABLES

Breakfast Egg Caprese Cups

Total Time: 15 minutes | **Servings:** 2

Ingredients

2 eggs
2 thin ham slices
3 tsp grated mozzarella cheese

2 cherry tomatoes, halved
1 tsp dried basil
Salt and black pepper to taste

Directions

Pour 1 cup water into your Instant Pot and fit in a trivet. Line 2 ramekins with a slice of ham each, crack in an egg into each and divide mozzarella, basil, and tomatoes on top; season. Place on the trivet, seal the lid, select Pressure Cook, and cook for 3 minutes. Do a quick release and serve.

Mediterranean Eggs with Feta Cheese

Total Time: 20 minutes | **Servings:** 4

Ingredients

3 tbsp butter
1 small red onion, chopped
½ red bell pepper, chopped
2 garlic cloves, chopped
Salt and black pepper to taste
28 oz canned diced tomatoes

½ tsp coriander, ground
½ tsp smoked paprika
½ tsp red chili flakes
4 eggs
¼ cup crumbled feta cheese
2 tbsp fresh dill, chopped

Directions

Set your Instant Pot to Sauté, melt the butter, and sauté onion, bell pepper, and garlic. Season with salt and cook for 2 minutes until the veggies are fragrant and beginning to soften. Stir in tomatoes, coriander, paprika, chili flakes, pepper, and 1 cup of water. Seal the lid, select Pressure Cook on High, and set the cooking time to 4 minutes.

When ready, do a quick pressure release. Gently crack the eggs onto tomato sauce in different areas. Set on Sauté and cook until the eggs are set, 4-5 minutes; don't stir. Sprinkle with feta cheese and dill. Dish into a platter and serve.

Gruyere-Onion Egg Scramble

Total Time: 15 minutes | **Servings:** 2

Ingredients

1 tbsp butter
1 large yellow onion, sliced
1 tsp Worcestershire sauce
½ tsp chopped rosemary

4 large eggs
3 tbsp milk
¼ cup grated Gruyère cheese
Salt and black pepper to taste

Directions

Melt butter in your Instant Pot on Sauté, and stir-fry onion for 10 minutes. Season with Worcestershire sauce and rosemary. Beat eggs with milk and pour them into onion mixture.

Scramble until eggs solidify. Turn the pot off and add Gruyere cheese; stir the mixture until cheese melts and season with salt and pepper. Serve immediately.

Kale-Sausage Egg Scramble

Total Time: 15 minutes | **Servings:** 2

Ingredients

¼ cup Italian sausage, casing removed
½ cup finely chopped kale
4 large eggs
3 tbsp milk

½ tsp chopped thyme
Salt and black pepper to taste
A pinch of red pepper flakes

Directions

Set your Instant Pot to Sauté, add sausage and brown with frequent stirring while breaking into small pieces, 5 minutes. Top with kale and cook until wilted, 3 minutes. Beat eggs with milk. Pour onto kale mixture and scramble until eggs solidify, 1 minute. Turn off and season eggs with thyme, salt, pepper, and chili flakes. Plate and serve.

Morning Egg Burritos

Total Time: 30 minutes | **Servings:** 2

Ingredients

¾ cup grated Monterey Jack cheese
4 eggs
½ cup heavy cream
½ tsp garlic powder
Salt and black pepper to taste
1 red bell pepper, diced

1 yellow onion, diced
2 tbsp chopped chives
¾ cup chopped turkey ham
1 cup water
2 whole-wheat tortillas

Directions

In a bowl, whisk the eggs with heavy cream, garlic, salt, and pepper. Mix in bell pepper, onion, chives, and ham. Transfer mixture to a large ramekin and cover with aluminum foil. Pour water in the pot, fit in a trivet, and place the ramekin on top. Seal the lid, select Pressure Cook on High, and set to 10 minutes.

After cooking, allow a natural release for 10 minutes. Unlock the lid, remove ramekin and stir eggs until broken into small pieces. Lay tortilla wraps on a clean, flat surface, divide eggs on top and sprinkle with cheese. Roll and slice wraps into halves. Serve.

Guacamole Stuffed Eggs

Total Time: 20 minutes | **Servings:** 4

Ingredients

8 eggs
1 cup guacamole
Salt and black pepper to taste

½ tsp paprika
1 tbsp cilantro, chopped

Directions

Pour 1 cup of water into the pot and fit in a trivet. Place the eggs on the trivet. Seal the lid, select Pressure Cook, and cook for 6 minutes. When done, do a quick pressure release. Open the lid and put the eggs to icy-cold water. When cooled, peel the eggs and slice them in half, lengthwise. Scoop out the yolks into a bowl. Mash with a fork and add in guacamole; stir until smooth; season. Stuff the whites with guacamole. Sprinkle with paprika and cilantro to serve.

Garam Masala Eggs

Total Time: 25 minutes | **Servings:** 2

Ingredients

3 tsp ghee
2 cups water
4 eggs, whole
Ice bath
¼ tsp fennel seeds
¼ tsp cumin seeds
4 cloves
1 tbsp cinnamon powder
3 long, red chilies, halved
1-star anise
2 white onions, finely chopped
2 tomatoes, finely chopped
¼ tsp garam masala
¼ tsp turmeric powder
½ tsp chili powder
Salt to taste
1 tbsp tomato paste
2 tbsp chopped cilantro

Directions

Pour water in your Instant Pot and place in eggs. Seal the lid, select Pressure Cook on High, and set to 5 minutes. After cooking, do a quick pressure release. Transfer eggs to an ice bath. Discard water and wipe clean the inner pot.

Peel eggs, cut in halves and set aside. Select Sauté, melt half of ghee and stir-fry fennel seeds, cumin, cloves, cinnamon, red chilies, and star anise, for 3 minutes or until fragrant.

Add half of onions, all tomatoes and sauté until softened, 5 minutes. Spoon mixture into a blender and process on low speed until smooth paste forms. Set aside.

Melt remaining ghee in the pot and sauté the remaining onions until softened. Add tomato paste, garam masala, turmeric, chili powder, and salt. Mix and cook for 3 minutes. Add eggs to coat in sauce, making sure not to break them. Allow heating for 1 to 2 minutes and spoon masala with eggs over bed rice. Garnish with cilantro and serve.

Cheese & Bacon Egg Bites

Total time: 15 minutes | **Servings:** 4

Ingredients

¾ cup shredded mozzarella
½ cup ricotta cheese
¼ cup crumbled cooked bacon
4 large eggs
¼ cup heavy cream
½ tsp salt
2 tbsp parsley, chopped

Directions

Mix eggs, mozzarella, ricotta, heavy cream, and salt in a bowl. Divide the bacon among ramekins, then fill with the cheese mixture. Pour 1 cup of water into the pot and fit in a trivet. Place the ramekins on the trivet.

Seal the lid, press Pressure Cook on High, and set to 8 minutes. Do a quick release. Garnish with parsley and serve.

Thyme Mushroom Frittata

Total Time: 30 minutes | **Servings:** 4

Ingredients

2 tbsp butter
1 cup sliced cremini mushrooms
Salt and black pepper to taste
1 cup water
8 large eggs
½ cup half and half
1 tsp dried thyme
1 cup shredded asiago cheese

Directions

Set your Instant Pot to Sauté, melt butter, and sauté mushrooms, 5 minutes. Season with salt and pepper; transfer to a plate. Clean the pot, pour in water, and fit in a trivet. Grease a springform pan and set aside.

In a bowl, beat eggs with half and half, salt, pepper, and thyme. Pour the mixture into a baking pan, sprinkle with asiago cheese, cover with aluminum foil, and place on the trivet. Seal the lid, select Pressure Cook on High, and set to 5 minutes. After cooking, allow a natural release for 10 minutes. Transfer frittata onto a wide plate, slice, and serve.

Tortilla de Patatas (Spanish Omelet)

Total Time: 35 minutes | **Servings:** 2

Ingredients

4 oz frozen hash browns, defrosted
1 tbsp butter, melted
6 large eggs
Salt and black pepper to taste
1 tsp tomato paste
¼ cup milk
¼ cup diced yellow onion
1 garlic clove, minced
4 oz grated cheddar cheese

Directions

Grease a ramekin with butter and spread hash browns at the bottom. In a bowl, whisk eggs, salt, and pepper until frothy. In another bowl, smoothly combine tomato paste with milk and mix into eggs along with onion and garlic. Pour mixture on top of hash browns. Add 1 cup water to inner pot, fit in a trivet, and place ramekin on top.

Seal the lid, select Pressure Cook on High, and set to 15 minutes. After cooking, allow a natural release for 10 minutes. Unlock the lid and remove ramekin. Sprinkle with cheddar cheese and place ramekin back on top of the trivet. Cover with the lid, without locking, to melt the cheese, for a minute or so. Once melted, slice, and serve.

Broccoli & Asparagus Eggs with Ricotta

Total Time: 15 minutes | **Servings:** 2

Ingredients

½ cup finely chopped broccoli
½ cup chopped asparagus
½ cup finely chopped spinach
½ tsp onion powder
½ tsp garlic powder
4 large eggs, beaten
¼ cup crumbled ricotta cheese
1 tbsp chopped scallions
Salt and black pepper to taste

Directions

Grease a ramekin with cooking spray. Lay ingredients in the following way: broccoli, asparagus, and spinach. Sprinkle with onion and garlic powders and create a hole in the center of the greens. Pour over the eggs and top with ricotta cheese. Season with salt and pepper. Pour 1 cup water into the inner pot, fit in a trivet, and place the ramekin on top.

Seal the lid, select Pressure Cook on High, and set to 5 minutes. After cooking, perform a quick pressure release to let out steam and unlock the lid. Carefully remove ramekin and serve eggs scattered with scallions.

Kale & Mozzarella Frittata

Total time: 30 minutes | **Servings**: 4

Ingredients

2 tbsp olive oil
2 cups kale
1 onion, chopped
2 garlic cloves, minced
8 large eggs

2 cups grated mozzarella cheese
2 tomatoes, chopped
¼ cup milk
Salt and black pepper to taste

Directions

Line a baking dish with aluminium foil and grease with cooking spray. Set your Instant Pot to Sauté and heat the olive oil. Cook the onion, kale, and garlic for 3 minutes until the onion is translucent and the kale soft; remove to a bowl. Stir in the eggs, 1 cup of cheese, tomatoes, milk, salt, and pepper. Mix until well combined.

Spoon the egg mixture into the baking dish and cover with aluminium foil. Add 1 cup water to the pot and fit in a trivet. Lay the dish on top, seal the lid, select Pressure Cook on High, and set to 5 minutes. After cooking, allow a natural release for 10 minutes, and remove the lid. Scatter the remaining cheese over, slice into wedges and serve.

Sausage & Bacon Frittata

Total Time: 40 minutes | **Servings**: 4

Ingredients

4 bacon slices, chopped
¼ cup chopped pork sausages
1 large yellow onion, chopped
1 red bell pepper, chopped

¼ cup chopped spinach
8 eggs, beaten
¾ cup milk
Salt and black pepper to taste

Directions

Set the pot to Sauté and cook bacon and sausages until crisp and brown, 5 minutes; set aside. Sauté onion and bell pepper in bacon fat until softened, 5 minutes. Add spinach to wilt for 2 minutes. Remove to the bacon plate.

Clean up the inner pot, pour in 1 cup water, and fit in a trivet. In a bowl, mix the eggs with milk and season with salt and pepper. Grease a cake pan with cooking spray and pour in eggs. Top with bacon, sausages and, vegetable mixture and sprinkle with salt and black pepper. Cover pan with foil and place on the trivet.

Seal the lid, select Pressure Cook on High, and set to 15 minutes. When ready, do a quick release, and unlock the lid. Remove cake pan, aluminum foil, and brown top of eggs under a broiler for 2 minutes. Plate frittata, slice, and serve.

Veracruz-Style Mixed Bell Peppers

Total Time: 15 minutes | **Servings**: 4

Ingredients

4 large mixed bell peppers, sliced into strips
1 (15 oz) can tomato sauce
2 tsp chili powder
2 large white onions, sliced

½ tsp Mexican seasoning
½ tsp garlic powder
Salt and black pepper to taste

Directions

In your Instant Pot, mix bell peppers, tomato sauce, chili powder, onions, Mexican seasoning, garlic powder, salt, black pepper, and 1 cup of water. Seal the lid, select Manual/Pressure Cook on High, and set the cooking time to 5 minutes. After cooking, do a quick pressure release, and unlock the lid. Stir well and serve warm.

Swiss Cheese & Mushroom Tarts

Total Time: 40 minutes | **Servings**: 4

Ingredients

2 tbsp melted butter, divided
1 small white onion, sliced
5 oz oyster mushrooms, sliced
Salt and black pepper to taste

¼ cup dry white wine
1 sheet puff pastry, thawed
1 cup shredded Swiss cheese
1 tbsp sliced green onions

Directions

On Sauté, add in 1 tbsp of butter, onion, and mushrooms and sauté for 5 minutes or until the vegetables are tender. Season with salt and pepper, pour in the white wine, and cook until evaporated, about 2 minutes; set aside. Unwrap the pastry and cut into 4 squares. Pierce the dough with a fork and brush both sides with the remaining butter. Share half of the Swiss cheese over the puff pastry squares. Also, share the mushroom mixture over the pastry squares and top with the remaining cheese. Place in a baking pan.

Pour 1 cup of water into the pot and place a trivet. Lay the pan on top of the trivet. Seal the lid, select Pressure Cook on High, and set the time to 20 minutes. After cooking, allow a natural release. Take the tart out of the pot and transfer to a plate. Garnish with the green onions and serve.

Hot Beans with Sweet Potatoes

Total time: 1 hour | **Servings**: 4

Ingredients

2 tbsp olive oil
8 oz dried kidney beans
3 cups vegetable broth
1 onion, quartered
1 garlic clove, minced
2 tsp chili powder

Salt to taste
¼ tsp cayenne pepper
4 sweet potatoes, scrubbed
½ cup crème fraîche
3 spring onions, chopped

Directions

Set your Instant Pot to Sauté and heat the olive oil. Cook onion and garlic for 3 minutes, until tender. Stir in chili, cayenne, and salt. Mix in beans with 3 cups broth. Seal the lid, select Pressure Cook on High, and set to 15 minutes. When done, allow a natural release for 10 minutes, and unlock the lid. Add in a tall trivet, and arrange the potatoes on the trivet. Lock the lid again; select Manual/Pressure Cook on High, and set the cooking time to 10 minutes.

When done, allow a natural release for 8 minutes. Remove the potatoes and let cool for a few minutes. To serve, make a hole in the middle of each potato and stuff with bean mixture; top with crème fraîche and spring onions.

Bacon & Spinach Egg Bites

Total Time: 35 minutes | **Servings:** 2

Ingredients

5 bacon slices, chopped
4 large eggs
¼ cup coconut cream

¼ cup chopped spinach
¾ cup grated Parmesan cheese
Salt and black pepper to taste

Directions

Set your Instant Pot to Sauté and brown bacon pieces until crispy, 5 minutes. Transfer to a paper towel-lined plate to drain grease. Clean the pot. In a bowl, beat eggs with coconut cream and fold in spinach, Parmesan cheese, salt, and pepper. Fill a silicone muffin tray (2/3 way up) with the mixture, cover with aluminum foil, and set aside.

Pour 1 cup water into the inner pot, fit in a trivet, and place the muffin tray on top. Seal the lid, select Manual/Pressure Cook on High, and set to 10 minutes. After cooking, allow a natural release for 10 minutes. Remove and uncover muffin mold. Invert tray onto a plate to release egg bites and serve with hot sauce or butter.

Herby Eggs in Avocados

Total Time: 10 minutes | **Servings:** 2

Ingredients

2 large ripe avocados, halved and pitted
½ cup Mexican four-cheese blend
1 cup water
4 small eggs

Salt and black peppers
1 ½ tsp dried Italian herb mix

Directions

Pour water In your Instant Pot. Spoon out half of the avocado flesh to make way for eggs and place in a steamer basket. Fill each hole with an egg, sprinkle with salt, pepper, herb mix, and cheese blend. Lower steamer basket into the pot. Seal the lid, select Pressure Cook on High, and set to 4 minutes. Do a quick release and serve with arugula.

Turkish Menemen (Turkish Baked Eggs)

Total Time: 25 minutes | **Servings:** 2

Ingredients

2 tbsp olive oil
1 onion, finely chopped
1 red bell pepper, chopped
1 green bell pepper, chopped
4 garlic cloves, minced

2 cups chopped tomatoes
2 scallions, chopped
4 large eggs
Salt and black pepper to taste

Directions

Heat olive oil in your Instant Pot on Sauté. Cook onion, garlic, and bell peppers for 4 minutes. Mix in tomatoes and scallions; sauté for 10 minutes until the sauce thickens. Transfer to a greased baking dish. Create 4 holes in the sauce and crack the eggs into them. Season with salt and pepper. Pour 1 cup of water into the pot and fit in a trivet. Place baking dish on top. Seal the lid, select Pressure Cook on High, and set to 3 minutes. After cooking, do a quick release. Serve.

Egg Tortilla Wraps with Ham

Total time: 30 minutes | **Servings:** 5

Ingredients

½ cup diced ham
1 ¼ cups frozen hash browns
3 large eggs, beaten
2 tbsp milk
3 tbsp crème fraîche

¼ cup cheddar cheese
Salt and black pepper to taste
5 flour tortillas
2 tbsp cilantro, chopped

Directions

Pour 1 cup water in your Instant Pot and fit in a trivet. Place the hash browns in a greased baking dish and top with ham. Combine eggs, milk, crème fraîche, cheddar, salt, and pepper in a bowl and pour the mixture over the hash browns; cover tightly with foil. Seal the lid, select Manual/Pressure Cook on High, and set the time to 10 minutes. When done, allow a natural release for 10 minutes. Remove the aluminium foil and stir the mixture. Warm tortillas for a few seconds in the microwave. Divide the egg mixture between tortillas, top with cilantro, and roll up to serve.

Prosciutto Egg Bake

Total Time: 30 minutes | **Servings:** 4

Ingredients

4 eggs
1 cup whole milk
Salt and black pepper to taste

1 cup grated Monterey Jack
1 orange bell pepper, chopped
8 oz prosciutto, chopped

Directions

Break the eggs in a bowl, pour in milk, salt, and pepper, and whisk until combined; stir in the cheese. Arrange bell pepper and prosciutto on a greased cake pan. Pour over the egg mixture, cover the pan with foil. Put a trivet in the Instant Pot and pour in 1 cup of water. Lay the pan on top. Seal the lid, select Manual/Pressure Cook on High, and set the time to 20 minutes. When done cooking, do a quick pressure release. Serve warm. Enjoy!

Smoked Kielbasa Baked Eggs

Total Time: 10 minutes | **Servings:** 2

Ingredients

½ cup diced smoked kielbasa sausages
½ cup hash brown potatoes
¼ cup shredded cheddar
4 eggs, cracked into a bowl

1 tbsp chopped scallions
Salt and black pepper to taste

Directions

Grease a large ramekin with cooking spray and lay in ingredients in this order: sausages, hash browns, and cheddar cheese. Create a hole in the center and pour in eggs. Scatter scallions on top and season with salt and pepper. Pour 1 cup water into the inner pot and fit in a trivet. Place ramekin on the trivet, seal the lid, select Manual/Pressure Cook on High, and set the time to 2 minutes. When done, do a quick release. Carefully remove ramekin and serve.

Goat Cheese Shakshuka

Total Time: 15 minutes | **Servings:** 2

Ingredients

1 cup tomato passata
¼ tsp coriander powder
½ tsp smoked paprika
¼ tsp cumin powder
¼ tsp red pepper flakes
1 garlic clove, minced
Salt and black pepper to taste
4 eggs
2 tbsp crumbled goat cheese

Directions

Grease a large baking pan with cooking spray; set aside. In a bowl, mix passata, coriander, paprika, cumin, red pepper flakes, garlic, salt, and black pepper. Spread mixture in the baking pan and, using the back of a spoon, create 4 pockets.

Break the eggs into each, scatter goat cheese on top, and season with salt and pepper. Pour 2 cups water into the inner pot, fit in a trivet, and place the ramekin on top. Seal the lid, select Pressure Cook on High, and set to 2 minutes. After cooking, do a quick pressure release. Serve warm.

Gyeran-Jjim (Korean Egg Custard)

Total Time: 25 minutes | **Servings:** 2

Ingredients

2 tbsp sesame oil
4 large eggs
¾ tsp fish sauce
2 chopped green onions

Directions

Beat eggs in a bowl until very smooth. Mix in fish sauce, 1 green onion, and 1 cup of water. Pour mixture into a ramekin and cover with foil. Pour 1 cup of water into the pot and fit in a trivet. Put the ramekin on the trivet.

Seal the lid, select Pressure Cook on Low, and set to 7 minutes. After cooking, allow a natural release for 10 minutes. Unlock the lid, carefully remove ramekin, top with remaining green onion. Drizzle with sesame oil to serve.

Colorful Risotto with Vegetables

Total Time: 30 minutes | **Servings:** 4

Ingredients

4 mixed bell peppers, chopped diagonally
2 tbsp ghee, divided
2 tbsp butter
1 garlic clove, minced
2 cups vegetable stock
¼ cup lemon juice
1 tsp grated lemon zest
1 cup Carnaroli rice
Salt and black pepper to taste
1 cup grated Parmesan cheese

Directions

Melt the ghee on Sauté and cook the garlic until fragrant, about 1 minute. Stir in the stock, lemon juice and zest, salt, and rice. Seal the lid, select Pressure Cook on High, and set the time to 7 minutes. In a bowl, toss the bell peppers with the remaining ghee, salt, and pepper. When ready, allow a natural release for 10 minutes. Stir butter into the rice until melted. Arrange bell peppers on top of rice and cook on Sauté for 5 minutes. Serve topped with Parmesan cheese.

Cheddar & Vegetable Tart

Total Time: 20 minutes | **Servings:** 4

Ingredients

2 cups broccoli, grated
1 onion, diced
3 zucchini, grated and drained
6 large carrots, grated
5 eggs, beaten
Salt and black pepper to taste
½ cup panko breadcrumbs
½ cup plain flour
½ tsp baking powder
½ cup grated cheddar cheese

Directions

Pour 1 cup of water and fit in a trivet. Lightly grease a springform pan with cooking spray and set aside. In a bowl, mix broccoli, onion, zucchini, carrots, eggs, salt, pepper, panko breadcrumbs, flour, baking powder, and cheddar cheese. Pour vegetable mixture into the pan, cover with foil, and place on the trivet.

Seal the lid, select Manual/Pressure Cook on High, and set the time to 10 minutes. After cooking, do a quick pressure release. Carefully remove the pan, take off the foil, and let cool. Release the pan, slice the cake, and serve. Enjoy!

Winter Vegetables with Miso Dressing

Total Time: 15 minutes | **Servings:** 4

Ingredients

1 cup Brussels sprouts, trimmed and halved lengthwise
1 head cauliflower, cut into bite-size pieces
1 tbsp olive oil
2 tbsp peanut oil
1 sweet potato, cubed
Salt and black pepper to taste
1 ½ tsp yellow miso paste
½ lemon, juiced

Directions

Pour 1 cup of water, fit in a steamer basket, and place in Brussels sprouts, cauliflower, and sweet potato. Seal the lid, select Pressure Cook on High, and set the cooking time to 8 minutes. After cooking, do a quick pressure release. In a bowl, whisk olive oil, salt, black pepper, miso paste, lemon juice, and peanut oil. Toss vegetables in dressing to serve.

Mixed Vegetable Soup

Total Time: 20 minutes | **Servings:** 4

Ingredients

3 cups vegetable broth
4 garlic cloves, minced
1 medium sweet onion
5 Yukon gold potatoes, diced
4 celery stalks, chopped
4 medium carrots, chopped
1 cup chopped tomatoes
1 tsp dried oregano
1 tsp dried thyme
2 bay leaves
1 bunch parsley, chopped
Salt and black pepper to taste

Directions

In your Instant Pot, add broth, 1 ½ cups of water, garlic, onion, potatoes, celery, carrots, tomatoes, oregano, thyme, bay leaves, parsley, salt, and pepper. Seal the lid; select Pressure Cook on High, and set the time to 10 minutes. After cooking, do a quick pressure release. Unlock the lid. Stir and adjust the taste with salt and pepper. Serve.

Mushroom Risotto with Swiss Chard

Total Time: 30 minutes | **Servings:** 4

Ingredients

3 tbsp olive oil
1 bunch Swiss chard, chopped
1 cup short-grain rice
½ cup white wine
2 cups vegetable stock
Salt to taste
½ cup mushrooms, sliced
½ cup caramelized onions
½ cup grated Pecorino Romano

Directions

Heat olive oil in your Instant Pot on Sauté. Stir-fry mushrooms for 5 minutes. Add and cook Swiss chard for 2 minutes until wilted. Spoon into a bowl and set aside. Stir in the rice for about 1 minute. Add the white wine and cook for 2 to 3 minutes, with occasional stirring until the wine has evaporated. Add in stock and salt; stir to combine.

Seal the lid, select Manual/Pressure Cook on High, and set the time to 8 minutes. When ready, perform a quick pressure release and unlock the lid. Stir in mushroom mixture and caramelized onions and cook for 1 minute on Sauté. Mix the Pecorino cheese into the rice until melted and serve.

Baked Potatoes with Broccoli & Cheese

Total time: 30 minutes | **Servings:** 4

Ingredients

4 bacon slices
1 tbsp butter
1 head broccoli, cut into florets
4 small russet potatoes
¾ cup half and half
2 cups Gruyere cheese, grated
1 tsp cornstarch
¼ cup chopped fresh chives

Directions

Set your Instant Pot to Sauté and cook the bacon for 4 minutes until crispy; crumble with a spatula and reserve.

Pour 1 cup of water and fit in a steamer basket. Place in the broccoli. Seal the lid, select Manual/Pressure Cook on High, and set the time to 1 minute. When ready, do a quick pressure, unlock the lid and remove the broccoli to a bowl.

In the steamer basket, place the potatoes. Seal the lid again, select Pressure Cook on High, and set to 15 minutes. When done, do a quick pressure release. Unlock the lid and let the potatoes cool. Take out the steamer basket and discard the water. Press Sauté and warm half and half and butter.

In a bowl, mix the cheese with cornstarch and pour it into the pot. Stir until the cheese melts. Toss broccoli with cheese sauce. Cut a slit into each potato and stuff it with the broccoli mixture. Scatter with bacon and chives to serve.

Cauliflower Tots

Total Time: 40 minutes | **Servings:** 4

Ingredients

3 tbsp olive oil
1 large cauliflower
1 egg, beaten
1 cup almond meal
2 garlic cloves, minced
1 cup grated Gruyere cheese
1 cup grated Parmesan cheese
Salt to taste

Directions

Pour 1 cup of water, fit in a trivet, and place cauliflower on top. Seal the lid, select Pressure Cook on High, and set the time to 3 minutes. Do a quick pressure release. Remove the cauliflower to a food processor and blend it until rice-like. Transfer the "rice" to a bowl. Add in egg, almond meal, garlic, cheeses, and salt. Form 2-inch oblong balls out of the mixture, place them on a sheet and chill for 20 minutes. Heat the olive oil on Sauté. Fry the tots on all sides (in batches) until golden brown, about 6. Place on a paper towel-lined plate to drain grease and serve. Enjoy!

Marjoram Potato Carrot Medley

Total Time: 20 minutes | **Servings:** 4

Ingredients

2 tbsp olive oil
1 cup potatoes, peeled, chopped
3 carrots, peeled and chopped
3 garlic cloves, minced
1 cup vegetable broth
1 tsp Italian seasoning
1 tbsp chopped parsley
1 tbsp chopped marjoram

Directions

Set your Instant Pot to Sauté, heat olive oil and sauté potatoes and carrots until sweaty, 5 minutes. Add garlic and cook until fragrant, 30 seconds. Pour in vegetable broth and season with Italian seasoning. Seal the lid, select Pressure Cook on High, and set the time to 5 minutes. After cooking, do a quick pressure release, and unlock the lid. Spoon carrots and potatoes into a serving bowl and mix in parsley and marjoram. Serve warm.

Pesto Minestrone with Cheesy Bread

Total Time: 30 minutes | **Servings:** 4

Ingredients

3 tbsp vegetable oil
3 tbsp butter, softened
1 red onion, chopped
1 celery stalk, chopped
1 large carrot, chopped
1 small yellow squash, chopped
1 (14-oz) can diced tomatoes
1 (27-oz) can cannellini beans
1 cup chopped zucchini
1 bay leaf
1 tsp mixed herbs
¼ tsp cayenne pepper powder
Salt and black pepper to taste
1 rind of Pecorino Romano
¼ cup grated Pecorino Romano
1 garlic clove, minced
4 slices white bread
¼ cup pesto

Directions

Heat the oil in your Instant Pot on Sauté. Cook onion, celery, and carrot for 5 minutes. Stir in the yellow squash, tomatoes, beans, 4 cups of water, zucchini, bay leaf, mixed herbs, cayenne pepper, salt, and Pecorino Romano rind.

Seal the lid, select Manual/Pressure Cook on High, and set the cooking time to 4 minutes. In a bowl, mix the butter, shredded cheese, and garlic. Spread the mixture on the bread slices. Place under the broiler for 4 minutes on high.

After cooking the soup, allow a natural release for 10 minutes. Adjust the taste with salt and black pepper, and remove the bay leaf. Ladle the soup into serving bowls and drizzle the pesto over. Serve with the garlic toasts.

Pea Mix with Bacon & Ham

Total Time: 15 minutes | **Servings**: 2

Ingredients

2 bacon slices, chopped
3 ham slices, chopped
1 cup chicken broth
1 cup frozen peas
1 tsp garlic powder
1 tsp onion powder
Salt and black pepper to taste
1 tbsp chopped parsley

Directions

Set your Instant Pot to Sauté and brown bacon until crispy, 5 minutes. Mix in ham and heat through, 1 minute. Top with broth, peas, garlic powder, onion powder, salt, and pepper. Seal the lid, select Pressure Cook on High, and set the time to 1 minute. After cooking, do a quick pressure release, and unlock the lid. Garnish with parsley and serve.

Spaghetti a la Puttanesca

Total time: 20 minutes | **Servings**: 4

Ingredients

2 tbsp olive oil
1 lb dried spaghetti
3 garlic cloves, minced
1 (32-oz) jar pasta sauce
1 tsp crushed chilies
1 tbsp capers
½ cup pitted black olives, sliced
Salt and black pepper to taste
2 tsp grated lemon zest
Grated Grana Padano cheese

Directions

In the pot, mix spaghetti and 6 cups water. Seal the lid, select Pressure Cook on High, and set to 5 minutes. When done, perform a quick release. Drain the spaghetti and set aside. Press Sauté and heat olive oil. Cook the garlic, chilies, capers, and olives for 2 minutes. Pour in the pasta sauce and stir. Once the sauce is ready, adjust the seasoning and add in spaghetti; toss to coat. Divide between plates and sprinkle with Grana Padano cheese and lemon zest. Serve warm.

Peanut Brussels Sprouts

Total Time: 20 minutes | **Servings**: 4

Ingredients

3 tbsp sesame oil
1 ½ lb Brussels sprouts, halved
2 tbsp fish sauce
1 cup chicken stock
½ cup chopped roasted peanuts

Directions

Set your Instant Pot to Sauté and warm sesame oil in the inner pot and fry Brussels sprouts until golden around edges, 5 minutes. Mix in fish sauce and chicken stock. Seal the lid, select Manual/Pressure Cook on High, and set the time to 3 minutes. After cooking, do a quick pressure release, and unlock the lid. Mix in peanuts, dish, and serve.

Cinnamon & Maple Coated Squash

Total Time: 10 minutes | **Servings**: 4

Ingredients

1 acorn squash, cut into slices
2 tbsp maple syrup
1 tsp cinnamon powder

Directions

Pour 1 cup of water, fit in a steamer basket, and put in acorn squash. Seal the lid, select Manual/Pressure Cook on High, and set the time to 2 minutes. After cooking, do a quick pressure release, and unlock the lid; set aside. Combine maple syrup and cinnamon powder in a deep plate and coat each squash slice in syrup mixture. Plate and serve.

Steamed Cabbage with Spicy Vinaigrette

Total Time: 20 minutes | **Servings**: 10

Ingredients

2 tbsp butter, melted
1 head cabbage wedges
Salt and black pepper to taste
1 lemon, juiced
¼ tsp red chili flakes

Directions

Pour 1 cup of water, fit in a trivet, and place cabbage on top. Seal the lid, select Manual/Pressure Cook on High, and set the cooking time to 2 minutes. After cooking, do a quick pressure release, and unlock the lid. Place cabbage on a plate. In a bowl, whisk butter, salt, pepper, lemon juice, and chili flakes. Drizzle mixture all over cabbage and serve.

Scrambled Eggs with Broccoli & Pepper

Total Time: 15 minutes | **Servings**: 2

Ingredients

2 tsp olive oil
½ cup finely chopped broccoli
1 orange bell pepper, diced
1 garlic clove, minced
4 large eggs
3 tbsp milk
¼ cup crumbled goat cheese
½ tsp dried oregano
Salt and black pepper to taste

Directions

Set your Instant Pot to Sauté, heat olive oil and sauté broccoli and bell pepper until softened, 4 minutes. Add garlic and keep cooking until fragrant, 1 minute. Beat the eggs with milk and pour the mixture onto the vegetables.

Using a spatula, begin scrambling the eggs immediately until set and soft, 2 minutes. Press Cancel and mix in goat cheese, oregano, salt, and pepper until well-combined. Transfer scrambled eggs to plates and serve warm.

Autumn Veggie Mix

Total Time: 10 minutes | **Servings**: 4

Ingredients

2 tbsp butter
1 carrot, sliced
1 head cauliflower florets
½ cup celeriac, sliced

Directions

Pour 1 cup of water into the pot and fit in a steamer basket. Place the carrots, cauliflower, and celeriac in the basket. Seal the lid, select Steam, and set the cooking time to 2 minutes. When done, perform a quick pressure release. Unlock the lid and transfer the veggies to a bowl. Add in the butter and stir until melted. Adjust the taste and serve.

Almond Mushroom & Broccoli Side

Total Time: 15 minutes | **Servings**: 4

Ingredients

1 large head broccoli, cut into bite-size pieces
2 tbsp olive oil   2 tsp hot sauce
1 cup sliced mixed mushrooms   2 tbsp chopped almonds

Directions

Pour 1 cup of water, fit in a steamer basket, and put in broccoli. Seal the lid, select Pressure Cook on High, and set the time to 2 minutes. Do a quick pressure release and unlock the lid. Transfer broccoli to a bowl and empty the pot. Wipe clean with a clean napkin and select Sauté.

Heat the olive oil and sauté mushrooms until softened, 5 minutes. Add broccoli and hot sauce. Sauté until well coated in hot sauce. Stir in almonds. Serve and enjoy!

Homestyle Ketchup with Potatoes

Total Time: 30 minutes | **Servings**: 4

Ingredients

2 tbsp slurry (1 tbsp cornstarch mixed with 1 tbsp water)
1 lb potatoes, peeled, chopped   ¼ tsp garlic powder
1 ½ lb tomatoes, quartered   ½ tsp Dijon mustard
1 cup chicken broth   ¼ tsp celery seeds
¼ tsp cinnamon powder   1 tbsp honey
1 tbsp paprika   ¼ cup raisins
Salt to taste   1 onion, cut into wedges
¼ tsp clove powder   6 tbsp apple cider vinegar

Directions

Cover the potatoes with salted water. Seal the lid, select Pressure Cook, and cook for 10 minutes. Once the time is done, do a quick release. Drain potatoes and set aside.

Add tomatoes, chicken broth, cinnamon, paprika, salt, clove powder, garlic powder, Dijon mustard, celery seeds, honey, raisins, onion, and apple cider vinegar to the pot. Seal the lid, select Pressure Cook on High, and cook for 5 minutes. After cooking, perform a quick pressure release. Puree the ingredients with an immersion blender. Select Sauté, mix in the slurry and cook until thickened, 5 minutes. Let cool the ketchup for a few minutes and serve with potatoes.

Mediterranean Green Beans with Nuts

Total Time: 15 minutes | **Servings**: 4

Ingredients

2 tbsp olive oil   1 lemon, juiced
1 lb green beans, trimmed   2 tbsp toasted peanuts, chopped

Directions

Pour 1 cup of water, fit in a steamer basket, and arrange green beans on top. Seal the lid, select Pressure Cook on High, and set the time to 1 minute. After cooking, do a quick pressure release to let out steam, and unlock the lid. Remove green beans onto a plate and mix in lemon juice, olive oil, and peanuts. Serve immediately.

Green Mash with Greek Yogurt

Total Time: 15 minutes | **Servings**: 4

Ingredients

2 avocados, halved, pitted, and peeled
2 tbsp butter   2 tbsp chopped parsley
1 head broccoli, cut into florets Salt and black pepper to taste
2 cups spinach   3 tbsp Greek yogurt
1 cup vegetable broth   2 tbsp toasted pine nuts

Directions

In your Instant Pot, add broccoli, spinach, and broth. Seal the lid, select Pressure Cook on High, and set the cooking time to 3 minutes. After cooking, do a quick pressure release. Add avocado, butter, parsley, salt, pepper, and Greek yogurt. Using an immersion blender, puree ingredients until smooth. Spoon into bowls and top with pine nuts. Serve.

Tomato & Rice Stuffed Zucchini Boats

Total Time: 25 minutes | **Servings**: 4

Ingredients

2 tbsp melted butter, divided   ½ cup chopped tomatoes
2 small zucchinis   ½ cup chopped toasted cashews
½ cup cooked short-grain rice   ½ cup grated Parmesan cheese
½ cup canned white beans   Salt and black pepper to taste

Directions

Cut each zucchini in half, lengthwise, and scoop out the pulp. Chop the pulp and set it aside. In a bowl, combine rice, beans, tomatoes, cashew nuts, half of Parmesan, 1 tbsp of melted butter, salt, and pepper. Spoon the mixture into the zucchini boats and arrange them in a single layer on the pot bottom. Pour in 1 cup of water and the remaining butter. Seal the lid, select Pressure Cook on High, and set to 6 minutes. After cooking, allow a natural release for 10 minutes. Top the zucchini boats with Parmesan and serve.

Roasted Squash with Rice & Tofu

Total Time: 20 minutes | **Servings**: 4

Ingredients

2 tbsp melted butter, divided   15 oz extra-firm tofu, cubed
1 butternut squash, chopped   2 tsp arrowroot starch
Salt and black pepper to taste   1 cup jasmine rice
1 tbsp coconut aminos   2 tbsp cilantro, chopped

Directions

Pour the rice, salt, pepper, cilantro, and 2 cups of water into the pot and mix well. Put in a trivet. In a bowl, toss the butternut squash with 1 tbsp of melted butter and season with salt and pepper. Transfer to a baking pan. In another bowl, mix the remaining butter with coconut aminos and toss the tofu in the mixture. Pour arrowroot starch over tofu. Put over the squash. Place the pan on the trivet. Seal the lid, select Pressure Cook on High, and set to 6 minutes. When done, perform a quick pressure release. Fluff the rice and top with tofu and squash to serve.

RICE & GRAINS

One-Pot Herbed Chicken with Rice

Total Time: 35 minutes | **Servings**: 4

Ingredients

1 tbsp olive oil	½ cup white wine
1 tbsp butter	1 cup chicken broth
4 chicken breasts	2 tbsp chopped parsley
Salt and black pepper to taste	2 tbsp chopped dill
1 yellow onion, diced	1 tbsp chopped scallions
2 garlic cloves, minced	1 lemon, zested and juiced
2 leeks, chopped	1 lemon, cut into wedges
1 ½ cups basmati rice, rinsed	

Directions

Set your Instant Pot to Sauté and heat olive oil. Season chicken with salt and black pepper, and fry in oil until golden on both sides, 6 minutes. Set aside. Add butter to the inner pot and sauté onion, garlic, and leeks until softened and leeks bright green, 4 minutes. Mix in rice, cook for 1 minute and stir in white wine, chicken broth; return the chicken.

Seal the lid, select Manual/Pressure Cook, and set the cooking time to 5 minutes. Allow sitting (covered) for 10 minutes and then perform a quick pressure release to let out all the steam. Unlock the lid, fluff with a fork, and mix in chopped parsley, dill, scallions, lemon zest, and lemon juice. Dish rice into bowls and garnish with lemon wedges.

Coconut Rice with Cashews

Total Time: 25 minutes | **Servings**: 4

Ingredients

1-inch piece of root ginger, chopped	
1 cup jasmine Thai rice, rinsed	Salt to taste
1 cup canned coconut milk	
½ cup roasted unsalted cashews	2 tbsp cilantro, chopped
	2 tbsp almonds, chopped

Directions

Mix the rice, ginger, coconut milk, 1 cup of water, and salt in your Instant Pot. Seal the lid, select Pressure Cook on High, and cook for 8 minutes. When off, do a natural pressure release for 10 minutes. Remove the lid and stir in cashews, cover, and let stand for a few minutes. After, fluff the rice with a fork and scatter cilantro and all over to serve.

Shrimp & Scallop Paella

Total Time: 25 minutes | **Servings**: 4

Ingredients

1 pinch saffron threads, soaked in 2 tbsp hot water	
4 tbsp butter	¼ cup white wine
Salt and black pepper to taste	1 cup chicken broth
1 large white onion, chopped	1 cup short-grain rice, rinsed
4 garlic cloves, minced	12 scallops
1 tsp turmeric powder	1 lb jumbo shrimp, deveined
1 tsp sweet paprika	½ cup frozen peas, thawed
¼ tsp red pepper flakes	1 lemon, cut into wedges

Directions

Set your Instant Pot to Sauté and melt butter. Stir-fry onion until softened, 4 minutes. Add garlic and cook until fragrant, 1 minute. Add turmeric, paprika, salt, black pepper, and saffron liquid. Cook for 1 minute to release flavor. Pour white wine and let it reduce by one-third.

Follow up with chicken broth and rice; stir well. Seal the lid, select Pressure Cook, and set the timer to 5 minutes. Perform a quick pressure release, and unlock the lid. Select Sauté and mix in scallops, shrimp, and peas. Cook for 5 to 7 minutes or until scallops and shrimp are opaque. Adjust taste with salt, black pepper, and stir in red pepper flakes. Plate paella and garnish with lemon wedges. Serve and enjoy!

Pork & Rice Casserole

Total Time: 35 minutes | **Servings**: 4

Ingredients

2 tbsp olive oil	
½ cup chopped orange bell peppers	
1 lb pork tenderloin, cubed	1 tsp smoked paprika
Salt and black pepper to taste	1 cup basmati rice
½ cup chopped brown onion	1 ¾ cups chicken broth

Directions

Set your Instant Pot to Sauté, heat 1 tbsp olive oil and brown pork on both sides, 6 minutes. Transfer to a plate and set aside. Heat the remaining olive oil and sauté onion and bell peppers until softened. Season with salt, pepper, and paprika, and cook to release flavors for 1 minute. Stir in rice and pork, cook for 1 minute, and add chicken broth.

Seal the lid, select Pressure Cook, and set the timer to 5 minutes. After cooking, perform a natural release for 10 minutes, then a quick pressure release. Unlock the lid, fluff the rice with a fork. Serve and enjoy!

Kheer (Rice Pudding)

Total Time: 35 minutes | **Servings**: 4

Ingredients

½ cup dried cherries, chopped, soaked	
3 cups milk	1 tsp ground cardamom
½ cup basmati rice	¼ cup sugar
2 large eggs	

Directions

Set your Instant Pot to Sauté and place in milk and sugar. Cook for 3 minutes until the sugar dissolves. Stir in basmati rice. Seal the lid, select Pressure Cook on High, and set the timer to 5 minutes. Do a quick pressure release.

In a bowl, whisk the eggs. Gradually pour 1 cup of the rice pudding into eggs, whisking constantly. Add the egg mixture to the remaining pudding in the pot. Select Sauté and cook for 3 minutes, moving continually with a spatula, until it thickens. Stir in cardamom and cherries. Divide between bowls and let chill for 15 minutes before serving.

Caribbean Jerk Chicken Rice

Total Time: 35 min + marinating time | **Servings:** 4

Ingredients

Chicken marinade

4 chicken thighs, boneless and skinless
3 tbsp olive oil
4 garlic cloves, pressed
1 tbsp grated ginger
2 tbsp tamarind sauce
1 tbsp balsamic vinegar

1 tbsp squeezed lemon juice
½ tbsp honey
½ tbsp allspice powder
½ tsp cinnamon powder
1 tsp dried rosemary
¼ tsp chili powder
Salt and black pepper to taste

Rice

1 cup chopped green onions
1 cup diced red bell pepper
1 cup coconut milk

1 cup jasmine rice
1 cup fresh pineapple chunks
1 cup water

Directions

Place chicken in a large zipper bag. In a medium bowl, combine 1 tbsp of olive oil, garlic, ginger, tamarind sauce, vinegar, lemon juice, honey, allspice, cinnamon, rosemary, chili powder, salt, and black pepper. Pour mixture over the chicken, seal the bag, and massage to coat chicken with marinade. Sit in the fridge for 3 hours.

Set your Instant Pot to Sauté and heat the remaining olive oil. Remove chicken from marinade and brown in oil on both sides, 8 minutes; reserve. Sauté green onions and bell pepper for 3 minutes or until tender, and mix in coconut milk, water, and rice. Cook for 1 minute and stir in pineapple. Place chicken thighs on top. Seal the lid, select Pressure Cook, and set the timer to 15 minutes. Do a quick pressure release. Stir rice and dish into plates. Serve.

Mexican Rice with Peas & Carrots

Total Time: 35 minutes | **Servings:** 6

Ingredients

2 tbsp olive oil
3 baby carrots, chopped
2 large celery stalks, diced
1 small yellow onion, chopped
2 cups hot water
2 cups white rice

2 tomatoes, peeled, chopped
Salt to taste
1 serrano pepper, minced
1 cup grated Monterey Jack
¼ cup chopped cilantro
1 cup green peas

Directions

Set Sauté and heat the oil. Cook onion, carrots, serrano pepper, and celery for 5 minutes. Add in the water, rice, tomatoes, and salt, and stir. Seal lid, select Pressure Cook on High, and cook for 10 minutes. When done, perform a natural pressure release for 10 minutes. Fluff the rice, add in the cheese and peas, stir and top with cilantro to serve.

Mustard Rice with Pecans

Total Time: 30 minutes | **Servings:** 4

Ingredients

2 tsp ghee
Salt to taste

1 tsp mustard powder
1 brown onion, finely chopped

1 green chili, finely chopped
½ tsp turmeric powder

1 cup jasmine rice
¼ cup chopped pecans

Directions

Set your Instant Pot to Sauté and melt ghee. Stir-fry mustard powder, onion, and chili for 3 minutes until the onion is softened. Stir in rice and add 1 ¼ cups of water. Season with salt. Seal the lid, select Pressure Cook, and set the time to 5 minutes. After cooking, perform natural pressure release for 10 minutes. Unlock the lid and stir in pecans. Plate the rice. Serve and enjoy!

Teriyaki Rice with Turkey

Total Time: 40 minutes | **Servings:** 4

Ingredients

1 tbsp olive oil
1 tbsp sesame oil
1 lb turkey breast, cubed
Salt and black pepper to taste
1 red bell pepper, chopped
1 red onion, finely chopped

1 garlic clove, minced
1 cup jasmine rice, rinsed
1 cup chicken broth
¾ cup teriyaki sauce
1 cup fresh snow peas
1 tbsp sesame seeds

Directions

Set your Instant Pot to Sauté and heat olive oil. Season turkey with salt and pepper and fry it until golden, 7 minutes. Set aside. Add sesame oil to the pot and sauté bell pepper and onion until softened, 4 minutes. Stir in garlic and cook until fragrant, 30 seconds. Mix in the rice for 1 minute and stir in broth, teriyaki sauce, and turkey cubes.

Seal the lid, select Pressure Cook on High, and set the cooking time to 5 minutes. Allow sitting (covered) for 10 minutes and then perform quick pressure release to let out all the steam. Unlock the lid and press Sauté. Mix in snow peas and cook until softened, 5 minutes. Dish rice into serving bowls and garnish with sesame seeds.

Yellow Pepper & Beef Rice with Cheddar

Total Time: 40 minutes | **Servings:** 4

Ingredients

1 tbsp olive oil
1 lb ground beef
Salt and black pepper to taste
1 yellow bell pepper, diced
1 yellow onion, diced
2 garlic cloves, minced
1 cup basmati rice, rinsed

1 cup beef broth
1 tbsp Italian seasoning
¼ cup tomato sauce
2 cups chopped kale
½ cup grated cheddar cheese,
¼ cup grated Parmesan cheese
2 tbsp chopped parsley

Directions

Set your Instant Pot to Sauté and heat the olive oil. Cook the beef until no longer pink, 6 minutes. Season with salt and black pepper. Add in bell pepper, onion, and garlic and cook for 3 minutes, stirring frequently until the vegetables soften. Stir in rice for 1 minute. Pour in beef broth, Italian seasoning, and tomato sauce. Seal the lid, select Pressure Cook, and set the cooking time to 6 minutes. Allow sitting (covered) for 10 minutes and then do a quick pressure release. Unlock the lid and select Sauté.

Stir in kale to wilt, 2 minutes, then half of cheddar and Parmesan cheeses; let melt. Dish rice into serving plates. Garnish with the remaining cheddar and Parmesan cheese. Garnish with parsley and serve warm.

Vegetarian Taco Rice

Total Time: 35 minutes | **Servings:** 4

Ingredients

1 tbsp olive oil	3 green chilies, chopped
1 yellow onion, diced	1 ¾ cups vegetable broth
1 green bell pepper, diced	1 cup frozen corn kernels
1 red bell pepper, diced	1 (15 oz) can black beans, rinsed
1 yellow bell pepper, diced	Salt and black pepper to taste
2 garlic cloves, minced	½ cup sour cream
2 tbsp taco seasoning	¼ cup guacamole
1 ½ cups basmati rice, rinsed	4 tbsp chopped cilantro
1 (20 oz) can diced tomatoes	1 lime, cut into wedges

Directions

Set your Instant Pot to Sauté and heat olive oil. Sweat onion and bell peppers until softened, 4 minutes. Stir in garlic and stir-fry until fragrant, 30 seconds. Add rice and taco seasoning and cook for 1 minute. Pour in tomatoes, green chilies, and vegetable broth. Stir and seal the lid. Select Manual/Pressure Cook and set the cooking time to 6 minutes. Allow sitting for 10 minutes and then perform quick pressure release to let out all the steam.

Unlock the lid. Press Sauté. Stir in corn and black beans and season with salt and pepper. Heat through for 1-2 minutes. Turn the pot off and dish rice onto serving plates. Top with sour cream, guacamole, cilantro, and lime wedges. Serve.

Mascarpone & Mushroom Risotto

Total Time: 50 minutes | **Servings:** 4

Ingredients

4 tbsp olive oil	4 tbsp butter
1 oz grated Parmesan cheese, plus more for serving	
1 ½ lb mixed mushrooms, sliced	1 ½ cups arborio rice
4 cups vegetable stock	1 tbsp miso paste
1 oz dried porcini mushrooms	3/4 cup dry white wine
1 cup hot water	¼ cup heavy cream
Salt and black pepper to taste	2 tbsp mascarpone, softened
1 onion, chopped	A handful of minced chervil
2 cloves garlic, minced	

Directions

Soak the porcini mushrooms in hot water for 20 minutes. Then, drain them, reserving the liquid, and chop roughly; set aside. Set the pot to Sauté mode and melt butter and olive oil. Place in the fresh mushrooms, sprinkle with salt and pepper and cook for 8 minutes until browned.

Add in onion, garlic, porcini, salt, and pepper, and cook for 5 minutes until onion is tender and fragrant. Stir often. Put in the rice and miso paste and cook for 3-4 minutes, until well combined. Pour in the white wine and scrape off any browned bits at the bottom of the pot and add in the stock.

Seal the lid, select Pressure Cook on Low, and set the timer to 5 minutes. Do a quick pressure release and unlock the lid. Stir in heavy cream, mascarpone cheese, Parmesan, and chervil. Serve topped with some more Parmesan cheese.

Rice Stuffed Zucchini Flowers

Total Time: 35 minutes | **Servings:** 4

Ingredients

1 tbsp olive oil	1 tbsp chopped cilantro
1 brown onion, chopped	½ cup tomato sauce
¼ tsp coriander powder	½ cup vegetable broth
Salt and black pepper to taste	1 cup short-grain rice
2 tbsp chopped dill	20 zucchini flowers
2 tbsp chopped mint leaves	2 cups water

Directions

Set your Instant Pot to Sauté and heat the olive oil. Sauté the onion for 4 minutes. Add the coriander, salt, pepper, dill, mint, cilantro, and tomato sauce. Cook for 3-4 minutes to allow the flavors to incorporate. Mix in broth and rice.

Seal the lid, select Pressure Cook on High, and set the timer to 5 minutes. After cooking, do a natural pressure release for 10 minutes. Prepare a large ramekin on the side. Fluff the rice and spoon 2 to 3 tbsp of rice into each zucchini flower; lay stuffed flowers side by side in the ramekin.

Clean the pot and pour in water. Fit a trivet over water and sit ramekin on top. Seal the lid, select Pressure Cook on High, and set the cooking time to 2 minutes. Once done cooking, perform a quick pressure release to let out all the steam, and unlock the lid. Carefully remove the ramekin and plate the food. Serve warm with hot tomato sauce.

Tasty Lemon Risotto with Salmon

Total Time: 35 minutes | **Servings:** 4

Ingredients

2 tbsp olive oil	1 cup Arborio rice
3 tbsp butter	½ cup white wine
4 salmon fillets	1 tbsp squeezed lemon juice
Salt and black pepper to taste	2 cups vegetable broth
2 garlic cloves, minced	2 tbsp chopped parsley
1 white onion, finely chopped	2 lemons, cut into wedges

Directions

Set your Instant Pot to Sauté and heat olive oil. Season salmon with salt and black pepper, and fry (skin side down) until cooked to the touch. Transfer to a plate and set aside. Add garlic and onion to the oil and stir-fry them for 3 minutes. Stir in rice until transparent, 1 minute. Add wine and cook until reduced by two-thirds. Pour in lemon juice and broth. Seal the lid, select Pressure Cook, and set the time to 10 minutes. When done, perform natural pressure release for 10 minutes. Unlock the lid, add butter and mix vigorously until risotto is sticky. Adjust taste with salt and pepper. Spoon onto plates, top with fried salmon, and garnish with parsley and lemon wedges. Serve and enjoy!

Garlicky Broccoli & Pea Rice

Total Time: 40 minutes | **Servings**: 4

Ingredients

2 tbsp olive oil
1 yellow onion, chopped
1 head broccoli, cut into florets
2 garlic cloves, minced
Salt and black pepper to taste
1 tsp dried oregano

¼ cup white wine
1 ½ cups chicken broth
1 cup short-grain rice
½ cup frozen peas, thawed
¼ cup chopped parsley

Directions

Set your Instant Pot to Sauté, heat olive oil, and stir-fry the onion and garlic until softened, 5 minutes. Season with salt and black pepper. Pour in oregano and white wine.

Cook until wine reduces by one-third. Mix in chicken broth, broccoli, and rice. Seal the lid, press Pressure Cook on High, and set the cooking time to 8 minutes.

Allow sitting (covered) for 10 minutes and then perform a quick pressure release to let out the remaining steam.

Select Sauté and mix in peas; cook until warmed through, 3 to 5 minutes. Garnish with parsley and serve warm.

Tarragon Chicken with Brown Rice

Total Time: 50 minutes + cooling time | **Servings**: 4

Ingredients

1 tbsp coconut oil
1 cup brown rice
2 cups water
1 lb ground chicken
Salt and black pepper to taste

½ cup frozen mixed vegetables
2 tbsp soy sauce
2 eggs, beaten
1 tbsp chopped tarragon

Directions

Add rice and water to the inner pot. Seal the lid, select Manual/Pressure Cook, and set the timer to 22 minutes. Let sit for 10 minutes, then perform a quick pressure release.

Unlock the lid. Fluff and spoon rice into a medium bowl. Set aside until completely cool for 1 to 2 hours or overnight. Set the cooker to Sauté and heat coconut oil.

Add chicken, season with salt and pepper, and cook until no longer pink, 6 minutes. Stir in rice, vegetables, and cook until heated through, 3 minutes. Mix in soy sauce and create a hole at the center of rice. Pour in eggs and scramble until set. Mix into rice and tarragon. Serve and enjoy!

Red cabbage & Brown Rice Tray

Total Time: 30 minutes | **Servings**: 4

Ingredients

1 cup brown rice
1 ¼ cups water
Salt and black pepper to taste
½ cup shredded red cabbage
½ cup shredded carrots
1 red bell pepper, chopped
1 tbsp tamarind sauce

1 tbsp peanut butter
½ lemon, juiced
1 tsp honey
½ tsp grated ginger
1 garlic clove, minced
¼ tsp red chili flakes
2 tbsp chopped cilantro

Directions

Add rice, water, and salt to the inner pot. Seal the lid, select Pressure Cook and set the timer to 22 minutes. Do a quick pressure release, and unlock the lid. Fluff and spoon rice into a bowl and mix in cabbage, carrots, and bell pepper.

In a bowl, mix tamarind sauce, peanut butter, lemon juice, honey, ginger, garlic, and chili flakes. Pour dressing over rice mixture, adjust taste with salt and black pepper, and spread on a serving tray. Garnish with cilantro and serve.

California Sushi Rolls

Total Time: 40 minutes | **Servings**: 4

Ingredients

1 cup Japanese rice, rinsed
1 tbsp sugar

¼ cup apple cider vinegar
1 tsp salt

Sushi

4 tbsp black and white sesame seeds, on a plate
Bamboo sushi mat
4 nori sheets
1 cucumber, julienned

1 medium avocado, julienned
3 oz crabmeat, julienned

Directions

Combine rice and 2 cups of water in the inner pot. Seal the lid, select Pressure Cook, and set the cooking time to 7 minutes. Do a natural pressure release for 10 minutes, then a quick pressure release. In a medium bowl, combine sugar, vinegar, and salt. Spoon rice into a bowl and mix until well-coated. Spread on a wide tray and allow complete cooling.

Lay bamboo sheet on a flat surface and line with plastic wrap. Spoon a quarter of rice onto the sheet and press firmly. Lay 1 nori sheet on top and arrange a quarter of cucumber, avocado, and crabmeat at one end of nori sheet.

Holding bamboo sheet (at the side with the cucumber topping), roll rice over the filling while compressing as you roll. Remove mat, roll sushi in sesame seeds, and set aside on a tray. Repeat assembling the remaining sushi rolls. When done, slice each roll into 8 pieces using a sharp knife and plate. Serve with soy sauce, wasabi, and ginger slices.

Wild Rice Pilaf with Mixed Mushrooms

Total Time: 60 minutes | **Servings**: 4

Ingredients

2 tbsp olive oil
1 white onion, chopped
1 cups sliced mixed mushrooms
2 garlic cloves, minced
Salt and black pepper to taste
¼ cup white wine

½ tsp dried rosemary
1 cup wild rice
3 cups vegetable broth
½ cup sliced almonds
1 tbsp chopped parsley

Directions

Set your Instant Pot to Sauté, heat olive oil, and stir-fry onion, garlic, and mushrooms until softened, 5 minutes. Season with salt and black pepper. Mix in wine, rosemary; allow reduction by one-third. Add rice, broth, and season with salt and black pepper. Seal the lid, select Pressure Cook on High, and set the timer to 28 minutes. After cooking, perform a natural pressure release for 15 minutes, and then a quick pressure release to let out the steam. Stir in half of the parsley and all of the almonds. Dish rice into plates and garnish with parsley to serve.

Jalapeño Rice with Cilantro

Total Time: 30 minutes | **Servings**: 4

Ingredients

2 tbsp olive oil
1 cup white rice
1 garlic clove, minced
1 red onion, chopped
1 jalapeño pepper, minced
2 cups vegetable broth
Salt to taste
¼ cup chopped fresh cilantro
Zest and juice from 1 lemon

Directions

Set your Instant Pot to Sauté and heat olive oil. Cook garlic, onion, jalapeño pepper, and rice for 3 minutes until the vegetables are softened. Pour in broth and season with salt. Seal the lid, select Pressure Cook on High, and set the timer to 8 minutes. When done, perform a natural pressure release for 10 minutes. Stir in lemon juice and lemon zest. Cover the pot and leave the rice to rest for a few minutes. Fluff the rice with fork. Sprinkle with cilantro before serving.

Raspberry Risotto

Total Time: 25 minutes | **Servings**: 4

Ingredients

1 cup fresh raspberries, chopped (leave 3 for garnishing)
2 tbsp butter
1 small carrot, chopped
1 celery stalk, chopped
A pinch of salt
1 cup Arborio rice
½ cup sparkling wine
2 cups water
1 cup grated Pecorino Romano

Directions

Set your Instant Pot to Sauté, melt butter, and sauté carrot and celery for 6 minutes; season with salt. Stir in rice, cook for 1 minute, and stir in wine and water. Pour in raspberries. Seal the lid, select Pressure Cook, and set time to 10 minutes. After cooking, do a quick release. Mix in cheese until it is sticky. Garnish with the remaining raspberries and serve.

Coconut-Cashew Purple Rice

Total Time: 35 minutes | **Servings**: 4

Ingredients

1 tbsp coconut oil
½ cup raw cashews
2 garlic cloves, minced
1-inch ginger, grated
1 cup purple rice, well-rinsed
½ cup coconut milk

Directions

Set your Instant Pot to Sauté and heat coconut oil. Fry cashews for 2 minutes; set aside. Add garlic and ginger to the oil and sauté for 2 minutes. Stir in rice, coconut milk, and 1 ½ cups water. Seal the lid, select Manual/Pressure Cook, and set the timer to 22 minutes. After cooking, perform a quick pressure release. Stir in cashews. Serve warm.

Mediterranean-Style Lamb with Rice

Total Time: 30 minutes | **Servings**: 4

Ingredients

1 tbsp butter
¼ cup blended onion
2 tsp fresh ginger paste
2 tsp fresh garlic paste
1 lb ground lamb
Salt and black pepper to taste
1 cup basmati rice, rinsed
¼ cup chopped tomatoes
¼ cup green peas
1 cup water
¼ cup whole milk
1 tbsp chopped cilantro

Directions

Set your Instant Pot to Sauté and melt butter. Sauté onion, ginger, and garlic paste for 2 minutes. Stir in lamb, season with salt and pepper, and cook for 6 minutes or until no longer pink. Stir in rice, tomatoes, green peas, and cook for 3 minutes. Pour in water and milk and stir. Seal the lid, select Pressure Cook, and set the cooking time to 5 minutes. After cooking, do a natural pressure release for 10 minutes. Fuff the rice and plate; serve garnished with cilantro.

Chorizo & Rice Stuffed Bell Peppers

Total Time: 25 minutes | **Servings**: 4

Ingredients

4 bell peppers, tops and seeds removed
½ cup grated Mexican blend cheese
2 tsp olive oil
¾ lb chorizo
1 onion, chopped
1 cup chopped fresh tomatoes
1 ½ cups cooked rice

Directions

Select Sauté and heat olive oil. Cook the chorizo while breaking the meat with a spatula. Cook until just starting to brown, about 2 minutes. Add the onion and sauté for 3 more minutes. Scoop the chorizo and onion into a medium bowl. Add in the tomatoes, rice, and cheese and mix to combine well. Spoon the filling mixture into the peppers. Clean the pot with paper towels. Pour in 1 cup of water and fix in a trivet. Put the peppers on the trivet and cover with foil. Seal the lid, select Manual/Pressure Cook on High, and set the time to 12 minutes. After cooking, perform a quick pressure release. Remove the foil from the peppers and let cool for a few minutes before serving.

Walnut & Banana Oat Cups

Total Time: 25 minutes | **Servings**: 2

Ingredients

½ cup steel-cut oats
1 banana, mashed
1 tsp sugar
1 tbsp walnuts, chopped

Directions

Spread the banana onto the bottom of the inner pot. Pour 1 ½ cups water, steel-cut oats, and sugar over the banana. Seal the lid, select Pressure Cook, and cook for 6 minutes on High. When done, do a natural pressure release for 10 minutes, then a quick release. Unlock the lid and stir the oatmeal. Divide between cups. Top with walnuts and serve.

Blue Cheese-Parmesan Risotto

Total Time: 30 minutes | **Servings:** 4

Ingredients

2 tbsp olive oil
1 small shallot, minced
1 cup Arborio rice
¼ cup Sauvignon Blanc
2 cups chicken stock

1 cup crumbled blue cheese
½ cup heavy cream
¼ cup grated Parmesan cheese
½ cup frozen peas, thawed

Directions

Set cooker to Sauté, heat olive oil, and sauté shallot until softened, 2 minutes. Mix in rice and cook until transparent. Add wine and cook until reduced by two-thirds; stir in stock. Seal the lid, select Pressure Cook, and set to 10 minutes.

When done cooking, perform natural pressure release for 10 minutes. Add in blue cheese, heavy cream, and Parmesan cheese; mix until risotto is sticky and cheese melts. Stir in peas. Turn Instant Pot off and serve risotto.

Arborio Rice with White Beans

Total Time: 25 minutes | **Servings:** 4

Ingredients

1 (15 oz) canned white beans, drained and rinsed
2 tbsp olive oil
2 tbsp butter
1 yellow onion, chopped
3 garlic cloves, minced
¼ tsp fresh thyme leaves

2 cups chicken stock
½ cup Pinot Grigio (white wine)
1 cup Arborio rice
½ cup grated Parmesan cheese
Salt and black pepper to taste

Directions

Heat the olive oil in your Instant Pot on Sauté. Stir-fry onion, garlic, and thyme leaves until fragrant, 2 minutes. Add in chicken stock, white wine, and Arborio rice. Seal the lid, select Pressure Cook, and set the timer to 10 minutes.

When done cooking, perform natural pressure release for 10 minutes, then a quick pressure release to let out the remaining steam. Unlock the lid. Add butter, Parmesan cheese, salt, and black pepper to the pot. Stir the rice until sticky and the cheese melts. Fold in white beans and warm through on Sauté mode, 3 minutes. Plate risotto and serve.

Gouda & Parmesan Risotto

Total Time: 35 minutes | **Servings:** 4

Ingredients

¼ cup grated Parmesan cheese + 2 tbsp for garnishing
2 tbsp butter
½ cup short vermicelli
1 cup Arborio rice
2 tsp cinnamon powder

1 cup whole milk
1 ½ cups chicken broth
2 oz Gouda cheese, grated
Salt and black pepper to taste

Directions

On Sauté, melt butter and fry vermicelli until light brown, 5 minutes, stirring occasionally. Stir in rice and cinnamon, and cook until transparent. Add milk and broth. Seal the lid, select Pressure Cook, and set the timer to 10 minutes.

After cooking, do a natural pressure release for 10 minutes. Stir in cheeses, salt, and pepper and allow the cheese to melt on Sauté for 2 minutes. Stir and dish risotto-pilaf. Garnish with the remaining Parmesan and serve.

Pork & Buckwheat Cabbage Rolls

Total Time: 65 minutes | **Servings:** 4

Ingredients

1 head Savoy cabbage, leaves separated (scraps kept)
2 tbsp butter
½ sweet onion, finely chopped
2 garlic cloves, minced
1 lb ground pork
Salt and black pepper to taste

1 cup buckwheat groats
2 cups beef stock
2 tbsp chopped cilantro
1 (23 oz) canned diced tomatoes

Directions

Set your Instant Pot to Sauté, melt butter and sauté onion and garlic until slightly softened, 4 minutes. Stir in pork, season with salt and pepper, and cook until no longer pink, 5 minutes. Stir in buckwheat and beef stock. Seal the lid, select Pressure Cook on High, and set the time to 6 minutes. After cooking, do a quick pressure release.

Add cilantro and give the buckwheat mixture a good stir. Spread large cabbage leaves on a clean flat surface and spoon 3-4 tbsp of the mixture onto each leave center; roll. Clean the pot and spread cabbage scrap inside. Pour in tomatoes with liquid and arrange the cabbage rolls on top. Seal the lid, select Pressure Cook on Low and set the time to 25 minutes. Perform natural pressure release for 10 minutes. Remove the cabbage rolls onto serving plates. Enjoy!

Peanut Oatmeal with Strawberries

Total Time: 20 minutes | **Servings:** 2

Ingredients

1 cup old-fashioned rolled oats
2 cups milk
2 tbsp strawberry jam

3 tbsp peanut butter
¼ cup fresh strawberries
2 tbsp chopped roasted peanuts

Directions

Pour oats and milk into your Instant Pot. Stir in jam and peanut butter until well mixed. Pour in 1 cup of water. Seal the lid, select Pressure Cook on High, and set the time to 3 minutes. After cooking, do a natural pressure release for 10 minutes. Unlock the lid, stir, and spoon oatmeal into bowls. Top with strawberries, peanuts, and serve.

Feta & Mushroom Oatmeal

Total Time: 30 minutes | **Servings:** 2

Ingredients

1 tbsp butter
1 cup sliced cremini mushrooms
1 garlic clove, minced
1 tsp thyme leaves
Salt and black pepper to taste

1 cup chopped baby kale
1 cup old fashioned rolled oats
2 cups vegetable broth
¼ tsp red pepper flakes
¼ cup crumbled feta cheese

Directions

Set your Instant Pot to Sauté, melt butter and sauté mushrooms until slightly softened, 4 to 5 minutes. Stir in garlic, thyme, salt, and black pepper. Cook until fragrant, 3 minutes. Mix in kale to wilt; stir in oats, vegetable broth, and red pepper flakes. Seal the lid, select Pressure Cook on High, and set the time to 3 minutes. After cooking, do a natural pressure release for 10 minutes. Unlock the lid, stir, and adjust the. Dish oatmeal into bowls and top with feta.

Quick Oatmeal Bowls with Raspberries

Total Time: 15 minutes | **Servings:** 3

Ingredients

1 cup steel-cut oats	½ tsp vanilla extract
1 ½ cups milk	Fresh raspberries, for topping
2 tbsp honey	Toasted Brazil nuts, for topping

Directions

Add the oats, milk, honey, vanilla, and 1 cup of water into the inner pot. Seal the lid, select Pressure Cook, and set the time to 6 minutes on High. When done, do a quick pressure release to let out the steam. Unlock the lid and stir the oatmeal. Divide the porridge between serving bowls and top with raspberries and toasted Brazil nuts to serve.

Chocolate Oatmeal with Walnuts

Total Time: 20 minutes | **Servings:** 2

Ingredients

2 cups milk	½ cup dried cherries
1 cup old fashioned rolled oats	Greek Yogurt for topping
1 tbsp cocoa powder	¼ cup chopped walnuts
3 tbsp maple syrup	

Directions

Pour milk, oats, cocoa powder, maple syrup, and cherries into the inner pot. Seal the lid, select Pressure Cook on High, and set the cooking time to 3 minutes. After cooking, do a natural release for 10 minutes, then a quick release.

Unlock the lid, stir, and spoon oatmeal into serving bowls. Top with Greek yogurt, walnuts, and serve warm.

Maple Oatmeal with Dates & Pecans

Total Time: 20 minutes | **Servings:** 2

Ingredients

1 cup shredded carrots + extra for garnishing	
2 cups milk	1/8 tsp grated nutmeg
1 cup old fashioned rolled oats	1 tsp vanilla extract
2 tbsp maple syrup	¼ cup chopped dates
1 tsp cinnamon	¼ cup chopped pecans
¼ tsp ground ginger	

Directions

Pour milk, oats, carrots, maple syrup, cinnamon, ginger, nutmeg, 1 cup of water, and vanilla into your Instant Pot. Seal the lid, select Pressure Cook, and cook for 3 minutes.

After cooking, do a natural release for 10 minutes. Unlock lid, stir in dates and pecans, and spoon oatmeal into bowls. Top with remaining carrots and serve.

Black Currant-Coconut Rye Porridge

Total Time: 20 minutes | **Servings:** 2

Ingredients

1 cup rye flakes	1 tsp vanilla extract
A pinch of salt	2 tbsp maple syrup
1 ¼ cups coconut milk	¾ cup frozen black currants

Directions

In your Instant Pot, combine rye flakes, salt, coconut milk, water, vanilla, and maple syrup. Seal the lid, select Pressure Cook on High, and set the time to 5 minutes. After cooking, perform a natural pressure release for 10 minutes. Stir and spoon porridge into serving bowls. Top with black currants and serve warm.

Parmesan Barley Risotto with Mushrooms

Total Time: 40 minutes | **Servings:** 4

Ingredients

¼ cup grated Parmesan cheese + extra for garnishing	
3 tbsp butter, divided	Salt and black pepper to taste
1 red onion, finely chopped	1 cup pearl barley
2 garlic cloves, thinly sliced	½ cup dry white wine
½ lb Bella mushrooms, sliced	2 ½ cups beef broth, hot
2 tsp fresh thyme leaves	

Directions

On Sauté melt 2 tbsp of butter, and sauté red onion and garlic until softened, 5 minutes. Stir in mushrooms, salt, and pepper. Cook until mushrooms are tender, 4 minutes. Stir in barley and the remaining butter. Mix in wine until absorbed, 4 minutes. Pour broth, seal the lid, select Pressure Cook on High, and set the cooking time to 7 minutes.

After cooking, perform natural pressure release for 10 minutes. Mix in Parmesan cheese to melt, adjust taste with salt and black pepper, and spoon risotto into serving bowls. Garnish with Parmesan cheese and thyme. Serve warm.

Sesame Seed Topped Corn Oatmeal

Total Time: 20 minutes | **Servings:** 2

Ingredients

2 cups vegetable broth	1 cup fresh corn kernels
2 tbsp soy sauce	4 scallions, sliced and divided
1 cup old fashioned rolled oats	Salt and black pepper to taste
1 tsp hot sauce	½ tsp black sesame seed

Directions

Pour broth, soy sauce, oats, hot sauce, corn, and scallions into your Instant Pot. Seal the lid, select Pressure Cook on High, and set the time to 3 minutes. After cooking, do a natural release for 10 minutes. Season with salt and pepper, stir, and spoon the oatmeal into bowls. Garnish with sesame seeds. Serve with sunny side eggs. Enjoy

Chicken & Ginger Congee

Total Time: 30 minutes | **Servings:** 4

Ingredients

6 oz ground chicken
1 ½-inch piece ginger, grated
2 garlic cloves, minced
1 tbsp rice wine
½ tsp sugar
1 ½ tbsp soy sauce
½ cup jasmine rice, rinsed
2 cups water
Salt and black pepper, to taste
Peanuts, chopped for garnish
2 tbsp spring onions, chopped

Directions

Combine all the ingredients in your Instant Pot. Seal the lid, select Manual/Pressure Cook, and cook for 20 minutes on High. When done, do a quick pressure release. Unlock the lid and select Sauté. Cook until the desired thickness is reached (if too watery). Season to taste. Top with peanuts, spring onions, and soy sauce to serve.

Speedy Morning Oatmeal

Total Time: 15 minutes | **Servings:** 4

Ingredients

1 tbsp butter
1 tbsp flaxseed
3 cups rolled oats
1 chocolate square, grated

Directions

Combine butter, oats, flaxseed, and 6 cups of water in your Instant Pot; mix well. Seal the lid, select Pressure Cook, and set the time to 4 minutes. When done, do a quick release. Serve in bowls topped with chocolate.

Pecan & Pumpkin Buckwheat Porridge

Total Time: 25 minutes | **Servings:** 4

Ingredients

1 cup raw buckwheat groats
1 ½ cups milk
¼ cup pumpkin puree
1 tbsp maple syrup
1 tsp cinnamon powder
½ tsp vanilla extract
3 tbsp raisins
2 tbsp pumpkin seeds
¼ cup chopped pecans

Directions

Pour buckwheat, milk, pumpkin puree, maple syrup, cinnamon, ½ cup of water, and vanilla into your Instant Pot. Stir until pumpkin puree is well-spread. Seal the lid, select Pressure Cook on High, and set the cooking time to 6 minutes. After cooking, perform natural pressure release for 10 minutes. Unlock the lid, stir in raisins, and spoon porridge into serving bowls. Top with more milk as desired and garnish with pumpkin seeds and pecans. Serve.

Buckwheat Pilaf with Apricots & Figs

Total Time: 30 minutes | **Servings:** 4

Ingredients

1 tbsp olive oil
1 red bell pepper, diced
4 garlic cloves, minced
1 cup roasted buckwheat groats
½ cup yellow lentils
2 ¼ cups chicken broth
Salt and black pepper to taste
¾ tsp dried thyme
1 cup dried figs, chopped
½ cup dried apricots, chopped
½ cup toasted walnuts
½ cup chopped cilantro

Directions

Set your Instant Pot to Sauté, heat oil, and sauté bell pepper and garlic for 5 minutes. Mix in buckwheat, lentils, broth, salt, pepper, and thyme. Seal the lid, select Pressure Cook on High, and set time to 6 minutes. Do a natural pressure release for 10 minutes. Unlock lid, stir in figs, apricots, walnuts, and cilantro. Spoon pilaf into bowls and enjoy!

Morning Barley & Spinach Bowls

Total Time: 25 minutes | **Servings:** 4

Ingredients

1 tbsp olive oil
1 cup pearl barley
¼ cup chopped red onions
1 ½ cups chicken broth
Salt and black pepper to taste
4 oz ham, chopped
4 oz baby spinach, chopped
2 scallions, chopped
¼ tsp red chili flakes

Directions

Set your Instant Pot to Sauté, heat olive oil and sauté onion and barley until fragrant. Stir in broth and ½ cup water; season to taste. Seal the lid, select Pressure Cook on High, and set the time to 18 minutes. After cooking, do a quick pressure. Select Sauté. Stir in ham and spinach until spinach wilts. Garnish with scallions and chili flakes and serve.

Oatmeal with Berries

Total Time: 30 minutes | **Servings:** 4

Ingredients

2 cups old fashioned oats
¼ cup plain vinegar
½ tsp nutmeg powder
1 tbsp cinnamon powder
½ tsp vanilla extract
½ cup dried cranberries
2 raspberries, sliced
¼ tsp salt
Honey, for topping

Directions

Combine the oats, 4 cups of water, vinegar, nutmeg, cinnamon, vanilla, cranberries, raspberries, and salt in your Instant Pot. Seal the lid, select Pressure Cook on High, and set the time to 11 minutes. When done, perform a natural pressure release for 10 minutes. Stir the oatmeal, drizzle with honey and and serve.

Chicken & Corn Chowder with Potatoes

Total Time: 35 minutes | **Servings:** 4

Ingredients

8 bacon strips, chopped
4 garlic cloves, minced
1 white onion, chopped
2 jalapeños, minced
2 medium potatoes, chopped
3 cups frozen sweet corn kernels
1 chicken breast, cut into cubes
2 cups chicken broth
1 tsp dried thyme
1 tsp smoked paprika
Salt and black pepper to taste
¾ cup heavy cream
3 tbsp all-purpose flour
¼ cup chopped chives

Directions

Set your Instant Pot to Sauté and cook bacon in rendering fat for 5 minutes. Transfer to a paper towel-lined plate. Add chicken, garlic, onion, and jalapeño peppers to the pot and sauté for 6 minutes. Pour in potatoes, corn, broth, thyme, paprika, salt, and pepper; mix well. Seal the lid, select Pressure Cook on High, and set the timer to 10 minutes.

Meanwhile, in a bowl, combine heavy cream with flour and set aside. After cooking, do a quick pressure release. Unlock the lid. Stir in the heavy cream mixture and half of the bacon. Cook on Sauté for 5 minutes or until chowder thickens. Mix in chives, spoon soup into serving bowls, top with the remaining bacon, and serve warm.

Spicy Beef Quinoa

Total Time: 25 minutes | **Servings:** 4

Ingredients

1 tbsp olive oil	1 tbsp chili seasoning
1 lb ground beef	1 (8 oz) can black beans, rinsed
Salt and black pepper to taste	1 cup quick-cooking quinoa
1 onion, finely diced	1 (14 oz) can diced tomatoes
2 garlic cloves, minced	2 ½ cups chicken broth
1 red bell pepper, chopped	1 cup grated cheddar cheese
1 jalapeño pepper, minced	2 tbsp chopped cilantro
1 cup corn, fresh or frozen	2 limes, cut into wedges
1 tsp ground cumin	

Directions

Set your Instant Pot to Sauté, heat olive oil, and cook beef until no longer pink, 5 minutes. Season with salt and pepper. Add onion, garlic, bell pepper, and jalapeño, and corn and cook for 5 minutes until bell pepper softens. Stir in cumin, chili seasoning, and add black beans, quinoa, tomatoes, and broth. Seal the lid, select Pressure Cook on High, and set the time to 1 minute. After cooking, do a quick pressure, and unlock the lid. Select Sauté and sprinkle the food with cheddar cheese. Cook until cheese melts, 3 minutes. Spoon quinoa into serving bowls and garnish with cilantro and lime wedges. Serve and enjoy!

South American Style Quinoa

Total Time: 55 minutes | **Servings:** 4

Ingredients

1 cup dried black beans, soaked	1 tsp cumin powder
4 cups vegetable broth	1 tsp coriander powder
3 sweet potatoes, peeled, cubed	1 tsp cayenne pepper
1 cup white quinoa, rinsed	1 tsp garlic powder
1 cup corn kernels, thawed	Salt and black pepper to taste
½ tsp dried thyme	½ cup chopped scallions

Directions

Pour beans and broth into your Instant Pot. Seal the lid, select Pressure Cook on High, and cook for 30 minutes. After cooking, do a quick pressure release. Mix in potatoes and quinoa. Seal the lid again, and cook further 10 minutes on Pressure Cook.

When done, perform a quick pressure release. Select Sauté. Stir in the remaining ingredients and cook for 5 minutes. Garnish with scallions and serve warm.

Basil Chicken Quinoa with Parmesan

Total Time: 20 minutes | **Servings:** 4

Ingredients

2 chicken breasts, cut into bite-size pieces	
2 tbsp butter	Salt and black pepper to taste
2 leeks, sliced	1 ½ cups green peas
3 garlic cloves, minced	1 cup ricotta cheese
1 ½ cups quick-cooking quinoa	2 tbsp lemon zest
1 tbsp chopped rosemary	2 tbsp lemon juice
3 cups chicken broth	¼ cup fresh parsley, chopped
1 tsp dried basil	1 cup grated Parmesan cheese

Directions

Set your Instant Pot to Sauté, melt butter and sauté leeks until bright green and softened, 3 minutes. Mix in garlic and sauté until fragrant. Add quinoa, rosemary, broth, chicken, basil, salt, and pepper; give ingredients a good stir. Seal the lid, select Pressure Cook on High, and set time to 1 minute. Do a quick release and unlock the lid. Stir in ricotta cheese, green peas, lemon zest, lemon juice, and Parmesan cheese. Press Sauté and cook until cheese melts and chicken cooks through, 6 minutes. Adjust the taste. Spoon quinoa into bowls and garnish with parsley. Serve.

Sausage & Shrimp Grits

Total Time: 45 minutes | **Servings:** 4

Ingredients

1 lb jumbo shrimp, peeled and deveined	
1 tbsp olive oil	1 cup whole milk
1 tbsp butter	1 (8 oz) canned diced tomatoes
6 oz andouille sausage, diced	1 tbsp Cajun seasoning
1 yellow onion, diced	1 tsp cayenne pepper
2 garlic cloves, minced	¼ cup chopped chives
1 cup white wine	1 tbsp chopped parsley
1 cup corn grits	¼ cup heavy cream
1 cup chicken broth	

Directions

Set your Instant Pot to Sauté, heat olive oil, and fry sausage until slightly brown on all sides, 5 minutes. Add onion and garlic; cook until softened and fragrant. Stir in white wine and cook until reduced by one-third, 3 minutes. In a heatproof bowl, mix grits with chicken broth and milk. Stir in tomatoes, Cajun seasoning, and cayenne pepper.

Fit a trivet over the sausage mixture and place the grit bowl on top of the trivet. Seal the lid, select Pressure Cook on High, and set the time to 10 minutes. Do a natural release for 10 minutes. Unlock the lid and take out grit bowl. Mix in butter and set aside. Take out the trivet also. Select Sauté and stir in chives, parsley, and shrimp. Cook for 5 minutes and stir in heavy cream. Let cool for 2 minutes. Spoon grits into bowls and top with shrimp and sauce. Serve.

Milk & Honey Corn on the Cob

Total Time: 25 minutes | **Servings:** 4

Ingredients

1 stick butter, sliced thinly
2 cups whole milk
4 cups water
3 tbsp Creole seasoning
¼ cup honey
6-8 ears corn, shucked

Directions

Set your Instant Pot to Sauté and add milk, water, and butter, and begin warming with frequent stirring until butter melts, 3 minutes. Pour in Creole seasoning and honey; mix again until evenly combined. Place in corn pieces. Seal the lid, select Pressure Cook on High, and set the cooking time to 4 minutes. After cooking, do a natural release for 10 minutes. Unlock lid, stir, and using tongs, lift corn onto serving plates and allow slight cooling. Serve warm.

Carrot & Mushroom Beef Barley Soup

Total Time: 45 minutes | **Servings:** 4

Ingredients

1 cup cremini mushrooms, quartered
2 tbsp olive oil
1 lb stewing beef, cubed
Salt and black pepper to taste
3 celery stalks, chopped
2 carrots, chopped
1 yellow onion, diced
2 garlic cloves, minced
2 tsp Italian seasoning
1 cup pearl barley
½ cup diced tomatoes
4 cups beef broth
2 tbsp chopped parsley
1 bay leaf

Directions

Set your Instant Pot to Sauté. Heat the oil. Season beef with salt and pepper, and sear until brown, 4 minutes. Add celery, carrots, onion, garlic, mushrooms, and Italian seasoning; sauté until softened, 4 minutes. Stir in barley, tomatoes, bay leaf, and broth. Seal the lid, select Pressure Cook on High, and cook for 20 minutes. After cooking, do a natural release for 10 minutes. Unlock the lid, discard the bay leaf, and stir in parsley. Spoon soup into bowls to serve.

Artichoke & Zucchini Corn Risotto

Total Time: 35 minutes | **Servings:** 4

Ingredients

1 (6 oz) can artichokes, drained and chopped
2 tbsp olive oil
2 large white onion, chopped
4 garlic cloves, minced
1 medium zucchini, chopped
Salt and black pepper to taste
1 cup Arborio rice
½ cup white wine
2 cups corn kernels
2 ½ cups chicken stock
1 cup grated Parmesan cheese
1 tbsp lemon zest
3 tbsp lemon juice
½ cup chopped basil

Directions

Set your Instant Pot to Sauté. Heat the olive oil and sauté onion, garlic, and zucchini until softened, 5 minutes. Season with salt and pepper. Stir in rice and cook until translucent, 2 minutes. Mix in wine and allow reduction by one-third.

Add in corn and chicken stock. Seal the lid, select Pressure Cook on High, and set time to 6 minutes.

After cooking, do a natural release for 15 minutes. Unlock the lid. Add artichokes, Parmesan cheese, lemon zest, and lemon juice to the pot and stir until the risotto is sticky. Spoon the risotto into bowls and top with basil. Serve.

Tasty Shrimp Quinoa

Total Time: 20 minutes | **Servings:** 4

Ingredients

1 lb jumbo shrimp, peeled and deveined 2 tbsp butter
1 white onion, finely diced
1 red bell pepper, chopped
4 garlic cloves, minced
2 tsp smoked paprika
1 ½ cups quick-cooking quinoa
3 cups chicken broth
2 cups broccoli florets
Salt and black pepper to taste
1 lemon, zested and juiced
3 scallions, chopped

Directions

Melt the butter in your Instant Pot on Sauté. Stir-fry the onion and bell pepper for 4 minutes. Add garlic and paprika and cook for 1 minute. Stir in quinoa and pour in broth; season with salt and pepper. Seal the lid, select Pressure Cook on High, and set the timer to 1 minute.

Do a quick release. Mix in shrimp and broccoli, sprinkle with lemon zest and juice, and continue cooking on Sauté for 5 minutes. Garnish with scallions and serve in bowls.

Enchilada Chicken Quinoa

Total Time: 35 minutes | **Servings:** 4

Ingredients

1 lb chicken breasts, sliced
1 cup sweet onion, chopped
¾ cup poblano pepper, minced
1 cup frozen corn kernels
¾ cup mixed bell peppers, diced
1 (15 oz) can black beans
1 (15 oz) can tomatoes, diced
2 cups beef broth
1 (15 oz) can red enchilada sauce
3 garlic cloves, minced
1 pack taco seasoning
1 cup quinoa, rinsed

Topping

½ cup grated cheddar cheese
½ cup pico de gallo
3 tbsp cilantro leaves
1 avocado, pitted and sliced
1 jalapeño pepper, sliced into rings and deseeded

Directions

Season the chicken with taco seasoning and add it to your Instant Pot pot. Top with onion, poblano pepper, corn, mixed bell peppers, black beans, tomatoes, beef broth, enchilada sauce, quinoa, and garlic.

Seal the lid, select Pressure Cook on High, and set the cooking time to 10 minutes. After cooking, do a natural pressure release for 10 minutes. Unlock the lid, top with cheddar cheese, pico de gallo, cilantro, avocado, and jalapeño pepper. Serve warm and enjoy!

CHICKEN RECIPES

Juicy Lemon-Garlic Chicken

Total Time: 30 minutes | **Servings**: 4

Ingredients

2 tbsp olive oil
3 tbsp butter
4 chicken breasts
1 white onion, finely chopped
2 garlic cloves, minced

1 cup milk
½ cup chicken broth
½ lemon, juiced
1 lemon, sliced
2 tbsp chopped parsley

Directions

Set your Instant Pot to Sauté, heat olive oil and fry the chicken until golden brown on both sides, 4 minutes; set aside. Melt butter in the pot and sauté onion and garlic until softened, 3 minutes. Stir in milk, broth, and place chicken in sauce. Seal the lid, select Pressure Cook on High, and set the time to 4 minutes.

Do a natural release for 10 minutes. Unlock the lid, stir in lemon juice, stick in lemon slices, and simmer on Sauté for 2 minutes. Dish chicken with sauce into bowls, garnish with parsley, and serve with mashed potatoes.

Chicken & Sausage Rice

Total Time: 40 minutes + marinating time | **Servings**: 4

Ingredients

Marinade

1 tbsp olive oil
½ tsp dried minced onion
½ tsp cayenne pepper
1 tsp salt
1 tsp garlic powder
1 ½ tsp paprika

½ tsp chili pepper
½ tsp dried basil
¼ tsp red pepper flakes
1 tsp lemon juice
4 chicken thighs

Rice

2 tbsp olive oil
1 link andouille sausages, sliced
1 jalapeño, deseeded and diced
1 medium yellow onion, diced
2 celery stalks, diced
A pinch of red pepper flakes

¼ tsp cayenne pepper
1 cup basmati rice
2 ¼ cups chicken broth
Salt and black pepper to taste
2 tbsp scallions, for garnishing
2 tbsp chopped parsley

Directions

In a bowl, combine onion, cayenne, salt, garlic powder, paprika, chili pepper, basil, red flakes, lemon juice, and olive oil. Place in chicken, coat in marinade, cover with plastic wrap and chill in the fridge for 1 hour.

Set your Instant Pot to Sauté and heat olive oil. Remove chicken from marinade and sear until golden brown, 6 minutes; set aside. Brown sausages in the pot for 5 minutes and spoon next to the chicken.

To the pot, add jalapeño, onion, and celery. Sauté until softened, 3 minutes. Stir in red pepper flakes, cayenne pepper, rice, broth, salt, and pepper. Place chicken and sausages on top.

Seal the lid, select Pressure Cook on High, and set the time to 5 minutes. Let sit for 10 minutes and then perform a quick pressure release. Top with scallions and parsley.

Chicken Drumsticks in Adobo Sauce

Total Time: 35 min + marinating time | **Servings**: 4

Ingredients

3 tbsp olive oil
1 lb chicken drumsticks
½ cup plain vinegar
½ cup soy sauce
1 bay leaf, ground
10 Ancho chilies, seeded
Guajillo dried chilies, seeded

8 garlic cloves, peeled
½ tsp Mexican oregano
½ tsp cumin powder
A pinch clove powder
Salt and black pepper to taste
¼ cup apple cider vinegar
2 tbsp chopped cilantro

Directions

In a bowl, combine chicken, vinegar, soy sauce, and bay leaf. Cover the bowl with a plastic wrap and marinate the chicken in the fridge for 1 hour. Set your Instant Pot to Sauté. Remove chicken from fridge and marinade. Fry in oil on both sides until golden brown, 6 minutes. Transfer to a paper towel-lined plate and set aside to drain fat.

Meanwhile, in a blender, grind chilies, garlic, Mexican oregano, half of the olive oil, cumin and clove powders until smooth paste forms. Pour mixture into the oil and stir-fry until fragrant, 3 minutes. Add salt, pepper, vinegar, and 1 cup water; stir and arrange chicken in the sauce. Seal the lid, select Pressure Cook on High, and set the time to 4 minutes. After cooking, do a natural pressure release for 10 minutes. Unlock the lid, stir, and adjust taste with salt and black pepper. Spoon chicken with sauce into serving bowls and garnish with cilantro. Serve warm with rice.

Buttery Caper & Chicken Piccata

Total Time: 25 minutes | **Servings**: 4

Ingredients

1 ½ tbsp all-purpose flour + ½ cup for dipping
3 tbsp butter, softened
2 tbsp olive oil
4 chicken breasts
Salt and black pepper to taste
¼ cup dry white wine

1 cup chicken broth
2 lemons, juiced
¼ cup drained capers
¼ cup chopped cilantro

Directions

Place chicken between two plastic wraps and. using a meat pounder, lightly pound until about ¼-inch thickness. Take off the plastic wrap and season with salt and pepper. In a bowl, combine 1 tbsp butter with 1 ½ tbsp flour until smooth. Pour remaining flour on a plate. Set your Instant Pot to Sauté and heat olive oil.

Dip chicken in flour, and fry until golden brown, 8 minutes; set aside. Pour the wine, chicken broth, and lemon juice into the inner pot, allow boiling, and stir in butter mixture. Stir in capers, remaining butter, cilantro, and cook until sauce thickens, 2 minutes. Adjust the taste. Plate chicken and spoon sauce all over. Serve warm with mashed potatoes.

West Country Chicken with Vegetables

Total Time: 35 minutes | **Servings:** 4

Ingredients

½ lb baby russet potatoes, quartered
2 tbsp olive oil
1 lb chicken thighs
Salt and black pepper to taste
½ lb asparagus, stems removed
2 large carrots, chopped
½ lb radishes, halved

2 cups chicken broth
2 tbsp smoked paprika
1 tsp garlic powder
1 tsp onion powder
3 fresh rosemary sprigs

Directions

Set your Instant Pot to Sauté. Heat olive oil, season chicken with salt and pepper, and fry until golden brown on both sides, 6 minutes; set aside. Sweat asparagus and carrots in the pot for 1 minute. Add potatoes, radishes, broth, paprika, garlic powder, onion powder, rosemary, and chicken. Seal the lid, select Pressure Cook, and set the time to 4 minutes.

After cooking, do a natural pressure release for 10 minutes. Unlock the lid, discard rosemary sprigs, stir, and adjust the taste. Spoon chicken and vegetables onto serving plates; set aside. Select Sauté and cook the remaining sauce until reduced and thickened, 2 minutes. Drizzle sauce over chicken and vegetables and serve warm.

Red Cili & Mango Glazed Chicken

Total Time: 30 minutes | **Servings:** 4

Ingredients

1 tbsp butter
1 lb chicken breasts, halved
Salt and black pepper to taste
1 medium mango, chopped

1 small red chili, minced
2 tbsp spicy mango chutney
1 cup chicken broth
2 scallions, thinly sliced

Directions

Set Sauté, melt butter, season chicken with salt and pepper, and cook until golden brown, 8 minutes. Plate chicken and set aside. To the pot, add mango, red chili, mango chutney, and broth. Seal the lid, select Pressure Cook on High, and set the time to 1 minute. After cooking, do a natural pressure release for 10 minutes. Unlock the lid, stir the sauce, and season to taste. Spoon sauce over chicken, garnish with scallions and serve with steamed spinach.

Cumin Chicken Pozole

Total Time: 35 minutes | **Servings:** 4

Ingredients

1 pound chicken thighs, skinless and boneless
1 tbsp olive oil
1 medium onion, chopped
6 garlic cloves, minced
1 tbsp tomato paste
2 green chilis, minced
2 tsp cumin powder
1 tbsp chili powder
2 tsp dried oregano
½ tsp chipotle paste

Salt and black pepper to taste
4 cups chicken broth
3 cups cooked hominy
1 lime, juiced
½ cup shredded red cabbage
1 cup sour cream
1 avocado, pitted and sliced
1 lime, cut into wedges
½ cup grated cheddar cheese

Directions

Set your Instant Pot to Sauté, heat olive oil, and sauté onion, garlic, tomato paste, and green chilies. Cook until softened, 3 minutes. Mix in cumin and chili powders, oregano, chipotle paste, salt, and pepper; cook until fragrant, 30 seconds. Add chicken, broth, and hominy. Seal the lid, select Pressure Cook on High, and set the time to 12 minutes. Do a natural pressure release for 10 minutes. Remove chicken to a plate, shred into strands, return to sauce, and stir in lime juice; adjust the taste. Dish into bowls and top with cabbage, sour cream, avocado, lime wedges, and cheddar. Serve.

Gruyere Chicken with Bell Peppers

Total Time: 35 minutes | **Servings:** 4

Ingredients

1 tbsp olive oil
1 large white onion, chopped
2 red bell peppers, chopped
2 green bell peppers, chopped
Salt and black pepper to taste
2 garlic cloves, minced
¾ cup marinara sauce

2 tbsp basil pesto
4 chicken breasts
1 cup chicken broth
1 cup sliced Bella mushrooms
1 cup grated Gruyere cheese
4 flatbreads, warmed
2 tbsp chopped parsley

Directions

Set your Instant Pot to Sauté, heat olive oil, and sauté onion, bell peppers, salt, and pepper until softened, 3 minutes. Stir in garlic and cook until fragrant, 30 seconds. Add marinara sauce, pesto, chicken, and chicken broth. Seal the lid, select Pressure Cook on High, and set the time to 12 minutes. After cooking, do a natural pressure release for 5 minutes.

Remove chicken to a plate; shred into strands. Fetch out a two-thirds cup of liquid in the inner pot, making sure to leave in vegetables. Select Sauté and mix in mushrooms. Cook until softened, 3 minutes. Stir in chicken, adjust the taste, and mix in Gruyere cheese to melt. Spoon mixture onto flatbread, garnish with parsley, and serve.

Chicken Shawarma Wraps

Total Time: 30 minutes + marinating time | **Servings:** 4

Ingredients

3 tbsp olive oil
1 lb chicken breasts
½ cup + 2 tbsp yogurt
2 tbsp lemon juice
3 garlic cloves, minced
1 tsp ground cumin
¼ tsp cinnamon powder
1 tsp smoked paprika
¼ tsp turmeric

Salt and black pepper to taste
¼ tsp cayenne pepper
4 lettuce leaves
2 tbsp Italian herb mix
1 tbsp chopped fresh cilantro
2 large tomatoes, sliced
½ medium cucumber, sliced
1 cup water

Directions

In a bowl, mix 2 tbsp of olive oil, 2 tbsp of yogurt, lemon juice, half of the garlic, cumin, cinnamon, paprika, turmeric, salt, pepper, and cayenne pepper. Pour the marinade and chicken in a plastic zipper bag. Seal the bag and massage to coat thoroughly. Refrigerate for 1 hour.

Pour water into the pot and insert a trivet. Place chicken on top, seal the lid, select Pressure Cook, and cook for 15 minutes. When ready, do a quick release. Shred the chicken.

Whisk the remaining olive oil, salt, remaining yogurt, Italian herb mix, cilantro, and remaining garlic in a bowl until combined. Spread 1 to 2 tbsp of yogurt sauce onto a lettuce leaf. Spoon in some chicken and add the tomato and cucumber slices. Wrap the leaf over the filling, repeat the assembling process for the remaining leaves and serve.

Teriyaki Chicken with Brussels Sprouts

Total Time: 35 minutes | **Servings**: 4

Ingredients

1 tbsp honey	4 chicken breasts
1 cup teriyaki sauce	1 cup Brussels sprouts, halved
1 cup chicken broth	2 tbsp chopped scallions

Directions

In your Instant Pot, mix honey and teriyaki sauce until combined. Stir in broth and place in chicken. Seal the lid, select Pressure Cook on High, and set the time to 12 minutes. When ready, do a natural release for 10 minutes. Remove chicken onto a plate and shred into strands. Fetch out two-thirds of cooking liquid and return chicken with Brussels sprouts to the pot. Select Sauté. Cook until Brussels sprouts soften, 5 minutes. Stir in scallions and serve.

Chicken & Egg Noodle One-Pot

Total Time: 20 minutes | **Servings**: 4

Ingredients

2 tbsp butter	12 oz frozen egg noodles
1 lb chicken breast strips	6 cups chicken stock
Salt and black pepper to taste	1 tsp chicken seasoning
1 small onion, chopped	½ tsp dried thyme
1 garlic clove, minced	1 tbsp cornstarch
16 oz bag mixed vegetables	1 tsp dried parsley

Directions

Set your Instant Pot to Sauté. Melt the butter, season chicken with salt and pepper, and fry until golden, 4 minutes. Add onion and garlic cook until softened, 3 minutes. Pour in mixed vegetables, top with noodles, stock, seasoning, and thyme; stir. Seal the lid, select Pressure Cook on High, and set the time to 3 minutes.

After cooking, perform a quick pressure release, and unlock the lid. Stir in cornstarch, select Sauté, and allow the sauce to thicken for 1 minute. Adjust taste with salt and pepper. Spoon into bowls, garnish with parsley and serve.

Chicken with Salsa Verde

Total Time: 30 minutes | **Servings**: 4

Ingredients

1 large yellow onion, chopped	Salt and black pepper to taste
1 cup salsa verde	4 chicken breasts, cut into
1 cup chicken broth	1-inch cubes

Directions

In your Instant Pot, combine onion, salsa verde, broth, salt, pepper, and chicken. Seal the lid, select Pressure Cook on High, and set the time to 12 minutes. Do a natural pressure release for 10 minutes. Plate chicken and serve warm.

Paprika Chicken with Pomegranate

Total Time: 45 minutes | **Servings**: 4

Ingredients

2 tbsp olive oil	2 tbsp ras el hanout
4 chicken thighs, bone-in	1 tsp smoked paprika
Salt and black pepper to taste	1 tsp cumin powder
2 carrots, peeled and chopped	½ tsp cinnamon powder
1 large onion, chopped	1 cup chicken broth
1 tsp fresh ginger puree	½ lemon, juiced
3 garlic cloves, minced	½ cup frozen peas
15 oz canned diced tomatoes	1 tbsp fresh parsley, chopped
1 tbsp balsamic vinegar	1 tbsp pomegranate to garnish

Directions

Set your Instant Pot to Sauté, heat olive oil, season chicken with salt and pepper, and cook until brown on both sides, 6 minutes. Transfer to a plate and set aside. Stir-fry carrots and onion until softened, 3 minutes. Add ginger, garlic, and cook until fragrant, 30 seconds. Mix in tomatoes, vinegar, ras el hanout, paprika, cumin, cinnamon, and cook until tomatoes begin to soften 3 minutes. Add chicken broth, lemon juice, salt, black pepper, and the chicken. Seal the lid, select Pressure Cook on High, and set the time to 10 minutes. After cooking, do a natural pressure release for 10 minutes. Unlock the lid, stir in peas and parsley, and adjust taste with salt and pepper. Cook on Sauté to warm the peas, 2 minutes. Spoon tagine into serving bowls, garnish with pomegranate, and serve warm with pita bread.

Kale Chicken Cacciatore with Mushrooms

Total Time: 40 minutes | **Servings**: 4

Ingredients

2 tbsp olive oil	½ cup short-grain rice
4 chicken breasts	15 oz can diced tomatoes
Salt and black pepper to taste	1 cup chicken broth
1 white onion, chopped	1 tbsp Italian seasoning
1 cup sliced button mushrooms	¼ cup grated Parmesan cheese
¼ tsp ginger paste	2 cups kale, steamed

Directions

Set the pot to Sauté, heat olive oil, season chicken with salt and pepper, and sear in oil on both sides until golden brown, 4 minutes. Remove onto a plate. Add onion and mushrooms to the oil and cook until softened, 4 minutes. Add ginger and allow releasing of fragrance, 1 minute. Stir in rice, tomatoes, broth, and Italian seasoning. Adjust the taste; return chicken to pot. Seal the lid, select Pressure Cook on High, and set the time to 10 minutes. After cooking, do a natural release for 10 minutes. Spoon cacciatore over a bed of steamed kale. Garnish with Parmesan and serve.

Orange Chicken with Sesame Seeds

Total Time: 40 minutes | **Servings:** 4

Ingredients

2 tbsp olive oil
2 tbsp cornstarch mixed with 2 tbsp orange juice
4 chicken breasts, cubed
Salt and black pepper to taste
1 cup orange juice
6 garlic cloves, minced
2 tbsp ginger puree
1 tbsp dry white wine
¼ cup honey
¼ cup brown sugar
¼ cup coconut aminos
1 tbsp hot sauce
1 cup chicken broth
1 orange, zested
4 scallions, chopped
1 tbsp sesame seeds

Directions

Set your Instant Pot to Sauté, heat olive oil, season chicken with salt and pepper, and sear until golden, 5 minutes. In a bowl, mix orange juice, garlic, ginger, wine, honey, sugar, coconut aminos, hot sauce, broth, and orange zest.

Pour mixture onto chicken and stir. Seal the lid, select Pressure Cook on High, and set the time to 12 minutes. After cooking, do a natural release for 10 minutes, and unlock the lid. Mix in cornstarch mixture and cook on Sauté until syrupy, for 3 minutes. Dish food onto serving plates, garnish with scallions and sesame seeds, and serve.

Lemony Chicken Rice with Asparagus

Total Time: 40 minutes | **Servings:** 4

Ingredients

1 tbsp olive oil
4 chicken breasts
1 tsp garlic salt
½ cup onion, finely diced
2 garlic cloves, minced
1 cup jasmine rice
1 lemon, zested and juiced
2 ¼ cups chicken broth
1 cup asparagus, chopped
1 tbsp parsley for garnish
Black pepper to taste
Lemon slices to garnish

Directions

Set your Instant Pot to Sauté, heat olive oil, season chicken with garlic salt and pepper, and sear until golden brown, 6 minutes; set aside. Add onion and garlic to the pot and cook until softened, 3 minutes.

Stir in rice and cook until translucent, 3 minutes. Add lemon zest, lemon juice, broth, asparagus, salt, pepper, and place chicken on top. Seal the lid, select Pressure Cook on High, and set the time to 5 minutes. After cooking, perform natural release for 15 minutes. Unlock the lid, fluff rice, and plate. Garnish with parsley and lemon slices to serve.

Spicy Chicken Manchurian

Total Time: 30 minutes | **Servings:** 4

Ingredients

½ cup olive oil
2 tbsp sesame oil
4 tbsp cornstarch, divided
2 eggs, beaten
2 tbsp soy sauce, divided
Salt and black pepper to taste
4 chicken breasts, cubed
1 tbsp fresh garlic paste
1 tbsp fresh ginger paste
1 red chili, sliced
2 tbsp hot sauce
½ tsp honey
1 cup chicken broth
2 scallions, sliced

Directions

Set your Instant Pot to Sauté and heat olive oil. Whisk cornstarch, eggs, soy sauce, salt, and pepper. Pour chicken into mixture and stir to coat well. Fry coated chicken until golden brown on all sides, 8 minutes. Transfer to a paper towel-lined plate to drain grease. Empty the inner pot, wipe clean with a paper towel, and return to base.

Heat in sesame oil and sauté garlic, ginger, and red chili until fragrant and chili softened, 1 minute. Stir in hot sauce, honey, broth, and arrange chicken in sauce.

Seal the lid, select Pressure Cook mode on High, and set the time to 3 minutes. After cooking, do natural pressure release for 10 minutes. Garnish with scallions. Serve warm.

Maple-Mustard Chicken

Total Time: 35 minutes | **Servings:** 4

Ingredients

¼ cup balsamic vinegar
2 tbsp maple syrup
1 tbsp Dijon mustard
1 cup chicken broth
1 brown onion, chopped
2 garlic cloves, minced
½ tsp dried thyme
4 chicken breasts

Directions

In your Instant Pot, mix balsamic vinegar, maple syrup, mustard, broth, onion, garlic, thyme, and chicken. Seal the lid, select Pressure Cook, and set the time to 12 minutes. After cooking, do a natural release for 10 minutes. Remove chicken to a plate and shred it with two forks. Return to the pot and press Sauté. Cook until sauce thickens, 5 minutes.

Mushroom & Spinach Chicken with Rotini

Total Time: 30 minutes | **Servings:** 4

Ingredients

2 tbsp butter
4 chicken breasts, cubed
Salt and black pepper to taste
1 small yellow onion, diced
2 cups sliced white mushrooms
1 garlic clove, minced
1 lb rotini pasta
6 cups chicken broth
1 tsp chopped oregano
4 cups chopped baby spinach
½ cup crumbled goat cheese

Directions

Set your Instant Pot to Sauté, melt butter, season chicken with salt and pepper, and sear until golden brown, 4 minutes; set aside. Add onion, garlic, and mushrooms and cook until softened, 4 minutes.

Return chicken to the pot, stir in rotini, chicken broth, and oregano. Seal the lid, select Pressure Cook on High, and set the time to 3 minutes.

After cooking, do a natural pressure release for 10 minutes. Select Sauté and unlock the lid. Stir in spinach, allow wilting, and mix in goat cheese until adequately incorporated. Adjust taste with salt, black pepper, and serve warm.

Traditional Coq Au Vin

Total Time: 45 minutes | **Servings:** 4

Ingredients

1 tbsp olive oil	½ cup chicken stock
4 chicken leg quarters, skin on	1 ½ tsp tomato puree
4 serrano ham, cut into thirds	½ tsp brown sugar
1 onion, sliced	½ cup mushrooms
1 ¼ cups dry red wine	¾ cup shallots, sliced

Directions

Set your Instant Pot to Sauté. Heat the olive oil. Place the ham in a single layer and brown for 4 minutes; remove to a plate. Add in the chicken and cook for 5 minutes, until the skin is golden brown; set aside. Stir in onion, mushrooms, and shallots and cook until the onion begins to brown, 4 minutes. Add ½ cup of wine and scrape the bottom off any browned bits. Boil the mixture until the wine reduces by 1/3, for 2 minutes. Pour in the remaining wine, stock, tomato puree, and sugar; boil for 1 minute. Return in the chicken, skin-side up, seal the lid, select Pressure Cook on High, and set the time to 12 minutes. After cooking, allow a natural release. Plate and crumble the ham on top.

Chicken Stroganoff with Fettucini

Total Time: 35 minutes | **Servings:** 4

Ingredients

2 tbsp butter	4 cups chicken stock
2 chicken breasts, cubed	8 oz fettucini
Salt to taste	½ tsp Worcestershire sauce
½ cup sliced onions	1 cup white mushrooms, sliced
1 tbsp flour	¼ cup heavy cream
½ cup dry white wine	2 tbsp chopped dill

Directions

On Sauté, melt the butter and cook the chicken for 5-6 minutes, stirring occasionally; reserve. Sauté the onion in the pot for 3 minutes until tender. Add in the flour and stir to make a roux. Gradually pour in the dry white wine while stirring and scraping the bottom of the pot to release any browned bits. Allow the wine to reduce by two-thirds.

Pour in stock and mushrooms and return the chicken; adjust the taste with salt. Seal the lid, select Pressure Cook on High, and set the time to 15 minutes. When done, do a quick pressure release. Unlock the lid and add fettucini. Seal the lid again and cook for 4 minutes on Manual. Do a quick release.

Open the lid and stir in the Worcestershire sauce and heavy cream and cook until for 3 minutes on Saut´´e. Ladle the stroganoff into bowls and garnish with dill. Serve.

Curry Chicken with Basmati Rice

Total Time: 40 minutes | **Servings:** 4

Ingredients

2 tbsp olive oil	Salt and black pepper to taste
4 chicken thighs	2 medium carrots, julienned
1 red bell pepper, thinly sliced	1 cup basmati rice
2 tbsp red curry paste	1 ½ cups chicken broth
1 garlic clove, minced	1 cup coconut milk
1 tsp ginger paste	1 lime, cut into wedges

Directions

Set your Instant Pot to Sauté, heat olive oil, season chicken with salt and pepper, and sear until golden brown on both sides, 6 minutes; set aside. Add carrots and bell pepper to oil and cook until softened, 4 minutes. Stir in curry paste, garlic, and ginger; sauté for 1 minute. Add rice, broth, and coconut milk and give ingredients a good stir. Arrange chicken on top. Seal the lid, select Pressure Cook on High, and set the time to 10 minutes. After cooking, do a natural release for 10 minutes. Unlock the lid, fluff rice, and adjust the taste. Garnish with lime wedges and serve.

Tamarind Chicken

Total Time: 25 minutes | **Servings:** 4

Ingredients

2 tbsp olive oil	1 tbsp honey
4 chicken thighs, bone-in	1 cup chicken broth
3 tbsp Dijon mustard	3 garlic cloves, minced
1 tbsp tamarind sauce	1 tbsp chopped parsley

Directions

Set your Instant Pot to Sauté and heat olive oil. Sear the chicken until golden brown on both sides, 6 minutes. In a bowl, combine mustard, tamarind sauce, honey, chicken broth, and pour into pot along with garlic. Seal the lid, select Pressure Cook on High, and set the cooking time to 2 minutes.

After cooking, do a natural pressure release for 10 minutes, then quick pressure release to let out the remaining steam. Unlock the lid. Dish the chicken and sauce. Sprinkle with parsley and serve. Enjoy!

Chicken Taco Bowls

Total Time: 35 minutes | **Servings:** 4

Ingredients

2 tbsp olive oil	2 ½ cups chicken broth
4 chicken breasts, cubed	Salt and black pepper to taste
1 tbsp taco seasoning	½ cup grated cheddar cheese
1 ½ cups salsa	2 scallions, chopped
½ cup sweet corn kernels	½ cup chopped cilantro
1 (15 oz) can black beans	1 avocado, pitted and chopped
1 ¼ cups basmati rice, rinsed	1 cup sour cream

Directions

Set your Instant Pot to Sauté, heat olive oil, season chicken breasts with taco seasoning, and sear it until golden, 5 minutes. Mix in salsa, corn kernels, black beans, rice, and broth and season with salt and pepper. Seal the lid, select Pressure Cook on High, and set the time to 8 minutes. Allow sitting (covered) for 10 minutes and then perform a quick pressure release. Top with cheddar cheese, scallions, cilantro, avocado, and sour cream and serve.

Louisiana-Style Chicken Quinoa

Total Time: 15 minutes | **Servings:** 4

Ingredients

2 tbsp olive oil
4 chicken breasts, thinly sliced
1 tsp Creole seasoning
2 green bell peppers, sliced
1 cup dry rainbow quinoa
2 cups chicken broth
1 lemon, zested and juiced
2 chives, chopped

Directions

Set your Instant Pot to Sauté, heat olive oil, season chicken with Creole seasoning, and fry it with bell peppers for 5 minutes until the chicken is golden brown on all sides, and peppers soften. Stir in quinoa and broth. Seal the lid, select Pressure Cook on High, and set the time to 1 minute.

After cooking, do a quick pressure release, and press Sauté. Fluff quinoa and stir in lemon zest, lemon juice, and chives. Dish meal into bowls and serve with hard-boiled eggs.

Creamy Ranch Chicken

Total Time: 35 minutes | **Servings:** 4

Ingredients

2 bacon slices, chopped
1 oz pack ranch seasoning
1 cup chicken broth
4 chicken breasts
4 oz cream cheese, softened
2 tbsp chopped scallions

Directions

Set your Instant Pot to Sauté and cook bacon until crispy and brown, 5 minutes. Stir in ranch seasoning, broth, and chicken. Seal the lid, select Pressure Cook on High, and set the time to 12 minutes. After cooking, do a natural pressure release for 10 minutes. Unlock the lid and remove chicken onto a plate and select Sauté mode. Shred chicken with two forks and return to sauce. Stir in cream cheese until melted and mix in scallions. Dish and serve warm.

Asiago Chicken with Thyme Sauce

Total Time: 30 minutes | **Servings:** 4

Ingredients

2 tbsp olive oil
4 chicken breasts
Salt and black pepper to taste
1 small white onion, diced
2 tbsp all-purpose flour
1 ½ cups chicken broth
2 tsp chopped thyme leaves
½ cup grated Asiago cheese

Directions

Set your Instant Pot to Sauté and heat olive oil. Season chicken with salt and pepper and sear it for 4 minutes; set aside. Add onion to the pot and sauté for 3 minutes. Stir in flour until light brown and mix in broth and thyme. Allow reduction by one-third and stir in cheese to melt. Place chicken in sauce and turn over a few times until well-coated.

Seal the lid, select Pressure Cook on High, and set the cooking time to 3 minutes. Do a natural release for 10 minutes. Unlock the lid, stir, and place chicken on serving plates. Spoon sauce all over and serve with mashed potatoes.

Chicken Soup with Artichokes & Vermicelli

Total Time: 40 minutes | **Servings:** 4

Ingredients

2 tbsp olive oil
1 yellow onion, chopped
2 celery stalks, chopped
2 large carrots, chopped
5 garlic cloves, minced
2 chicken breasts, cubed
4 cups chicken stock
2 tsp Italian seasoning
2 bay leaves
Salt and black pepper to taste
½ tsp chili powder
½ lemon, juiced
3 cups chopped artichoke hearts
¼ cup vermicelli

Directions

Set your Instant Pot to Sauté, heat olive oil, and sauté onion, celery, carrots, until softened, 3 minutes. Stir in garlic until softened, 3 minutes. Mix in chicken breasts, stock, Italian seasoning, bay leaves, salt, pepper, and chili powder.

Seal the lid, select Pressure Cook on High, and set the time to 10 minutes. After cooking, do a natural release for 10 minutes. Mix in lemon juice, artichoke, and vermicelli and cook further 5 minutes on Sauté. Serve warm.

Cajun Chicken with Rice & Vegetables

Total Time: 30 minutes | **Servings:** 4

Ingredients

1 tbsp olive oil
4 chicken breasts, cubed
1 tbsp Cajun seasoning
1 small white onion, chopped
3 garlic cloves, minced
1 tbsp tomato paste
1 cup basmati rice
2 cups chicken broth
1 cup frozen mixed vegetables

Directions

Set your Instant Pot to Sauté and heat olive oil. Season the chicken with Cajun seasoning and sear it until golden, 5 minutes. Mix in onion and garlic and cook for 3 minutes until fragrant. Stir in tomato paste and rice for 1 minute.

Pour in broth, seal the lid, select Pressure Cook on High, and set the time to 5 minutes. Once ready, do a quick pressure release. Select Sauté and mix in vegetables; cook until warmed through, 3-5 minutes. Serve warm.

Flavorful Chicken with Lemongrass

Total Time: 35 minutes | **Servings:** 4

Ingredients

2 lemongrass stalks, chopped
2 garlic cloves, minced
Salt and black pepper to taste
1 cup chicken broth
4 chicken breasts
1 lemon, juiced

Directions

In your Instant Pot, combine lemongrass, garlic, salt, pepper, broth, and chicken. Seal the lid, select Pressure Cook, and set the time to 12 minutes. After cooking, perform a natural pressure release for 10 minutes. Unlock the lid. Select Sauté and remove chicken onto a plate. Take out the lemongrass and discard. Shred chicken into strands and return to sauce. Stir in lemon juice and cook for 5 minutes. Serve warm.

Buffalo Chicken Breasts with Blue Cheese

Total Time: 35 minutes | **Servings**: 4

Ingredients

1 large white onion, chopped
2 celery stalks, chopped
½ cup buffalo sauce

1 cup chicken broth
4 chicken breasts
¼ cup crumbled blue cheese

Directions

In your Instant Pot, combine onion, celery, buffalo sauce, broth, and chicken. Seal the lid, select Pressure Cook on High, and set the time to 12 minutes. When done, allow a natural release for 10 minutes. Select Sauté and remove chicken to a plate. Shred into strands and return to sauce. Stir in blue cheese and cook further for 3 minutes. Serve.

Party BBQ Chicken

Total Time: 35 minutes | **Servings**: 4

Ingredients

1 ½ cups chopped sweet pineapples
1 cup chicken broth
¼ tsp salt

¾ cup BBQ sauce
4 chicken breasts, cubed

Directions

In your Instant Pot, combine pineapples, broth, salt, BBQ sauce, and chicken. Seal the lid, select Pressure Cook on High, and set the time to 12 minutes. After cooking, do a natural pressure release for 10 minutes. Remove chicken to a plate and press Sauté. Cook sauce until reduces by half, 4 minutes, and stir in chicken. Serve warm.

Chicken Drumsticks with Lime Sauce

Total Time: 30 minutes | **Servings**: 4

Ingredients

1 tbsp olive oil
4 large drumsticks
Salt and black pepper to taste
4 garlic cloves, minced

1 tsp red chili flakes
2 limes, juiced
¼ chopped cilantro
1 cup chicken broth

Directions

Set your Instant Pot to Sauté, heat olive oil, season chicken with salt, and pepper, and sear until golden on the outside, 5 minutes. Stir in garlic, red flakes, lime juice, cilantro, and broth. Seal the lid, select Pressure Cook on High, and set the time to 10 minutes. After cooking, do a natural release for 10 minutes. Serve warm.

Chicken Cordon Blue Casserole

Total Time: 25 minutes | **Servings**: 4

Ingredients

2 tbsp unsalted butter, melted
10 oz rotini pasta
5 cups chicken broth
4 chicken breasts, cut into strips
1 lb ham, cubed
1 tbsp Dijon mustard

1 tsp garlic powder
Salt and black pepper to taste
¼ cup shredded Gouda cheese
¼ cup shredded Parmesan
½ cup heavy cream
1 cup crushed pork rinds

Directions

In your Instant Pot, add rotini, broth, and mustard. Arrange chicken and ham on top. Sprinkle with garlic powder, salt, and pepper. Seal the lid, select Pressure Cook on High, and set the time to 10 minutes. After cooking, perform a quick pressure release. Unlock the lid. Mix in cheese and heavy cream. Cook on Sauté until the cheese melts, 5 minutes. Spoon cordon blue onto serving plates. In a bowl, mix butter with pork rinds and pour on cordon blue. Serve.

Chicken & Kale Quesadillas

Total Time: 15 minutes | **Servings**: 4

Ingredients

¼ cup grated Pecorino Romano cheese
¼ cup butter
1 tbsp olive oil
2 cups baby kale, chopped
1 jalapeño pepper, minced
1 onion, chopped

3 oz cottage cheese
2 tsp Mexican seasoning mix
1 cup shredded cooked chicken
6 oz shredded cheddar cheese
4 medium flour tortillas

Directions

On Sauté, melt 1 tbsp of butter and cook kale, jalapeño pepper, and onion, for 3-4 minutes, stirring occasionally, until the vegetables soften. Mix in the cottage cheese to melt and add the Mexican seasoning and chicken. Stir to combine. Spoon the filling into a large bowl and stir in cheddar cheese. Set aside.

Place a tortilla on a clean flat surface. Brush the top with olive oil and sprinkle 1 tsp of Pecorino cheese on top. Press the cheese down with the palm of your hand to stick. Spread about a 1/3 cup of filling over half tortilla. Fold the other half over the filling and press gently. Repeat the process with the remaining tortillas. Serve with guacamole.

Mushroom & Pancetta Chicken Pot

Total Time: 40 minutes | **Servings**: 4

Ingredients

1 pound bone-in, skinless chicken thighs
1 (10-oz) can condensed cream of mushroom soup
2 leeks, white part only, chopped
4 tbsp olive oil
2 pancetta slices, chopped
¼ cup flour
Salt and black pepper to taste

1 cup mushrooms, sliced
2 garlic cloves, minced
1 cup chicken broth
1 cup tomato sauce

Directions

Rub the thighs with salt and pepper and brush with half of the olive oil. Roll them in flour until evenly coated. Heat the remaining oil in your Instant Pot on Sauté and brown chicken for 6 minutes. Add in pancetta, mushrooms, leeks, and garlic. Cook for 5 minutes. Stir in broth and tomato sauce. Seal the lid and set on Pressure Cook for 15 minutes.

When done, perform a natural pressure release for 10 minutes, then a quick pressure release to let out the remaining steam. Unlock the lid. Select Sauté. Add the cream of mushroom soup and cook for 3 minutes. Serve.

Bourbon Chicken with Broccoli

Total Time: 15 minutes | **Servings:** 4

Ingredients

1 lb chicken breasts, cubed
2 cups broccoli florets
½ cup bourbon
½ cup teriyaki sauce
2 tbsp honey
1 Dijon mustard

1 tsp garlic powder
2 tsp onion powder
1/8 tsp ginger powder
½ cup brown sugar
1 tbsp cornstarch
1 tbsp water

Directions

Pour chicken and broccoli into the inner pot. In a bowl, mix bourbon, teriyaki sauce, honey, mustard, garlic, onion, and ginger powders, and brown sugar. Pour mixture all over chicken and broccoli and stir. Seal the lid, select Pressure Cook on High, and set the time to 6 minutes. When done, perform a quick pressure release and unlock the lid.

Combine cornstarch and water in a small bow. On the cooker, press Sauté, and pour cornstarch mixture over chicken. Stir and allow thickening for a minute. Spoon chicken over rice and serve warm.

Serrano & Jalapeño Peppered Chicken

Total Time: 35 minutes | **Servings:** 4

Ingredients

12 oz baby plum tomatoes, halved
1 tbsp olive oil
1 cup chicken stock
Salt to taste
½ tsp ground cumin
1 tsp Mexican seasoning mix
1 lb chicken breasts
2 jalapeño peppers, chopped

2 serrano peppers, chopped
2 garlic cloves, minced
1 onion, sliced
¼ cup minced fresh cilantro
½ cup grated cheddar cheese
½ lime, juiced

Directions

Set your Instant Pot to Sauté. Heat the olive oil. Add the tomatoes; cook without turning for 3-4 minutes. Add in the stock while scraping the bottom of the pot to dissolve any browned bits. Stir in cumin, Mexican seasoning, and salt.

Add chicken, jalapeños, serrano peppers, garlic, and onion. Seal the lid, select Pressure Cook on High, and set the time to 15 minutes. After cooking, perform a natural pressure release for 5 minutes; set the chicken aside.

With an immersion blender, purée the vegetables. Shred the chicken with two forks and return the pieces to sauce. Add the lime juice. Serve the chili in bowls, sprinkled with cheddar cheese and cilantro.

Orange Poblano Chicken Pot

Total Time: 30 minutes | **Servings:** 4

Ingredients

2 tbsp olive oil
4 chicken breasts
Salt and black pepper to taste
2 medium red onions, chopped

3 poblano peppers, sliced
3 garlic cloves, minced
1 cup orange juice
2 cups chicken broth

Directions

Set your Instant Pot to Sauté. Heat olive oil. Season chicken with salt and pepper, and sear on both sides until golden brown, 6 minutes. Stir in onion, poblano peppers, garlic, orange juice, and chicken broth. Seal the lid, select Pressure Cook on High, and set the time to 6 minutes. After cooking, do a natural release for 10 minutes. Unlock the lid. Stir and adjust the taste. Spoon into serving bowls and serve with tortilla chips, salsa, and taco toppings.

Mexican-Style Hot Chicken

Total Time: 35 minutes | **Servings:** 4

Ingredients

2 tbsp olive oil
1 white onion, chopped
1 red bell pepper, chopped
1 green bell pepper, chopped
Salt and black pepper to taste
2 tsp cumin powder

½ tsp chili powder
2 jalapeños, chopped
2 tsp garlic powder
1 (10 oz) can diced tomatoes
4 chicken breasts, cubed
1 lemon, juiced

Directions

Set your Instant Pot to Sauté, heat olive oil, and sauté onion, bell peppers until vegetables soften, 3 minutes. Mix in salt, pepper, cumin powder, chili powder, jalapeños, garlic powder, tomatoes, 1 cup of water, and chicken breasts. Seal the lid, select Pressure Cook on High, and set the time to 12 minutes. After cooking, do a natural pressure release for 10 minutes. Unlock the lid, select Sauté and stir in lemon juice. Cook for 3 minutes and adjust the taste. Serve warm.

Avocado Chicken Dip

Total Time: 20 minutes | **Servings:** 4

Ingredients

2 chicken breasts
½ cup chicken broth
Salt and black pepper to taste
1 large avocado, diced
1 shallot, finely chopped
2 tbsp chopped cilantro

1 tbsp lemon juice
2 tbsp sour cream
½ tsp garlic powder
¼ tsp cumin powder
¼ tsp hot sauce

Directions

Add chicken, broth, salt, and black pepper to the inner pot. Seal the lid, select Pressure Cook on High, and set the time to 10 minutes. After cooking, perform a quick pressure release, and unlock the lid. Using two forks, shred chicken into small strands. Add avocado, shallot, cilantro, lemon juice, sour cream, garlic and,cumin powders, hot sauce, salt, and pepper. Stir ingredients until well-combined. Spoon food into bowls and serve with pretzel chips.

Saucy Enchilada Chicken

Total Time: 20 minutes | **Servings:** 4

Ingredients

1 cup chicken broth
4 chicken breasts, cubed
1 ½ tsp dried oregano

1 ½ tsp cumin powder
1 ½ cups red enchilada sauce

Directions

In your Instant Pot, combine broth, chicken, oregano, cumin, and enchilada sauce. Seal the lid, select Pressure Cook on High, and set the cooking time to 10 minutes. After cooking, perform a natural pressure release for 5 minutes, then a quick pressure release to let out the remaining steam. Unlock the lid, stir, and serve the chicken with sauce.

Mustard Chicken with Potatoes

Total Time: 30 minutes | **Servings**: 4

Ingredients

2 tbsp olive oil
1 lb chicken thighs
Salt and black pepper to taste
1 cup chicken broth
Lemon juice from 1 lemon

2 tbsp Dijon mustard
2 tsp rosemary, chopped
3 garlic cloves, crushed
2 lb red potatoes, quartered

Directions

Rub the chicken with salt and pepper. Set your Instant Pot to Sauté, warm oil, and sear the chicken for 6 minutes until golden brown. In a bowl, place broth, lemon juice, mustard, rosemary, and garlic; mix to combine. Pour in the pot and add potatoes. Seal the lid, and set on Pressure Cook on High, for 15 minutes. Do a quick release. Serve warm.

Chicken with Mushrooms & Brussel Sprouts

Total Time: 35 minutes | **Servings**: 4

Ingredients

2 tbsp olive oil
4 chicken thighs, bone-in skin-on
1 small onion, sliced
½ cup dry white wine
½ cup chicken stock

1 lb halved Brussel sprouts
¼ tsp dried rosemary
Salt and black pepper to taste
1 cup mushrooms, sliced
¼ cup heavy cream

Directions

Season the chicken on both sides with salt and pepper. Heat olive oil in the Instant Pot on Sauté. Add the chicken and fry for 5 minutes or until browned, 5-6 minutes; reserve.

In the pot, sauté the onion for about 2 minutes. Stir in white wine and bring to a boil for 3 minutes or until reduced by half. Mix in stock, Brussel sprouts, mushrooms, rosemary, salt, and pepper. Arrange chicken thighs on top. Seal the lid, select Pressure Cook, and set the time to 15 minutes. Do a quick pressure release. Stir in heavy cream and serve.

Crispy Chicken with Carrots & Potatoes

Total Time: 30 minutes | **Servings**: 4

Ingredients

4 chicken thighs, bone-in skin-on
2 tbsp melted butter
1 tbsp olive oil
Salt to taste
2 tsp Worcestershire sauce
2 tsp turmeric powder
1 tsp dried oregano

½ tsp dry mustard
½ tsp garlic powder
¼ tsp sweet paprika
2 tsp hot sauce
1 cup chicken stock
1 lb potatoes, quartered
2 carrots, sliced into rounds

Directions

In a bowl, mix melted butter, Worcestershire sauce, turmeric, oregano, dry mustard, garlic powder, paprika, and hot sauce until well combined; stir in the stock. Heat olive oil in the cooker on Sauté. Stir-fry the chicken thighs for 4-5 minutes. Season with salt. Remove from the pot.

Add the potatoes and carrots. Pour in the hot sauce and mix to coat. Put the thighs on top. Seal the lid and cook on Pressure Cook for 15 minutes. Do a quick pressure release.

Easy Chicken Florentine

Total Time: 30 minutes | **Servings**: 4

Ingredients

1 lb chicken breasts, cut into bite-size pieces
2 tbsp butter
1 cup cremini mushrooms, sliced
½ tsp garlic powder
Sal and black pepper to taste
1 yellow onion, finely chopped
1 ½ cups chicken broth

1 cup heavy cream
1 tbsp lemon juice
4 oz baby spinach
8 oz linguine, broken in half
¾ cup Parmesan cheese, grated

Directions

Season the chicken with garlic powder, salt, and pepper. Set your Instant Pot to Sauté and melt the butter. Add in the onion, mushrooms, and chicken and sauté for 4-5 minutes. Pour in the chicken broth, scrape the bottom, and add the heavy cream. Stir to combine and season with salt and pepper. Mix in the linguine and stir to coat it in the sauce.

Seal the lid, select Pressure Cook on High, and set the time to 5 minutes. When done cooking, do a natural release for 10 minutes, then a quick pressure release to let out the remaining steam. Unlock the lid and select Sauté. Throw the spinach in the pot and stir. Slowly add in the Parmesan cheese and cook for 3-4 minutes, stirring often until the cheese melts and the sauce thickens. Drizzle with lemon juice and serve warm.

Chicken Meatballs with Tomato Sauce

Total Time: 20 minutes | **Servings**: 4

Ingredients

2 tbsp olive oil
1 lb ground chicken
3 tbsp breadcrumbs
1 garlic clove, minced
1 egg, beaten

2 tbsp fresh basil, chopped
2 ¼ tbsp Parmesan, grated
2 tbsp white wine
½ can (14.5-oz) tomato sauce
Salt and black pepper to taste

Directions

In a bowl, mix chicken, breadcrumbs, garlic, black pepper, salt, egg, and Parmesan cheese. Shape the mixture into medium-sized balls. Set the pot to Sauté and heat oil. Add in the meatballs and cook for 8 minutes; reserve. Pour in the white wine to scrape up any browned bits from the bottom of the pot. Stir in the tomato sauce, meatballs, and 1 cup water. Seal the lid, select Pressure Cook, and set the cooking time to 5 minutes. When done, perform a quick pressure release. Top with basil and serve.

Chicken Fajitas with Cherry Tomatoes

Total Time: 25 minutes | **Servings:** 4

Ingredients

1 lb chicken breasts
8 corn tortilla shells

1 avocado, sliced
½ cup cherry tomatoes, halved

Filling

1 can (10-oz) fire-roasted tomatoes, chopped
1 tbsp olive oil
½ yellow onion, chopped
1 garlic clove, minced
½ cup chicken broth

½ tbsp chili powder
1 tbsp taco seasoning
Salt and black pepper to serve
¼ tsp ground coriander

Directions

Add the chicken to your Instant Pot. In a bowl, mix all the filling ingredients. Pour the mixture over the chicken. Seal the lid, select Poultry on High, and cook for 15 minutes. When done, do a quick pressure release. Remove the chicken to a cutting board and let it cool for a few minutes before shredding it. Then, return to the pot and stir. Warm tortillas in the microwave. Divide the chicken mixture between the tortillas. Top with tomatoes and avocado.

Thai Sweet Chili Chicken

Total Time: 30 minutes | **Servings:** 4

Ingredients

4 chicken breasts
¼ cup soy sauce
2 tbsp teriyaki sauce
¼ cup ketchup
2 tbsp sweet chili sauce
2 ½ tbsp brown sugar

3 garlic cloves, minced
1 tbsp freshly grated ginger
½ tsp onion powder
1 ½ tbsp cornstarch
1 cup chicken broth
Salt and black pepper to taste

Directions

Place chicken In your Instant Pot. In a bowl, combine soy sauce, teriyaki sauce, ketchup, sweet chili sauce, brown sugar, garlic, ginger, onion powder, cornstarch, broth, salt, and pepper. Pour mixture over chicken. Seal the lid, select Pressure Cook on High, and set the time to 12 minutes. Perform a natural release for 10 minutes. Remove chicken to a plate and shred with two forks. Return to the sauce, pour in the cornstarch mixture, and stir. Select Sauté and cook until sauce is syrupy. Dish and serve warm.

Juicy Peanut Chicken with Rice Noodles

Total Time: 30 minutes | **Servings:** 4

Ingredients

4 chicken breasts
1 cup chicken broth
1 cup peanut sauce
Salt and black pepper to taste

5 oz rice noodles
1 cup green beans, halved
1 tbsp chopped peanuts
1 tsp chopped cilantro

Directions

In your Instant Pot, add chicken, broth, peanut sauce, and salt. Seal the lid, select Pressure Cook on High, and set the time to 12 minutes. After cooking, perform a quick pressure release to let out steam, and unlock the lid.

Meanwhile, in a bowl, pour the rice noodles and top with 2 cups of hot water. Allow sitting for 4 minutes. Strain noodles through a colander and divide between serving plates. Select Sauté and add green beans. Cook for 3 minutes and adjust taste with salt and pepper. Top with chicken and sauce, garnish with peanuts and cilantro and serve.

Tandoori Chicken Thighs

Total Time: 30 min + marinating time | **Servings:** 4

Ingredients

1 lb chicken thighs
Salt and black pepper to taste
1 cup plain Greek yogurt
1 ½ tsp garlic puree
1 tbsp ginger puree
1 tsp sweet paprika
½ tsp chili pepper powder

½ tsp garam masala
½ tsp ground cumin
1 tsp turmeric powder
1 cup long-grain rice
½ cup coconut milk
½ cup lima beans
1 tbsp chopped fresh parsley

Directions

In a bowl, mix the yogurt, salt, garlic, ginger, paprika, chili pepper, garam masala, cumin, turmeric, and black pepper. Pour the marinade with the chicken in a plastic zipper bag. Seal and shake to coat chicken. Refrigerate for 3 hours.

Add rice into your Instant Pot and mix in coconut milk, beans, 1 cup water, and salt. Place a trivet over the rice. Remove chicken from the marinade and put it on the trivet in a single layer. Seal the lid, select Pressure Cook on High, and set the time to 12 minutes. After cooking, allow a natural release for 10 minutes. Top with parsley to serve.

Honey-Lime Chicken Drumsticks

Total Time: 30 minutes | **Servings:** 4

Ingredients

1 tbsp olive oil
4 chicken drumsticks
Salt and black pepper to taste
¼ cup honey
3 limes, juiced

¼ cup soy sauce
2 garlic cloves, minced
1 tsp freshly grated ginger
2 scallions, thinly sliced

Directions

Set your Instant Pot to Sauté, heat olive oil, season chicken with salt and pepper, and sear until golden brown, 6 minutes. Pour in honey, lime juice, soy sauce, garlic, ½ cup water, and ginger and stir well.

Seal the lid, select Pressure Cook on High, and set the time to 5 minutes. After cooking, do a natural pressure release for 10 minutes. Unlock the lid, baste the chicken with sauce, and plate. Garnish with scallions and serve.

Chicken Breasts in Peanut-Soy Sauce

Total Time: 40 minutes | **Servings:** 4

Ingredients

1 tbsp olive oil
1 small red onion, chopped
½ red bell pepper, chopped
1 cup peanut sauce

2 tsp soy sauce
½ tsp miso paste
1 cup chicken broth
4 chicken breasts

Directions

Set your Instant Pot to Sauté. Heat olive oil and sauté the onion and bell pepper until softened, 3 minutes. Mix in peanut sauce, soy sauce, miso paste, and broth. Boil for 1 minute and stir in chicken. Seal the lid, select Pressure Cook on High, and set the time to 12 minutes. Do a natural release for 10 minutes. Remove the chicken to a plate, shred it with two forks, and return it to sauce. Press Sauté. Cook until the sauce thickens, 5 minutes. Serve with rice.

Traditional Hainanese Chicken with Rice

Total Time: 35 minutes | **Servings**: 4

Ingredients

2 tbsp sesame oil	1 tsp habanero hot sauce
2 lb chicken breasts	1 tbsp peanut butter
½ cup Thai sweet chili sauce	1 cup white rice
3 tbsp soy sauce	1 ½ cups chicken broth
1 ½ tsp minced fresh ginger	½ cup coconut milk
1 garlic clove, minced	2 tbsp fresh cilantro, chopped
1 lime, juiced	

Directions

Set the pot to Sauté and warm sesame oil. Place in the chicken and brown for 6 minutes on all sides. In a bowl, mix sweet chili sauce, soy sauce, ginger, garlic, lime juice, habanero sauce, and peanut butter; stir to combine.

Place rice in the pot and stir. Pour the sauce over. Add in broth and coconut milk. Seal the lid, select Pressure Cook on High for 10 minutes. When done, allow a natural release for 10 minutes. Remove the chicken to a plate; shred it with a fork. Fluff the rice and spoon it into four bowls. Top with chicken and cilantro and serve.

Smoky Chicken Pilaf

Total Time: 50 minutes | **Servings**: 4

Ingredients

½ lb boneless chicken thighs, skin on

2 tbsp olive oil	1 tsp cumin
1 leek, chopped	1 bay leaf
1 cup rice, rinsed	2 cups chicken stock
Salt and black pepper to serve	1 carrot, chopped
¼ tsp ground smoked paprika	1 celery stick, chopped
¼ tsp ground coriander	2 garlic cloves, minced

Directions

Set your Instant Pot to Sauté and heat the olive oil. Cook chicken for 10 minutes in total or until golden brown; reserve. Put leek, carrot, celery, and garlic in the pot and cook for 3 minutes. Stir in rice, salt, pepper, cumin, paprika, ground coriander, and bay leaf. Cook for 2 minutes. Pour in the stock and add stir. Return the chicken.

Seal the lid, select Pressure Cook and set the time to 15 minutes on High. When done, perform a natural pressure release for 10 minutes, then a quick pressure release to let out the remaining steam. Unlock the lid and remove the bay leaf. Fluff the rice with a fork and serve.

Bombay Chicken Tikka Masala

Total Time: 30 minutes | **Servings**: 4

Ingredients

4 chicken thighs, boneless and cut into bite-size pieces

2 tbsp butter	Salt to taste
1 (14 oz) can diced tomatoes	1 tsp garam masala
2 tsp ginger puree	1 tsp cumin powder
1 tsp turmeric powder	1 cup chicken broth
½ tsp cayenne powder	2 tbsp coconut milk
1 tsp sweet paprika	¼ chopped cilantro

Directions

To the inner pot, add tomatoes, ginger, turmeric, cayenne, paprika, salt, garam masala, cumin powder, chicken, butter, broth, and coconut milk. Seal the lid, select Pressure Cook on High, and set the cooking time to 12 minutes.

After cooking, perform a natural pressure release for 10 minutes, then a quick pressure release to let out the remaining steam. Unlock the lid. Stir and adjust taste with salt. Ladle into serving bowls, garnish with cilantro. Serve.

Parma-Style Cheesy Chicken

Total Time: 25 minutes | **Servings**: 4

Ingredients

4 chicken thighs	1 tsp garlic powder
5 cups tomato pasta sauce	1 tsp dried oregano
1 cup chicken broth	10 oz rigatoni
Salt and black pepper to taste	1 cup grated Parmesan cheese
¼ tsp red chili flakes	2 cups grated mozzarella
1 tsp dried thyme	

Directions

Add the chicken to your Instant Pot. Top with pasta sauce, broth, salt, pepper, red flakes, thyme, garlic powder, and oregano. Seal the lid, select Pressure Cook on High, and set the time to 12 minutes. Do a quick release. Stir in rigatoni. Seal the lid again, select Pressure Cook on High, and set the time to 5 minutes. Do a quick release and stir in Parmesan to melt. Plate, top with mozzarella cheese and serve.

Cilantro Chicken & Biscuit Chili

Total Time: 20 minutes | **Servings**: 6

Ingredients

1 tbsp olive oil	1 tbsp dried oregano
1 onion, chopped	4 cups chicken broth
2 garlic cloves, minced	Salt and black pepper to taste
1 ½ lb ground chicken	1 package refrigerated biscuits
1 tbsp ground cilantro	

Directions

On Sauté, heat olive oil and add the ground chicken, onion, and garlic; sauté until the onion is softened, about 3 minutes. Add in cilantro, oregano, broth, salt, and black pepper. Spread the biscuits in a single layer over the chili. Seal the lid, select Pressure Cook on High, and set the time to 10 minutes. When done, do a quick release and serve.

Sticky Sesame Chicken Wings

Total Time: 25 minutes | **Servings:** 4

Ingredients

2 tbsp sesame oil
2 lb chicken wings
2 tbsp hot garlic sauce
2 tbsp honey
2 garlic cloves, minced
1 tbsp toasted sesame seeds

Directions

Pour 1 cup of water into the inner pot and insert a trivet. Place the chicken wings on the trivet. Seal the lid, select Pressure Cook on High, and set the time to 10 minutes. After cooking, do a quick pressure release. Remove the trivet and discard the water. In a large bowl, whisk the sesame oil, hot garlic sauce, honey, and garlic. Toss the wings in the sauce and put them in the pot. Press Sauté and cook for 5 minutes. Sprinkle with the sesame seeds to serve.

Parsley Chicken & Vegetable Rice

Total Time: 30 minutes | **Servings:** 4

Ingredients

½ tbsp butter
4 chicken breast halves
1 bunch of parsley
2 cups water
1 cup pearl onions, halved
2 cloves garlic, minced
1 carrot, chopped
1 cup rice
1 cup celery, chopped
1 cup red bell peppers, diced
Salt and black pepper to taste
1 cup frozen peas

Directions

Set your Instant Pot to Sauté and melt the butter. Rub the chicken with salt and pepper on all sides; set aside. Place in onions and garlic and sauté for 3 minutes, until slightly brown. Pour in rice, salt, pepper, peas, and water and stir.

Put in the chopped vegetables and top with the chicken. Seal the lid, select Pressure Cook on High, and set the time to 8 minutes. When done, do a natural pressure release for 10 minutes. Unlock the lid and remove the chicken to shred it using two forks. Then, return it to the pot and mix well. Serve immediately topped with parsley.

Sweet Sriracha Chicken Drumsticks

Total Time: 25 minutes | **Servings:** 4

Ingredients

1 lb chicken drumsticks
4 tbsp soy sauce
2 tbsp Sriracha sauce
1 tbsp honey
1 garlic clove, minced
½ tsp crushed red pepper
1 tbsp cornstarch
1 green onion, chopped

Directions

In a bowl, combine sriracha sauce, soy sauce, honey, garlic, and red pepper and mix well. Place in chicken and toss to coat. Transfer to your Instant Pot. Add in 1 cup water. Seal the lid, select Poultry on High, and cook for 15 minutes. When done, perform a quick pressure release. Select Sauté. In a bowl, combine the cornstarch and 2 tbsp water. Stir in the pot. Cook for 2 minutes until the sauce thickens. Top with green onions to serve.

Fast Chicken Fried Rice with Vegetables

Total Time: 30 minutes | **Servings:** 4

Ingredients

1 (16-oz) bag frozen mixed vegetables
2 tbsp canola oil
1 onion, chopped
4 garlic cloves, minced
1 lb chicken breasts, chopped
Salt and black pepper to taste
2 cups chicken broth
¼ cup coconut aminos
1 cup long-grain rice

Directions

On Sauté, heat oil and cook the onion and garlic for 3 minutes, until fragrant. Put the chicken in the pot and season with salt and black pepper. Cook for 5 minutes, until browned. Pour in chicken broth, coconut aminos, and rice. Seal the lid, select Pressure Cook on High, and set the time to 8 minutes. When done, perform a quick pressure release. Pour in the frozen vegetables. Select Sauté and cook for 5 minutes, stirring occasionally. Serve immediately.

Restaurant-Style Chicken with Frijoles

Total Time: 50 minutes | **Servings:** 4

Ingredients

4 chicken thighs, bone-in skin-on
Salt and black pepper to taste
2 pancetta slices, cut into thirds
1 medium carrot, chopped
½ small onion, chopped
½ cup dry red wine
1 cup beans Frijoles, soaked
3 cups chicken stock

Directions

Season the chicken on both sides with salt and pepper. Select Sauté and brown the pancetta for 5 minutes. Remove to a paper towel-lined plate. Put the thighs in the pot and fry for 6-7 minutes or until golden brown; set aside.

Sauté carrot and onion in the same fat for 3 minutes. Stir in the wine while scraping off the brown bits at the bottom. Let boil until the wine reduces by one-third and stir in the beans and stock. Return the chicken. Seal the lid, select Pressure Cook on High, and set the time to 25 minutes. Do a quick pressure release. Scatter pancetta over and serve.

Sesame Seed Chicken & Broccoli Bulgur

Total Time: 20 minutes | **Servings:** 2

Ingredients

2 tbsp butter
1 cup bulgur
1 head broccoli, cut into florets
Salt and black pepper to taste
4 chicken tenders
1 tbsp sesame seeds
2 tbsp sliced green onions
2 cups water

Directions

Melt butter on Sauté and brown chicken for 5 minutes in total. Add in bulgur, then pour in water; season. Seal the lid, select Pressure Cook on High, and set the cooking time to 5 minutes. Perform a quick pressure release. Place a trivet over the bulgur and arrange the broccoli on top. Seal the lid, select Pressure Cook, and cook for 3 minutes on High. Do a quick pressure release. Spoon into plates and top with broccoli, sesame seeds, and green onions. Serve warm.

Hunter's Chicken

Total Time: 25 minutes | **Servings**: 4

Ingredients

4 chicken breasts, cut into bite-size pieces

2 cups tomato sauce	1 tsp garlic powder
1 medium onion, thinly sliced	½ cup chicken broth
3 red bell peppers, chopped	1 cup sliced oyster mushrooms
½ tsp cayenne pepper	1 cup Kalamata olives, pitted
Salt and black pepper to taste	2 tbsp chopped parsley

Directions

In your Instant Pot, add tomato sauce, chicken, onion, bell peppers, cayenne pepper, salt, pepper, garlic powder, broth, and mushrooms. Seal the lid, select Pressure Cook on High, and set the time to 10 minutes. After cooking, do a natural release for 5 minutes. Unlock the lid, stir in olives, and adjust the taste. Serve topped with parsley.

Rosemary Whole Chicken

Total Time: 50 minutes | **Servings**: 4

Ingredients

2 tbsp olive oil	3 lb whole chicken, cleaned
1 tbsp fresh rosemary leaves	4 tbsp balsamic vinegar
6 garlic cloves, minced	2 cups chicken broth
Salt and black pepper to taste	1 large white onion, diced
½ tsp smoked paprika	

Directions

In a bowl, mix rosemary, garlic, salt, pepper, and paprika. Rub spice mixture all over the chicken. Set your Instant Pot to Sauté. Heat olive oil in and sear chicken all around until golden, 7 minutes; remove to a plate. Pour vinegar and broth into the pot. Using a spatula, scrape the stuck bits at the bottom. Place onion and then chicken in the pot.

Seal the lid, select Pressure Cook on High, and set the time to 18 minutes. After cooking, do a natural pressure release for 10 minutes. Remove chicken to a plate and cover with foil for 5 minutes before slicing. Serve warm.

Mediterranean Chicken

Total Time: 50 minutes | **Servings**: 4

Ingredients

1 lb chicken thighs, bone-in, skin removed

2 tbsp olive oil	
Salt and black pepper to taste	1 cup chicken stock
2 red bell peppers, cut into strips	2 tbsp black olives, pitted
1 red onion, diced	½ tbsp capers, drained
1 garlic clove, minced	½ tsp dried rosemary
¼ cup dry white wine	1 tbsp parsley, chopped
1 ½ cups canned passata	1 tbsp basil, chopped

Directions

Set your Instant Pot to Sauté and heat olive oil. Season chicken with salt and pepper. Sear for 8 minutes until golden brown. Remove to a plate. Pour bell peppers, onion, and garlic into the pot. Cook for 6 minutes until softened.

Pour in white wine, passata, stock, and rosemary and cook for another 2 minutes; return the chicken. Seal the lid, select Pressure Cook, for 15 minutes on High.

When done, allow a natural release for 10 minutes. Stir in olives and capers, and adjust the seasoning. Garnish with parsley and basil. Serve warm and enjoy!

Roman-Style Chicken

Total Time: 25 minutes | **Servings**: 4

Ingredients

1 lb boneless, skinless chicken breasts, halved lengthwise

½ cup sun-dried tomatoes, chopped

2 tbsp butter	¾ cup heavy cream
1 tbsp Italian seasoning	¾ cup Parmesan cheese, grated
1 tbsp garlic powder	2 cups fresh spinach, chopped
1 cup chicken broth	2 tbsp fresh parsley, chopped

Directions

Flatten the chicken breasts with a meat mallet. Season with Italian seasoning and garlic powder. Set the pot to Sauté and melt butter. Place in the chicken, and brown for 4 minutes on all sides. Pour in the chicken broth and and seal the lid.

select Pressure Cook on High, and set the time to 10 minutes. When done, perform a quick pressure release. Unlock the lid and remove the chicken to a plate.

Select Sauté and add in the heavy cream. Cook for 2 minutes, stirring often. Pour in the cheese and sun-dried tomatoes, stir until the cheese is melted. Add in the spinach and stir until the spinach is wilted. Serve the chicken with parsley.

Easy Mango Chicken with Teriyaki Sauce

Total Time: 35 minutes | **Servings**: 4

Ingredients

2 tbsp sesame oil	2 tbsp soy sauce
1 lb chicken thighs	1 red bell pepper, chopped
Salt to taste	1 cup canned mango chunks
1 cup chicken broth	1 tsp sesame seeds for garnish
¼ cup teriyaki sauce	

Directions

Set your Instant Pot to Sauté and warm sesame oil. Salt the chicken. Cook the chicken until golden brown; remove to a plate. Pour in broth to scrape up any browned bits.

Stir in 2 tbsp of teriyaki sauce and soy sauce. Add in bell pepper and return the chicken. Seal the lid, select Pressure Cook on High, and set the time to 10 minutes.

When done, allow a natural release for 10 minutes. Transfer the chicken to a baking sheet. Drizzle with the remaining teriyaki sauce and place under the broiler for 4 minutes, until golden brown. Add mango chunks to the pot.

Press Sauté and cook for 3 minutes until the sauce thickens. Divide chicken among plates, top with bell pepper and mango, and spoon the sauce over the top. Sprinkle with sesame seeds before serving. Enjoy!

Pecorino-Romano Chicken with Potatoes

Total Time: 35 minutes | **Servings:** 4

Ingredients

3 tbsp grated Pecorino Romano cheese
3 tbsp olive oil   ½ tsp dried oregano
4 chicken breasts   1 tsp garlic powder
1 lb baby russet potatoes   1 tsp dried rosemary
3 tbsp ranch seasoning   1 cup chicken broth
Salt and black pepper to taste

Directions

In a bowl, add chicken, potatoes, olive oil, 2 tbsp of ranch seasoning, salt, pepper, oregano, garlic powder, and rosemary; toss well. Pour broth into your Instant Pot. Add potatoes, and place chicken on top. Seal the lid, select Pressure Cook on High, and set the cooking time to 15 minutes. After cooking, allow a natural release for 10 minutes. Plate chicken and potatoes, sprinkle with ranch seasoning, and scatter Pecorino cheese on top. Serve warm.

Thyme Chicken & Cannellini Bean Soup

Total Time: 35 minutes | **Servings:** 4

Ingredients

2 tbsp olive oil   2 chicken breasts, cubed
1 white onion, chopped   5 cups chicken stock
1 celery stalk, chopped   Salt and black pepper to taste
6 garlic clove, minced   1 lemon, juiced
2 tbsp thyme leaves   2 tbsp chopped parsley
1 cup dried cannellini beans

Directions

Set your Instant Pot to Sauté. Heat olive oil and sauté onion, celery, and garlic until softened, 3 minutes. Mix in thyme, beans, chicken, stock, salt, and pepper. Seal the lid, select Pressure Cook on High, and set the time to 13 minutes.

After cooking, perform a natural pressure release for 10 minutes, and unlock the lid. Stir in lemon juice and adjust the taste with salt and pepper. Garnish with parsley. Serve.

Tamari & Agave Chicken Thighs

Total Time: 30 minutes | **Servings:** 2

Ingredients

½ pound bone-in, skin-on chicken thighs
1 tbsp olive oil   3 tbsp agave nectar
1 tbsp tamari sauce   1 lemon, juiced and zested
1 tsp lemon pepper seasoning   2 cloves garlic, minced

Directions

Rub chicken with lemon pepper seasoning. Set your Instant Pot to Sauté and heat olive oil. Place in chicken and cook for 4-5 minutes on all sides, until lightly browned. Add in the garlic and cook for 1 minute, stirring often. In a bowl, combine lemon juice, lemon zest, agave nectar, ½ cup water, and tamari sauce. Pour over the chicken. Seal the lid, select Poultry, and set the time to 15 minutes. When done, do a quick pressure release. Serve hot with rice.

Sweet Chili Chicken Strips

Total Time: 15 minutes | **Servings:** 4

Ingredients

2 tbsp sesame oil   ½ cup soy sauce
¼ cup maple syrup   2 tbsp sweet chili sauce
2 tbsp cornstarch, divided   ¼ tsp red pepper flakes
Salt to taste   2 tsp sesame seeds
1 lb chicken tenders, sliced   3 scallions, chopped

Directions

Mix cornstarch with salt in a bowl. Add the chicken and toss to coat. Set the pot to Sauté and heat 1 tbsp of sesame oil; cook chicken for 4 minutes until golden brown. In a separate bowl, mix soy sauce, chili sauce, 1 cup water, and red flakes. Pour the mixture over the chicken. Seal the lid, select Pressure Cook on High, and set the time to 5 minutes. When done, do a quick release. Stir in the remaining sesame oil and maple syrup. Top with sesame seeds and scallions.

Stewed Chicken with Herby Dumplings

Total Time: 30 minutes | **Servings:** 4

Ingredients

1 tbsp coconut oil   2 cups chicken stock
½ cup butter, softened   Salt to taste
1 white onion, chopped   ½ cup half-and-half
2 carrots, chopped   1 cup flour
2 celery stalks, chopped   2 tbsp rosemary, chopped
1 lb chicken breasts, cubed

Directions

On Sauté, melt coconut oil and sauté onion, carrots, celery, and chicken and cook for 5 minutes, stirring frequently. Pour in stock and season with salt. Seal the lid, select Pressure Cook on High, and set the time to 6 minutes.

Whisk together the flour, rosemary, 2 tbsp of water, butter, and salt in a bowl. Mix with a wooden spoon until well combined. Shape the mixture into balls and set aside. When done cooking, perform a quick pressure release. Unlock the lid. Stir in the half-and-half. Drop the dumpling over the top and cook for 10 minutes on Sauté. Serve and enjoy!

Chicken Spinach Soup

Total Time: 30 minutes | **Servings:** 5

Ingredients

1 onion, chopped   ½ lb chicken breasts, cubed
1 carrot, chopped   5 cups chicken broth
½ cup celery, chopped   ¼ cup vermicelli
1 garlic clove, minced   1 cup spinach, chopped

Directions

Place the onion, carrot, celery, garlic, chicken, and broth into the inner pot Seal the lid, select Pressure Cook, and cook for 15 minutes on High. When done, do a quick pressure release; press Sauté. Stir in vermicelli and cook 5 minutes. Add in spinach and cook for another 5 minutes until wilted. Adjust the taste and serve.

Cheesy Macaroni with Chicken & Bacon

Total Time: 25 minutes | **Servings**: 4

Ingredients

2 tbsp olive oil
4 bacon slices, chopped
4 chicken breasts
1 tbsp ranch dressing mix
16 oz macaroni

3 cups chicken broth
Salt and black pepper to taste
4 oz cream cheese, softened
1 cup grated Monterey Jack

Directions

Set your Instant Pot to Sauté and cook bacon until brown and crispy; set aside. Heat olive oil in bacon fat, season chicken with ranch dressing mix, and sear for 5 minutes. Return bacon to pot and top with macaroni and broth. Season with salt and pepper.

Seal the lid, select Pressure Cook on High, and set the time to 6 minutes. After cooking, do a quick release. Select Sauté and mix in cream and Monterey Jack cheeses until melted, 3 minutes. Dish and serve.

Classic Chicken Caesar Salad

Total Time: 20 minutes | **Servings**: 4

Ingredients

4 tbsp olive oil
2 chicken breasts
Salt and black pepper to taste
1 cup water
1 bay leaf
1 lemon, quartered
1 head Iceberg lettuce, torn

¼ cup croutons
½ cup grated Parmesan cheese
1 garlic clove, minced
1 tsp Worcestershire sauce
¼ tsp grated lemon zest
2 tbsp white wine vinegar
3 tbsp mayonnaise

Directions

Season the chicken with salt and pepper. Place it in the inner pot. Add water, bay leaf, and lemon and stir. Seal the lid, select Pressure Cook, and set the time to 10 minutes. When done, do a quick pressure release. Remove the chicken to a plate to cool slightly and slice into strips. Place the lettuce in a bowl and toss with croutons and half of the cheese.

In another bowl, make the dressing by whisking garlic, Worcestershire sauce, lemon zest, remaining cheese, vinegar, mayonnaise, oil, and salt to taste. Split the mixture into bowls, top with chicken, and drizzle with the dressing.

Chicken Penne with Peas

Total Time: 25 minutes | **Servings**: 4

Ingredients

1 tbsp olive oil
1 ½ cups dried penne
4 chicken breasts, cubed
Salt and black pepper to taste

4 tbsp white wine
¼ cup heavy cream
¼ cup frozen peas
2 tbsp chopped parsley

Directions

Add penne and 5 cups of salted water to your Instant Pot. Seal the lid, select Pressure Cook, and cook for 3 minutes. After cooking, do a natural release for 10 minutes.

Unlock the lid. Drain the pasta through a colander. Place in a bowl and set aside. Wipe inner pot clean and set to Sauté.

Heat olive oil, season chicken with salt and pepper, and cook until golden brown, 6-8 minutes. Pour in the wine, cook further for 1 minute, and stir in heavy cream.

Heat for 1 minute. Stir in peas and penne until well coated. Season with salt and pepper. Spoon food into serving plates and garnish with parsley. Serve and enjoy!

Chinese Chicken with Noodles

Total Time: 25 minutes | **Servings**: 4

Ingredients

½ cup shiitake mushrooms, sliced
2 tbsp olive oil
1 ½ lb chicken breasts, sliced
1 garlic clove, minced
8 oz Chinese egg noodles
1 cup snap peas
11 ½ cups chicken broth

1 tbsp soy sauce
1 tbsp fish sauce
1 tbsp rice wine
1 tsp grated fresh ginger
1 tbsp brown sugar

Directions

Set your Instant Pot to Sauté mode and heat the olive oil. Add in the chicken and garlic and cook for 5 minutes, until browned. Add in the snap peas and mushrooms and stir.

In a bowl, combine broth, soy sauce, fish sauce, rice wine, ginger, and brown sugar. Whisk until the sugar is dissolved. Pour the mixture into the pot.

Seal the lid, select Pressure Cook on High, and set the time to 5 minutes. When done, perform a quick pressure release. Unlock the lid and stir in the noodles. Select Sauté and cook for 4 minutes. Ladle into individual bowls and serve.

Peruvian Arroz con Pollo

Total Time: 35 minutes | **Servings**: 4

Ingredients

4 tbsp olive oil
1 onion, chopped
3 chicken breasts, cubed
Salt and black pepper to taste
1 red bell pepper, chopped
2 garlic cloves, minced
1 cup white rice
2 tsp ground cumin

2 cups chicken broth
½ cup dry white wine
2 tbsp drained Spanish capers
1 (14-oz) can crushed tomatoes
1 cup frozen peas
½ cup green olives
¼ cup chopped parsley

Directions

Set your Instant Pot to Sauté and heat the olive oil. Sprinkle the chicken with salt and pepper and cook for 3 minutes per side, until browned; remove to a plate. In the pot, warm the remaining oil and sauté the onion, bell pepper, and garlic for 3 minutes. Add in the rice and stir. Pour in the broth, wine, cumin, capers, tomatoes, frozen peas, and olives.

Return the chicken. Seal the lid, select Pressure Cook on High, and set the time to 10 minutes. When done, allow a natural release for 10 minutes. Unlock the lid, fluff the rice with a fork and garnish with parsley to serve.

Tomato Chicken Pilaf

Total Time: 40 minutes | **Servings**: 4

Ingredients

2 tbsp avocado oil
1 red onion, chopped
1 yellow bell pepper, chopped
1 tbsp cayenne powder
1 tsp ground cumin
1 tsp Italian herb mix

Salt to taste
1 cup basmati rice
2 cups chicken broth
½ cup tomato sauce
1 lb chicken thighs
2 tbsp chopped cilantro

Directions

Heat avocado oil in your Instant pot on Sauté. Cook the onion, thighs, bell pepper, cayenne pepper, cumin, herb mix, and salt for 5 minutes, stirring occasionally.

Pour in the rice, broth, and tomato sauce. Seal the lid, select Pressure Cook on High, and set the time to 25 minutes. When done, do a quick pressure release. Garnish with cilantro and serve. Enjoy!

Pulled Chicken Carnitas

Total Time: 20 minutes | **Servings**: 4

Ingredients

4 chicken breast halves, cut into 1-inch strips
1 tbsp olive oil
2 tbsp soy sauce
1 tbsp rice vinegar
1 tsp sugar
½ head white cabbage, shredded
1 large carrot, shredded

1 bell pepper, sliced
3 spring onions, chopped
2 garlic cloves, minced
1 tsp fresh ginger, grated
1 cup chicken broth
4 tortillas, warmed

Directions

Mix soy sauce, vinegar, and sugar In your Instant Pot. Stir in cabbage, carrot, bell pepper, spring onions, garlic, ginger, and olive oil. Place the chicken on top and pour in broth. Seal the lid, select Pressure Cook, and set to 12 minutes.

When ready, do a quick pressure release. Remove the chicken to a plate. Let cool and shred into small pieces.

Bring back to the pot, select Sauté, and cook until the liquid has reduced by half. Divide the filling between tortillas with a perforated spoon. Roll up and serve immediately.

Juicy Chicken Breasts

Total Time: 35 minutes | **Servings**: 4

Ingredients

¼ cup chopped roasted red peppers
4 chicken breasts
1 cup chicken broth
1 tsp Italian seasoning
3 garlic cloves, minced

Salt and black pepper to taste
¼ cup heavy cream
1 ½ tbsp cornstarch
1 tbsp basil pesto

Directions

In your Instant Pot, add chicken, chicken broth, Italian seasoning, garlic, salt, black pepper, and roasted peppers and stir well. Seal the lid, select Pressure Cook on High, and set the cooking time to 10 minutes.

After cooking, allow a natural pressure release for 10 minutes, then quick pressure release to let out the remaining steam. Unlock the lid.

Select Sauté and remove chicken to a plate. Add heavy cream, cornstarch, and pesto to the pot and stir. Cook for 4 minutes until the sauce thickens. Return chicken to the pot, stir and cook for 2 minutes. Serve warm.

Kimchi Chicken

Total Time: 50 minutes | **Servings**: 4

Ingredients

1 lb boneless, skinless chicken thighs
2 tbsp olive oil
½ cup chili sauce
1 cup chicken broth
1 tsp kimchi spice

Salt and black pepper to taste
1 onion, chopped
4 green onions, sliced
2 tbsp sesame seeds

Directions

Set your Instant Pot to Sauté, heat olive oil and cook the chicken for 6-8 minutes on all sides until browned. Season with kimchi, salt, and pepper.

In a bowl, mix onion, chili sauce, and broth and pour over the chicken. Seal the lid, select Pressure Cook on High, and set the time to 25 minutes.

When cooking is complete, do a natural release for 10 minutes, then quick pressure release to let out the remaining steam. Unlock the lid. Garnish with green onions and sesame seeds. Serve immediately.

Southwestern Chicken in Green Salsa

Total Time: 25 minutes | **Servings**: 4

Ingredients

1 pound bone-in, skin-on chicken legs
1 cup canned green chiles, chopped
30 oz canned roasted bell peppers
1 (15-oz) jar green chile salsa
1 chopped serrano pepper
1 onion, chopped

4 tsp minced garlic
Salt and black pepper to taste
2 tbsp cilantro, chopped

Directions

Mix the chicken, salsa verde, bell peppers, green chiles, serrano, onion, garlic, 1 cup of water, salt, and pepper in your Instant Pot; stir to combine. Seal the lid, select Pressure Cook on High, and set the time to 15 minutes.

When done, perform a quick pressure release. Remove the chicken to a plate. Discard the bones and skin and let cool before cutting into small pieces. Bring the chicken back to the pot and stir. Serve scattered with cilantro.

TURKEY, DUCK & GOOSE

Rosemary Turkey in Wine-Mustard Sauce

Total Time: 60 minutes | **Servings:** 4

Ingredients

1 lb turkey thighs, boneless and skinless
1 tbsp avocado oil
Salt and black pepper to taste
2 white onions, thinly sliced
3 garlic, minced
½ cup white wine

½ cup chicken broth
2 tbsp Dijon mustard
1 tsp dried rosemary
1 tbsp all-purpose flour
1 tbsp chopped parsley

Directions

Set your Instant Pot to Sauté, heat avocado oil, season turkey with salt and pepper, and sear until golden brown, 6 minutes; set aside. Cook onion and garlic until softened, 3 minutes. Stir in white wine, broth, mustard, and rosemary. Once simmering, lay in turkey. Seal the lid, select Pressure Cook mode on High, and set the time to 30 minutes.

After cooking, allow a natural release for 10 minutes. Unlock the lid. Remove the turkey to serving plates and set aside. Press Sauté. Mix flour into the sauce in the pot and cook until thickened, 1 minute. Adjust the taste with salt and black pepper. Spoon the gravy all over the turkey. Sprinkle with parsley. Serve warm and enjoy!

Turkey & Lentil Chili

Total Time: 45 minutes | **Servings:** 4

Ingredients

1 (14.5 oz) can chopped tomatoes
1 (4 oz) can green chilies, chopped
1 tbsp olive oil
1 lb ground turkey
1 medium yellow onion, diced
2 garlic cloves, minced
2 tbsp tomato paste
Salt and black pepper to taste

1 cup dry green lentils
2 cups chicken broth
1 (8 oz) can tomato sauce
1 tsp cumin powder
2 tsp chili powder
¼ cup grated cheddar cheese

Directions

Set your Instant Pot to Sauté. Heat oil and brown turkey for 6 minutes. Top with onion, garlic, tomato paste, salt, and pepper. Stir and cook until onions soften, 3 minutes. Mix in lentils, broth, tomato sauce, tomatoes, green chilies, and cumin. Seal the lid, select Pressure Cook on High, and set the cooking time to 15 minutes. After cooking, do a natural release for 10 minutes and unlock the lid. Stir in chili and adjust the taste. Top with cheddar cheese and serve.

Hot Turkey in Orange-Ginger Sauce

Total Time: 25 min + marinating time | **Servings:** 4

Ingredients

3 tbsp olive oil
1 ¼ cups orange juice
¼ cup soy sauce

3 tbsp grated ginger
2 tbsp garlic paste
1 ½ tbsp plain vinegar

2 tsp orange zest
2 tsp honey
¼ tsp white pepper
2 tbsp hot sauce

1 lb turkey breast fillets
1 cup chicken broth
1 tbsp cornstarch
3 scallions, thinly sliced

Directions

In a bowl, combine orange juice, soy sauce, ginger, half olive oil, garlic, vinegar, orange zest, honey, white pepper, and hot sauce. Place the turkey in the marinade, cover with plastic wrap, and marinate in the refrigerator for 1 hour.

Set your Instant Pot to Sauté and heat the remaining olive oil. Remove turkey from the fridge and marinade (shaking off as much marinade as possible) and sear until golden brown on both sides, 6 minutes. Pour in remaining marinade and chicken broth; stir. Seal the lid, select Manual/Pressure Cook on High, and set the time to 4 minutes.

After cooking, perform a natural pressure release for 10 minutes. Stir in cornstarch and set to Sauté. Cook until the sauce thickens, 1 minute. Spoon turkey with sauce over beds of rice, garnish with scallions and serve warm.

Cilantro Turkey & Bean Casserole

Total Time: 25 minutes | **Servings:** 6

Ingredients

1 tbsp butter
1 yellow onion, chopped
2 garlic cloves, minced
1 lb turkey breast
2 cups enchilada sauce
Salt and black pepper to taste

1 (15-oz) can pinto beans
8 tortillas, each cut into 8 pieces
1 (16-oz) bag frozen corn
2 cups grated Monterey Jack
2 tbsp cilantro, chopped

Directions

On Sauté, melt the butter and stir-fry onion and garlic for 3 minutes. Put in the turkey, enchilada sauce, and 1 cup of water; season with salt and pepper; stir to combine. Seal the lid, select Pressure Cook on High, and set to 15 minutes.

When done, perform a quick pressure release and unlock the lid. Shred the turkey with two forks. Mix in the pinto beans, tortilla pieces, corn, and half of the cheese. Serve topped with the remaining cheese and cilantro.

Buffalo Turkey Sandwiches with Coleslaw

Total Time: 30 minutes | **Servings:** 4

Ingredients

1 lb turkey breasts, boneless
1 cup chicken broth
2 tbsp ranch seasoning
½ cup buffalo sauce

Salt and white pepper to taste
4 hamburger buns
1 cup seasoned coleslaw

Directions

Add the turkey, broth, ranch seasoning, buffalo sauce, salt, and white pepper to your Instant Pot. Seal the lid, select Manual/Pressure Cook on High, and cook for 10 minutes. After cooking, allow a natural release for 10 minutes. Using two forks, shred turkey and give food a good stir. Fill burger buns with turkey and coleslaw. Serve and enjoy!

Broccoli & Turkey Barley with Gouda

Total Time: 25 minutes | **Servings:** 4

Ingredients

1 cup pearl barley
2 cups chicken broth
Salt and black pepper to taste

1 lb turkey breasts, cubed
1 broccoli head, cut into florets
1 ½ cups shredded gouda

Directions

Place the broth, pearl barley, salt, pepper, and turkey in your Instant Pot. Seal the lid, select Manual/Pressure Cook on High, and set the time to 10 minutes. When done, perform a quick pressure release and unlock the lid. Press Sauté and add the broccoli; cook for 4 minutes. Scatter shredded gouda cheese over the top and serve.

Minestrone Turkey Soup

Total Time: 35 minutes | **Servings:** 4

Ingredients

2 tbsp olive oil
1 lb hot turkey sausage
3 celery stalks, chopped
3 garlic cloves, chopped
1 red onion, chopped
Salt to taste
½ cup dry white wine

4 cups chicken broth
½ tsp fennel seeds
1 (15-oz) can cannellini beans
9 oz refrigerated tortellini
1 Parmesan cheese rind
2 cups chopped spinach
½ cup grated Parmesan cheese

Directions

On Sauté, heat olive oil and cook the sausage for 4 minutes, until golden brown. Stir in the celery, garlic, and onion, season with salt, and cook for 3 minutes. Pour in the wine. Scrape the bottom of the pot to let off any browned bits. Add the chicken broth, fennel seeds, tortellini, Parmesan rind, cannellini beans, and spinach.

Seal the lid, select Manual/Pressure Cook on High, and set the time to 10 minutes. Once done, perform a natural pressure release for 10 minutes. Ladle the soup into bowls and sprinkle with the grated cheese and serve.

Classic Turkey Goulash

Total Time: 35 minutes | **Servings:** 4

Ingredients

2 tbsp olive oil
1 lb turkey breast, cubed
Salt and black pepper to taste
3 yellow onions, chopped
2 carrots, peeled and diced
3 red bell peppers, chopped
2 yellow bell peppers, chopped
2 garlic cloves, minced
2 tbsp tomato paste

1 tsp cumin powder
2 tbsp paprika powder
1 tsp caraway powder
1 tbsp dried mixed herbs
2 cups vegetable stock
1 ½ cups Guinness stout
2 tbsp all-purpose flour
2 tbsp tomato ketchup
¼ tsp chili powder

Directions

Set your Instant Pot to Sauté, heat olive, season turkey with salt and pepper, and sear until golden brown, 6 minutes; set aside. Sauté onions, carrots, and bell peppers until softened, 5 minutes. Add garlic and stir for 30 seconds.

Stir in tomato paste, cumin, paprika, and caraway. Allow flavors to combine, 1 minute while frequently stirring. Add mixed herbs, turkey, stock, and Guinness stout.

Seal the lid, select Pressure Cook on High, and set the time to 4 minutes. After cooking, perform natural pressure release for 10 minutes and unlock the lid. Mix in flour, tomato ketchup, chili powder, and adjust the taste. Select Sauté and cook until the sauce thickens. Serve over rice.

Holiday Turkey with Cranberry Gravy

Total Time: 50 minutes | **Servings:** 4

Ingredients

2 tbsp butter, melted
1 lb bone-in turkey breast
4 tsp poultry seasoning
Salt and black pepper to taste

1 cup chicken broth
2 tbsp flour
½ cup white wine
2 tbsp cranberry sauce

Directions

In a bowl, combine poultry seasoning, salt, and pepper. Rub half of the seasoning onto the turkey. In your Instant Pot, pour chicken broth and fit in a trivet. Lay turkey on the trivet. Seal the lid, select Manual/Pressure Cook on High, and cook for 15 minutes. When done, allow a natural release for 10 minutes. Carefully unlock the lid.

Preheat oven to 400 F. Combine the remaining seasoning mix with butter. Transfer the turkey to a baking sheet and brush with butter mixture. Bake for 10 minutes or until brown. Remove trivet from the pot and press Sauté.

In a bowl, combine flour, wine, cranberry sauce, and the ½ cup of the cooking juices from the pot; stir well. Throw the mixture into the pot and cook for 5 minutes until the sauce thickens. Remove turkey from the oven and let cool before slicing. Serve with the sauce.

White Wine Turkey with Pappardelle

Total Time: 25 minutes | **Servings:** 4

Ingredients

2 tbsp olive oil
1 lb ground turkey
1 red onion, thinly sliced
2 cups sliced mixed bell peppers
4 garlic cloves, minced
Salt and black pepper to taste

1 tsp Italian seasoning
½ cup white wine
1 (28 oz) can diced tomatoes
3 cups chicken broth
16 oz pappardelle noodles
¼ cup basil chiffonade

Directions

Set your Instant Pot to Sauté mode. Heat olive oil and brown turkey, while occasionally stirring and breaking any lumps that form, 5 minutes. Add red onion, bell peppers, and cook until softened, 3 minutes. Top with garlic and cook until fragrant, 30 seconds. Season with salt, pepper, and Italian seasoning. Stir and cook for 1 minute.

Pour in the wine and reduce by two-thirds. Stir in tomatoes, broth, and noodles. Seal the lid, select Pressure Cook on High, and set the time to 3 minutes. Do a quick pressure release, stir in basil, and adjust the taste. Dish and serve.

Delicious Turkey & Spinach Chowder

Total Time: 35 minutes | **Servings**: 4

Ingredients

2 tbsp olive oil
1 lb link turkey sausages, sliced
½ cup chopped green onions
2 tbsp red chili flakes
1 cup short-grain rice

2 cups chicken broth
1 tbsp Old Bay Seasoning
2 cups baby spinach
2 tbsp chopped basil

Directions

Set your Instant Pot to Sauté. Heat olive oil and fry sausages until brown on both sides, 5 minutes. Stir in onions and red chili flakes; cook until onions soften, 3 minutes. Mix in rice, allow heating for 1 minute, and stir in broth and Old Bay seasoning. Seal the lid, select Manual/Pressure Cook mode on High, and set the cooking time to 5 minutes.

After cooking, allow sitting (covered) for 5 minutes and then do a quick pressure release. Unlock the lid and press Sauté. Mix in spinach and cook until softened, 5 minutes. Dish chowder into serving bowls and garnish with basil.

Turkey Meatballs Macaroni in Red Sauce

Total Time: 20 minutes | **Servings**: 4

Ingredients

5 cups chicken broth
4 tbsp tomato paste
¼ cup chopped basil
1 tsp oregano
1 tsp onion powder
¼ tsp red chili flakes

5 garlic cloves, minced
24 frozen turkey meatballs
10 oz macaroni
1 (25 oz) jar tomato sauce
Salt and black pepper to taste
¼ cup grated Parmesan cheese

Directions

Add the chicken broth to your Instant pot and stir in tomato paste until properly combined. Add basil, oregano, onion powder, chili flakes, garlic, meatballs, macaroni, and tomato sauce. Stir, making sure not to break the meatballs.

Seal the lid, select Pressure Cook mode, and set the cooking time to 3 minutes. After cooking, perform a natural release for 10 minutes. Gently stir and adjust the taste with salt and pepper. Garnish with Parmesan and serve warm.

Rice & Turkey Salad with Apples & Peanuts

Total Time: 45 minutes | **Servings**: 4

Ingredients

3 tsp peanut oil
1 cup brown rice
1 lb turkey breast tenderloin
3 tbsp apple cider vinegar
Salt and black pepper to taste

¼ tsp celery seeds
½ cup peanuts, toasted
3 celery stalks, thinly sliced
1 apple, cored and cubed

Directions

Pour the 2 cups of water into the the inner pot. Stir in brown rice and salt. Seal the lid, select Manual/Pressure Cook on High, and set the cooking time to 8 minutes. After cooking, perform a natural pressure release for 10 minutes.

Unlock the lid and spoon the rice into a bowl to cool completely. Season the turkey with salt; set aside. Wipe the pot clean and set it to Sauté. Heat 2 tsp peanut oil and put in the turkey. Cook for 7-8 minutes. Pour the remaining peanut oil and vinegar in a jar with a tight-fitting lid. Add salt, pepper, and celery seeds. Close the jar and shake until the ingredients are combined. Transfer the turkey to a plate to cool for a few minutes. Cut it into bite-size chunks and add to the rice along with the peanuts, celery stalks, and apple. Coat the salad with the dressing. Serve and enjoy!

Teriyaki Turkey Meatballs

Total Time: 40 min | **Servings**: 4

Ingredients

1 tbsp cornstarch mixed with 1 tbsp water
2 tbsp canola oil
1 lb ground turkey
½ cup Panko breadcrumbs
1 shallot, chopped
1 large egg, lightly beaten

½ tsp garlic powder
Salt black pepper to taste
½ cup teriyaki sauce
2 tbsp soy sauce
½ tsp ground coriander

Directions

In a bowl, mix the ground turkey, breadcrumbs, shallot, egg, garlic powder, coriander, salt, and pepper. Shape the mixture into 2-inch meatballs. Warm the oil in your Instant Pot on Sauté. Add the meatballs and brown them for 6-8 minutes on all sides. Remove and set aside. In a small bowl, whisk together teriyaki sauce, soy sauce, and 1 cup of water.

Pour the sauce into the pot and scrape any browned bits from the bottom. Return the meatballs to the pot. Seal the lid, select Manual/Pressure Cook, and set the cooking time to 7 minutes on High. When done cooking, do a quick release. Stir in the cornstarch mixture and Press Sauté. Simmer until the sauce thickens, about 2 minutes, then press Cancel. Transfer the meatballs and sauce to a serving dish and serve warm.

Fettucine Turkey Bolognese with Parmesan

Total Time: 25 minutes | **Servings**: 4

Ingredients

1 tbsp olive oil
1 lb ground turkey
Salt and black pepper to taste
1 large yellow onion, chopped
1 celery stalk, chopped
1 carrot, peeled and chopped

1 garlic clove, minced
1 (25 oz) jar marinara sauce
5 cups chicken broth
16 oz fettuccine pasta
¼ cup grated Parmesan cheese
2 tbsp basil, chopped

Directions

Set your Instant Pot to Sauté, heat olive oil, season turkey with salt and pepper, and cook with frequent stirring until brown, 5 minutes. Add onion, celery, carrot, and garlic; cook until vegetables soften, 3 minutes. Stir in marinara sauce, broth, salt, pepper, and fettuccine. Seal the lid, select Pressure Cook, and set the time to 4 minutes. After cooking, do a quick pressure release. Unlock the lid, stir, and plate. Top with Parmesan cheese and basil and serve.

Turkey & Cauli Rice Stuffed Bell Peppers

Total Time: 35 minutes | **Servings:** 4

Ingredients

4 mixed bell peppers, top removed and deseeded
1 lb ground turkey
¾ cup cauliflower rice
¼ cup seasoned breadcrumbs
¾ cup tomato sauce
¼ cup chopped yellow onion

¼ cup grated Parmesan cheese
3 tbsp chopped parsley
Salt and black pepper to taste
¼ cup grated mozzarella

Directions

In a medium bowl, combine turkey, cauliflower rice, breadcrumbs, tomato sauce, yellow onion, Parmesan cheese, parsley, salt, and pepper. Stuff peppers with the mixture and cover with mozzarella cheese. Pour 1 cup water into the the inner pot, fit in a trivet, and place bell peppers on top. Seal the lid, select Manual/Pressure Cook, and set the time to 15 minutes. When done, perform a natural release for 10 minutes. Remove peppers. Plate and serve warm.

Saucy Turkey with Celery & Green Peas

Total Time: 55 minutes | **Servings:** 4

Ingredients

2 tbsp olive oil
1 (1 oz) package onion soup mix
1 lb turkey breast, sliced
2 ribs celery, chopped

1 onion, chopped
1 cup chicken broth
1 tbsp cornstarch
1 cup green peas

Directions

Set your Instant Pot to Sauté, heat olive oil, and stir-fry celery and onion for 3 minutes, until softened. Rub the turkey with the onion soup mix and add to the pot; cook for 5 minutes, stirring occasionally. Pour in broth. Seal the lid, select Poultry, and set the cooking time to 30 minutes.

When done, allow a natural release for 15 minutes. Remove the turkey to a plate. In a bowl, combine 2 tbsp water, cornstarch, and some hot liquid from the pot; stir until dissolved. Pour the slurry in the pot and cook for 3 minutes on Sauté until reduced to a thick consistency. Stir in peas and cook for 3 minutes. Top the turkey with gravy to serve.

Mediterranean Turkey with Ravioli

Total Time: 25 minutes | **Servings:** 4

Ingredients

1 tbsp olive oil
1 cup cheese ravioli
1 lb ground turkey
1 cup canned diced tomatoes
1 tbsp dried mixed herbs

3 cups chicken broth
1 cup baby spinach
¼ cup Kalamata olives, sliced
¼ cup crumbled feta cheese

Directions

Pour ravioli, 3 cups of salted water in your Instant Pot. Seal the lid, select Pressure Cook on High, and set the time to 3 minutes. After cooking, do a quick pressure release. Drain pasta through a colander and set aside.

Set your Instant Pot to Sauté, heat olive oil, and brown turkey for 5 minutes. Mix in tomatoes, mixed herbs, and chicken broth. Seal the lid, select Pressure Cook on High, and set the cooking time to 10 minutes. Do a quick release. Select Sauté and add in pasta, spinach, and olives. Stir and cook until spinach wilts. Stir in feta cheese and serve warm.

Jamaican-Style Turkey Tacos

Total Time: 35 minutes | **Servings:** 4

Ingredients

2 tbsp Jamaican jerk seasoning
¼ cup mayonnaise
2 tbsp honey
2 tbsp lime juice
1 tsp ginger puree
1 tsp dried thyme

1 cup chicken broth
1 lb turkey breast, cubed
½ cup celery, thinly sliced
1 cup chopped pineapple
4 flour tortillas
1 tbsp chopped cilantro

Directions

In your Instant Pot, mix Jamaican seasoning, mayonnaise, honey, lime juice, ginger puree, thyme, and broth. Place in turkey, celery, and pineapple. Coat well with the sauce. Seal the lid, select Pressure Cook on High, and set to 10 minutes.

After cooking, allow sitting for 5 minutes, then perform a natural release for 10 minutes. Unlock the lid and spoon taco filling into tortillas. Garnish with cilantro and serve.

Mushroom & Duck Soup with Rice

Total Time: 45 minutes | **Servings:** 4

Ingredients

2 tbsp melted duck fat
1 lb cremini mushrooms, sliced
¼ cup chopped green onions
2 garlic cloves, minced
½ lb smoked duck, cubed
4 cups chicken broth

½ cup short-grain rice
Salt and black pepper to taste
¾ cup mustard greens, chopped
1 lemon, juiced
1 tbsp ginger paste
2 tbsp parsley, chopped

Directions

Set your Instant Pot to Sauté. Heat duck fat and sauté garlic, mushrooms, ginger, and green onions until softened, 3 minutes. Toss duck in vegetables; allow releasing of flavor, and pour the chicken broth on top. Add rice, salt, and black pepper. Seal the lid, select Pressure Cook on High, and set the time to 10 minutes. Allow sitting for 10 minutes, perform natural pressure release for 10 minutes, and then a quick pressure release. Unlock the lid.

Set to Sauté and mix in mustard greens. Allow wilting for 1 to 2 minutes; adjust the taste and stir in lemon juice. Spoon soup into serving bowls and serve sprinkled with parsley.

Tender Duck in Lemon Sauce

Total Time: 25 minutes | **Servings:** 4

Ingredients

2 tbsp duck fat
1 lb duck breast, cut into cubes
½ tsp mixed herbs

Salt and black pepper to taste
1 yellow onion, chopped
2 celery stalks, chopped

8 garlic cloves, minced
1 fresh rosemary sprig
1 tbsp tomato paste
1 cup chicken stock
2 lemon, juiced
2 tbsp chopped parsley

Directions

Melt the duck fat in your Instant Pot on Sauté. Season the duck with mixed herbs, salt, and pepper and fry until golden brown on both sides, 8 minutes. Set aside. Add onion and celery to oil and sauté until softened, 3 minutes. Stir in garlic, rosemary, and cook until fragrant, 30 seconds.

Mix in tomato paste and pour in chicken stock. Let simmer for 1 minute and return the duck to the pot. Seal the lid, select Pressure Cook on High, and set to 5 minutes. When done, do a quick release. Stir in lemon juice and parsley, and serve the duck with gravy and some mashed potatoes.

Peking-Style Duck

Total Time: 15 minutes | **Servings:** 4

Ingredients

2 tbsp sesame oil
½ cup soy sauce
3 tbsp ketchup
3 tbsp balsamic vinegar
1 tbsp brown sugar
1 tbsp honey
1 tbsp minced ginger
1 tbsp minced garlic
½ tsp Chinese Five Spices
½ tsp red chili flakes
2 cups chopped smoked duck
1 medium red onion, quartered
2 cups broccoli florets
1 cup chicken broth
Salt and black pepper to taste
2 tbsp cornstarch
1 cup cashews
½ celery cup, chopped

Directions

In a bowl, whisk 1 tbsp of sesame oil, soy sauce, ketchup, vinegar, sugar, honey, ginger, garlic, Five Spice, and red chili flakes; set aside. Set your Instant Pot to Sauté and heat the remaining sesame oil. Cook duck to take on the flavor of sesame oil. Stir in onion, celery, and broccoli and cook for 3 minutes. Mix in ketchup mixture and chicken broth.

Seal the lid, select Manual, and set the time to 3 minutes. When done, do a quick pressure release. Adjust the taste and stir in cornstarch and cashews. Select Sauté and allow sauce thickening for 1-2 minutes. Spoon over rice to serve.

Thai Red Curry Duck

Total Time: 40 min | **Servings:** 4

Ingredients

1 tbsp sesame oil
1 lb duck breasts
2 tbsp Thai red curry paste
1 eggplant, chopped
1 tbsp garlic paste
1 tbsp ginger paste
8 oz snow peas
2 tbsp soy sauce
1 (13.5-oz) coconut milk
2 tbsp cilantro, chopped
2 cups basmati rice, cooked
4 lime wedges

Directions

Set your Instant Pot to Sauté, heat sesame oil, and fry duck for 8-10 minutes. Turn and cook for another 4 minutes. Set aside. Add eggplant, curry paste, garlic, and ginger to the cooker and sauté for 2 minutes. Pour in coconut milk, peas, soy sauce, and 1 cup water; return the duck.

Seal the lid, select Pressure Cook and set to 12 minutes. When done, allow a natural release for 10 minutes. Carefully unlock the lid and remove the duck to a plate. Let it sit for a few minutes, then slice.

Arrange the duck siles on a platter, add in the cooked rice and pour the sauce over. Garnish with cilantro and lime wedges and serve.

Alsatian-Style Goose Choucroute Garnie

Total Time: 35 minutes | **Servings:** 6

Ingredients

1 lb cooked knockwurst sausages, cubed
1 lb potatoes, pricked all over with a fork
4 bacon slices, chopped
2 yellow onions, thinly sliced
½ head savoy cabbage, sliced
4 garlic cloves, minced
1 lb sauerkraut, drained
1 tsp ground caraway powder
Salt and black pepper to taste
3 bay leaves
1 lb goose breast, cubed
1 cup mirin wine
2 cups chicken broth
1 tbsp whole-grain mustard

Directions

Set your Instant Pot to Sauté and cook bacon for 5 minutes; set aside. Melt goose fat in the pot and sauté onion, garlic, and cabbage for 4 minutes.

Add in sauerkraut, potatoes, caraway powder, salt, bay leaves, and bacon. Place goose on top and season with salt and pepper. Prick sausages all over with a fork and arrange them over the goose.

Pour in mirin wine and chicken broth. Seal the lid, select Pressure Cook, and set the time to 13 minutes. When done, do a quick release. Spoon sauerkraut and potatoes onto plates and top with meat. Garnish with mustard.

Stewed Goose with Egg Noodles

Total Time: 25 min + marinating time | **Servings:** 4

Ingredients

2 tsp olive oil
¼ cup butter, cubed
¼ cup coconut aminos
2 tsp lime juice
1 tsp garlic powder
1 tsp Worcestershire sauce
½ lb goose breast, cubed
1 cup all-purpose flour
4 cups chicken broth
1 pack onion soup mix
8 oz egg noodles

Directions

In a bowl, combine coconut aminos, olive oil, lime juice, garlic powder, and Worcestershire sauce.

Add in the goose, toss to coat, and marinate for 30 minutes. Set your Instant Pot to Sauté and melt the butter. Remove the goose from marinade (discard marinade). Toss in onion soup mix and brown in butter on both sides, 8 minutes.

Pour in the broth and egg noodles. Seal the lid, select Pressure Cook, and set the cooking time to 7 minutes. Allow a quick release. Serve and enjoy!

PORK RECIPES

Herbed Pork in Creamy Wine Sauce

Total Time: 45 minutes | **Servings:** 4

Ingredients

4 tbsp butter	2 garlic cloves, minced
1 tsp onion powder	½ cup dry white wine
2 tsp dried mixed herbs	½ cup chicken stock
¼ cup + 1 tbsp flour	½ lemon, juiced
Salt and black pepper to taste	½ cup heavy cream
4 boneless pork chops	4 thyme sprigs, leaves extracted

Directions

In a bowl, combine onion powder, mixed herbs, ¼ cup of flour, salt, and pepper. Dredge pork lightly in the mixture. Set your Instant Pot to Sauté and melt 2 tbsp of butter. Sear pork on both sides until golden brown, 10 minutes.

Add in chicken stock and seal the lid. Cook for 15 minutes on Manual/Pressure Cook on High. When ready, do a quick pressure release. Transfer pork with cooking liquid to a bowl, cover with foil and set aside.

Clean the pot with a paper towel and melt in the remaining butter. Add garlic and cook for 2 minutes until fragrant; stir in remaining flour. Pour in the wine, cook for 1 minute, and stir in cooking liquid and lemon juice. Cook further for 2 minutes. Stir in heavy cream and thyme, season to taste, and simmer for 3 minutes. Plate and drizzle sauce all over.

Pork Chops with Maple Glaze

Total Time: 20 minutes | **Servings:** 4

Ingredients

1 tbsp olive oil	3 tbsp ketchup
2 tbsp butter	1 tsp grated ginger
4 pork chops	2 tbsp soy sauce
Salt and black pepper to taste	1 tsp thyme leaves
1 ½ cups maple syrup	

Directions

Set your Instant Pot to Sauté and heat olive oil. Season the pork with salt and pepper and brown it in the pot until golden brown on both sides, 10 minutes. Transfer to a plate and set aside for serving. Melt butter in oil and stir in maple syrup, ketchup, ginger, soy sauce, and thyme; simmer for 1 minute. Spoon sauce all over the pork and serve warm.

Pork & Sweet Corn Chowder

Total Time: 40 minutes | **Servings:** 4

Ingredients

1 tbsp olive oil	4 cups chicken stock
1 lb pork tenderloin, cubed	½ lemon, juiced
2 shallots, chopped	Salt and black pepper to taste
2 garlic cloves, minced	3 tbsp heavy cream
1 (8 oz) can sweet corn kernels	3 tbsp chopped chives
½ tsp mustard powder	

Directions

Set your Instant Pot to Sauté, heat olive oil, season pork with salt and pepper, and sear in oil until golden brown, 8 minutes; set aside. Sauté shallots until softened, 2 minutes. Stir in garlic, cook for 30 seconds, follow up with corn kernels, mustard, and cook for 1 minute. Stir in stock and pork. Seal the lid, select Pressure Cook on High, and set the time to 10 minutes. When done, allow a natural release for 10 minutes. Spoon pork meat into bowls and set aside. Using an immersion blender, puree soup until smooth, and stir in lemon juice. Adjust taste with salt and black pepper. Mix in heavy cream and spoon soup over pork. Garnish with chives and serve warm.

Braised Pork Ragu

Total Time: 40 minutes | **Servings:** 4

Ingredients

8 oz fettuccine	2 tbsp tomato paste
8 cups water	2 (15-oz) cans diced tomatoes
1 lb pork shoulder, cubed	1 tsp dried oregano
1 white onion, chopped	1 tsp dried rosemary
2 large carrots, chopped	Salt and black pepper to taste
2 garlic cloves, minced	¼ grated Parmesan cheese

Directions

Pour fettuccine and water into your Instant Pot. Seal the lid, select Pressure Cook on High, and set the time to 2 minutes. After cooking, do a quick release. Drain pasta and set aside. Add pork, onion, carrots, garlic, tomato paste, tomatoes with juice, oregano, rosemary, salt, and pepper to the pot. Stir to coat the pork. Seal the lid, select Pressure Cook on High, and set the time to 30 minutes. After cooking, do a quick release, and unlock the lid. Stir in fettuccine and adjust taste with salt and pepper. Garnish with Parmesan.

Russian-Style Pork Stew with Rice

Total time: 35 minutes | **Servings:** 6

Ingredients

1 (10-oz) can condensed cream of mushroom soup	
3 tbsp olive oil	1 tbsp flour
3 cups beef broth	1 ½ cups brown rice
1 lb pork tenderloin strips	1 cup crème fraiche
1 onion, sliced	2 tsp yellow mustard
1 garlic cloves, minced	

Directions

Set your Instant Pot to Sauté and heat olive oil. Cook pork, onion, and garlic for 8 minutes, with a couple of water splashes until the meat is tender. Pour in the broth, cream of mushroom soup, and flour and stir until smooth. Place in the rice. Seal the lid, select Pressure Cook on High, and set the time to 10 minutes. When done, perform a natural pressure release for 10 minutes, then a quick pressure release to let out the remaining steam. Unlock the lid and pour in the crème fraiche and mustard and stir. Let it rest for a few minutes and serve warm.

Spice-Rubbed Baby Back Ribs

Total Time: 45 min + marinating time | **Servings**: 4

Ingredients

Seasoning

Salt and black pepper to taste	½ tbsp ground mustard
2 tbsp smoked paprika	½ tsp cayenne pepper
1 tbsp garlic powder	½ tsp cumin
1 tbsp onion powder	½ tsp ground fennel seeds
1 tbsp chili powder	½ tsp dried rosemary
1 tbsp white sugar	

Ribs

1 rack (2 pounds) pork baby back ribs, quartered	
1 tbsp oil	Hoisin sauce

Directions

In a bowl, combine all seasoning ingredients and coat the ribs with the mixture. Cover them with plastic wrap and refrigerate overnight. Set the Instant Pot to Sauté and heat the oil. Cook the ribs, meat-side down for 5 minutes, until browned; remove to a plate. Pour 1 cup of water into the inner pot and fit in a trivet. Arrange the ribs on the trivet.

Seal the lid, press Pressure Cook, and cook for 20 minutes on High. Do a quick pressure release. Transfer the ribs to a foil-lined baking dish. Brush with hoisin sauce and set under broiler for 7-10 minutes, until a nice crust is formed.

Pork Chops in Honey-Mustard Sauce

Total Time: 15 minutes | **Servings**: 4

Ingredients

1 tbsp olive oil	½ cup apple cider vinegar
2 tbsp butter	2 tbsp honey
4 pork chops	1 tbsp Dijon mustard
Salt and black pepper to taste	2 tbsp parsley, chopped

Directions

Pat pork chops dry with a paper towel and season with salt and pepper. Set your Instant Pot to Sauté, heat olive oil and brown pork until golden brown on both sides, and cooked through, 8 minutes. Transfer to a plate and set aside. Add butter to the oil and allow melting while stirring. Pour in apple cider vinegar, honey, and mustard. Continually stir until well-combined and simmering, 1 minute. Spoon sauce all over the pork and serve topped with parsley.

Pork Meatballs the Swedish Way

Total Time: 25 minutes | **Servings**: 4

Ingredients

2 tbsp olive oil	¼ tsp ground nutmeg
1 tbsp butter	Salt and black pepper to taste
1 lb ground pork	1 egg, beaten
½ cup breadcrumbs	2 tbsp flour
1 onion, chopped	1 cup vegetable broth
1 garlic clove, minced	½ tbsp Tabasco sauce
¼ tsp coriander seeds, mince	½ tsp mayonnaise
¼ tsp allspice	¼ cup heavy cream

Directions

Combine pork, breadcrumbs, onion, garlic, coriander seeds, allspice, nutmeg, pepper, salt, and egg; mix well. Shape the mixture into balls. Set the cooker to Sauté and heat oil. Cook the meatballs for about 5 minutes per side; reserve. Stir in the butter and flour and whisk until it is fully combined, about 2 minutes. Mix in broth, Tabasco sauce, and mayonnaise. Return the meatballs to the inner pot. Seal the lid, select Pressure Cook, and set it to 5 minutes. When done, do a quick release. Stir in heavy cream. Adjust the seasoning and serve with mashed potatoes.

Marsala Pork with Potatoes & Pancetta

Total Time: 50 minutes | **Servings**: 4

Ingredients

1 tbsp olive oil	2 cups chicken broth
6 pieces pancetta, chopped	1 ½ cups sweet corn kernels
4 boneless pork chops	2 small Yukon Gold potatoes,
Salt and black pepper to taste	peeled and diced
1 medium red onion, chopped	2 tsp chopped chives
2 garlic cloves, minced	3 tbsp heavy cream
1 red chili pepper, minced	¼ cup chopped parsley
½ cup marsala wine	

Directions

Set your Instant Pot to Sauté and fry the pancetta until brown and crispy, 5 minutes. Transfer to a paper towel-lined plate to drain grease. To the pot, add the olive oil to heat. Season pork with salt and pepper, and sear in oil on both sides until golden, 6 minutes; set aside. Sauté onion, garlic, and red chili pepper in oil until fragrant, 2 minutes. Add marsala wine and cook until reduced by one-third. Pour in broth, corn kernels, potatoes, pork, and pancetta. Seal the lid, select Pressure Cook, and set the time to 30 minutes. After cooking, allow a quick release. Fetch out pork onto serving plates. Mix in chives, heavy cream, and spoon masala all over pork. Garnish with parsley and serve.

Lemony Shredded Pork

Total Time: 40 minutes | **Servings**: 4

Ingredients

2 tbsp olive oil	1 tbsp dried oregano
1 lb pork shoulder	1 tbsp smoked paprika
1 ½ cups chicken broth	10 garlic cloves, minced
1 orange, juiced	Salt and black pepper to taste
1 lemon, juiced	1 white onion, cut into rounds
1 lime, juiced	Lime wedges to garnish

Directions

Place pork in the inner pot of your Instant Pot. In a bowl, combine olive oil, broth, orange juice, lemon juice, lime juice, oregano, smoked paprika, garlic, salt, and pepper. Pour the mixture all over the meat and top with onions. Seal the lid, select Pressure Cook on High, and set the time to 30 minutes. After cooking, do a quick release and unlock the lid. Using two forks, shred meat and stir well. Adjust the taste and plate. Garnish with lime wedges and serve.

Ground Pork Huevos Rancheros

Total Time: 45 minutes | **Servings:** 4

Ingredients

1 tbsp olive oil
1 lb ground pork
1 small white onion, chopped
1 garlic clove, minced
1 red bell pepper, chopped
2 tbsp tomato paste
4 cups tomatoes, chopped
1 tsp smoked paprika
1 tsp chili powder
Salt and black pepper to taste
4 eggs, cracked into a bowl
1 tbsp chopped parsley

Directions

Set your Instant Pot to Sauté, heat olive oil and brown pork for 5 minutes. Add onion, garlic, and bell pepper. Stir-fry until softened, 3 minutes. Stir in tomato paste, tomatoes, paprika, chili powder, salt, pepper, and 1 cup of water.

Seal the lid, select Pressure Cook on Low, and set the time to 15 minutes. Allow a natural release for 10 minutes, and unlock the lid. Select Sauté and stir. Create four holes in the sauce and pour each egg into each hole. Allow egg setting for 1 to 2 minutes. Spoon shakshuka into serving bowls, garnish with parsley and serve warm.

Pork with Spicy Red Sauce

Total Time: 35 minutes | **Servings:** 4

Ingredients

1 lb ground pork
2 tbsp chili powder
Salt and black pepper to taste
½ tsp dried oregano
2 tsp garlic, minced
¼ cup cilantro, chopped
1 cup diced red onion
2 (15-oz) cans stewed tomatoes
1 (19-oz) can enchilada sauce
1 cup chicken broth
2 (15-oz) cans red kidney beans

Directions

Into your Instant Pot, add pork, chili powder, salt, black pepper, oregano, garlic, cilantro, onion, tomatoes, enchilada sauce, chicken broth, and kidney beans. Seal the lid, select Pressure Cook on High, and set the time to 15 minutes.

Perform natural pressure release for 10 minutes, then a quick pressure release until remaining steam is out, and unlock the lid. Stir, adjust taste with salt and pepper, and dish the chili. Serve warm with tortillas and cheddar cheese.

Pork in Corn Field

Total Time: 45 minutes | **Servings:** 4

Ingredients

1 (21 oz) can cream of mushroom soup
8 slices bacon, chopped
6 half ears of corn
5 small potatoes, chopped
1 yellow onion, chopped
4 boneless pork chops
½ cup whole milk
Salt and black pepper to taste
¾ tsp dried rosemary

Directions

Set your Instant Pot to Sauté and cook bacon until crispy, 5 minutes. Spoon onto a paper towel-lined plate to drain grease. In the pot, arrange corn, potatoes, onion, and pork.

Pour mushroom soup on top, followed by milk, salt, pepper, rosemary, bacon, and 1 cup water. Seal the lid, select Pressure Cook on High, and set the time to 20 minutes. Once done cooking, perform natural pressure release for 10 minutes, then a quick pressure release until remaining steam is out. Unlock the lid. Serve warm topped with bacon.

Pork Ragu with Rigatoni Pasta

Total Time: 55 minutes | **Servings:** 6

Ingredients

4 oz Italian sausages, casings removed
½ cup grated Parmesan cheese + for serving
2 tbsp olive oil
1 lb boneless pork shoulder
Salt to taste
1 medium onion, chopped
2 garlic cloves, minced
1 medium carrot, chopped
1 celery stalk, chopped
½ cup dry red wine
¼ tsp red pepper flakes
1 (28-oz) can crushed tomatoes
2 tbsp tomato paste
2 tsp dried Italian herb mix
8 oz rigatoni

Directions

Set your Instant Pot to Sauté, heat olive oil, season the pork with salt, and sear for 4 minutes or until browned. Add in sausages, onion, garlic, carrot, and celery. Sauté for 2 minutes or until softened. Stir in wine and use a wooden spoon to scrape off the bottom of any browned bits. Cook for 2 to 3 minutes until the wine has reduced by half.

Add the red flakes, tomatoes, tomato paste, 1 cup of water, and Italian herbs; stir to combine. Seal the lid, select Manual/Pressure Cook on High, and set the time to 20 minutes. After cooking, allow a natural release for 10 minutes. Shred the pork with two forks and break the sausage apart. Add 4 cups of water and the rigatoni. Seal the lid, press Pressure Cook on High for 4 minutes. Do a quick pressure release. Sprinkle Parmesan over sauce and pasta to serve.

Agave BBQ Pulled Pork

Total Time: 65 minutes | **Servings:** 4

Ingredients

1 lb pork shoulder, cut into 4 chunks
1 (12-oz) can root beer
¼ cup agave syrup
1 ½ cups bbq sauce
½ lemon, juiced
2 tsp garlic powder
1 tsp onion powder
4 hamburger buns for serving

Directions

Place pork in your Instant Pot and pour beer all over. In a bowl, whisk agave syrup, 1 cup of bbq sauce, lemon juice, garlic and onion powders, and 1 cup of water. Spread the mixture all over the meat. Seal the lid, select Pressure Cook on High, and set the time to 45 minutes. After cooking, allow a natural release for 10 minutes, and unlock the lid.

Using two forks, shred pork into small pieces. Using tongs or slotted spoon, transfer to a serving bowl and stir in remaining bbq sauce. Spoon pulled pork into burger buns, top with coleslaw, mayonnaise, if desired, and serve.

Melt In Your Mouth Braised Pork

Total Time: 70 minutes | **Servings:** 4

Ingredients

2 tbsp olive oil
1 lb pork belly, cubed
Salt to taste
2 tbsp freshly grated ginger
2 leeks, chopped
1 red chili
2 bay leaves

1-star anise
2 tsp granulated sugar
1 ½ cups chicken broth
1 tbsp regular soy sauce
1 tbsp dark soy sauce
2 scallions, chopped
1 tbsp sesame seeds

Directions

Pour 3 cups of water and add pork and salt into your Instant Pot. Seal the lid, set to Pressure Cook on High, and set the time to 30 minutes. After cooking, allow a natural release for 10 minutes. Drain pork and set aside.

Clean inner pot and press Sauté. Heat olive oil and stir-fry ginger, leeks, red chili, bay leaves, star anise, until fragrant, 3 minutes. Add pork. In a bowl, mix sugar, broth, and soy sauces; pour mixture over pork.

Seal the lid, set on Pressure Cook on High, and set to 10 minutes. When done, allow a natural release for 10 minutes, then a quick pressure release; unlock the lid. Stir and spoon into plates. Garnish with scallions and sesame seeds.

Korean-Style Pork with Green Beans

Total Time: 30 minutes | **Servings:** 4

Ingredients

1 tbsp olive oil
8 oz egg noodles
1 lb green beans, trimmed
Salt and black pepper to taste

1 pork tenderloin, cubed
1 cup teriyaki sauce
Sesame seeds, for garnish
1 cup water

Directions

Pour the egg noodles in your Instant Pot and cover them with enough water. Seal the lid, select Pressure Cook on High, and set the time to 3 minutes. When ready, do a quick pressure release. Drain the noodles and set them aside.

In a bowl, toss green beans with oil, salt, and pepper. In the pot, toss the tenderloin with teriyaki sauce. Pour in water. Seal the lid, select Pressure Cook on High, and set to 12 minutes. Do a quick pressure release and select Sauté. Stir in beans and cook for 6 minutes. Serve the pork with green beans over egg noodles. Garnish with sesame seeds.

Sesame Pork Egg Roll Bowls

Total Time: 30 minutes | **Servings:** 4

Ingredients

1 tbsp olive oil
1 tbsp sesame oil
1 lb ground pork
Salt and black pepper to taste
1 garlic clove, minced
1 tbsp freshly grated ginger
½ red onion, thinly sliced

1 cup shredded carrots
1 small green cabbage, sliced
¼ cup soy sauce
1 tbsp hot sauce
1 cup chicken broth
1 scallion, thinly sliced
1 tbsp sesame seeds

Directions

Set your Instant Pot to Sauté, heat olive oil, add pork, season with salt, pepper, and cook until brown, 5 minutes. Add garlic, ginger, and cook until fragrant, 1 minute. Mix in sesame oil, onion, carrots, cabbage, soy sauce, hot sauce, and broth. Seal the lid, select Pressure Cook on High, and set the time to 15 minutes. After cooking, perform a quick pressure. Stir in scallion and adjust the taste. Dish food into serving bowls and garnish with sesame seeds.

Basil & Parsley Creamy Pork

Total Time: 55 minutes | **Servings:** 4

Ingredients

1 tbsp olive oil
1 tbsp butter
1 pork shoulder, cut into cubes
Salt and black pepper to taste
½ tsp dried mustard powder
1 small yellow onion, diced

3 garlic cloves, minced
1 ½ cups chicken broth
¾ cup heavy cream
1 tbsp cornstarch
1 tsp dried parsley
1 tsp dried basil

Directions

Set your Instant Pot to Sauté, heat olive oil and butter, and season pork with salt, pepper, and mustard powder. Sear in oil until golden on the outside, 7 minutes. Transfer to a plate. Sauté onion until softened, 3 minutes. Stir in garlic and cook until fragrant, 30 seconds. Pour in chicken broth and return meat to the pot. Seal the lid, select Pressure Cook on High, and set the time to 20 minutes. After cooking, allow a natural release for 10 minutes. Transfer the pork to a plate and press Sauté. Into sauce, whisk heavy cream, cornstarch, basil, and parsley. Cook for 2 minutes and return pork to sauce. Let heat for 3 minutes. Serve pork with sauce.

Pork & Veggie Rice

Total time: 45 minutes | **Servings:** 6

Ingredients

2 tbsp olive oil
1 onion, finely chopped
1 garlic clove, minced
2 lb pork loin filet, chopped
Salt and black pepper to taste
4 cups water

2 cups rice
1 large egg, beaten
3 tbsp soy sauce
1 carrot, chopped
1 cup green beans, chopped
2 scallions, finely chopped

Directions

Set your Instant Pot to Sauté and heat 1 tbsp of olive oil. Stir-fry onion and garlic for 3 minutes. Sprinkle pork with salt and pepper, and cook for 8-10 minutes with a splash of water. Pour in 1 cup of water to scrape any browned bits from the bottom. Place in rice and remaining water. Seal the lid, select Pressure Cook, and set to 8 minutes on High.

When done, allow a natural release for 10 minutes. Unlock the lid and fluff the rice with a fork. In a bowl, mix in the remaining oil and beaten egg. Add in the soy sauce and pork mixture and stir. Put in the green beans and carrots. Stir the resulting mixture in the rice and let sit until heated through, 6 minutes on Sauté. Sprinkle with scallions to serve.

Sage Pork with Caramelized Apples

Total Time: 45 minutes | **Servings:** 4

Ingredients

2 tbsp olive oil
3 tbsp butter
4 bone-in pork chops
Salt and black pepper to taste
2 garlic cloves, minced
2 tbsp chopped sage

1 lb apples, peeled and sliced
4 tbsp honey
½ cup apple cider vinegar
1 cup chicken broth
½ cup heavy cream
2 tbsp chopped parsley

Directions

Set your Instant Pot to Sauté, heat olive oil, season pork with salt and pepper, and sear until golden brown, 6 minutes; set aside. Add garlic and sage, and stir-fry until fragrant, 30 seconds. Pour in apples, butter, and honey; cook until apples caramelize, 5 minutes. Top with vinegar, broth, and pork. Seal the lid, select Pressure Cook on High, and set to 20 minutes. After cooking, allow a natural release for 10 minutes. Unlock the lid and stir in heavy cream. Simmer in Sauté mode for 2 to 3 minutes. Spoon food into serving plates with a generous topping of sauce. Garnish with parsley and serve.

Three-Pepper Pork Chili with Tomatillos

Total Time: 45 minutes | **Servings:** 4

Ingredients

2 tbsp olive oil
1 lb pork shoulder, cubed
Salt and black pepper to taste
2 jalapeño peppers
2 poblano peppers
2 Anaheim peppers

4 garlic cloves
6 tomatillos, husk removed
1 large white onion, quartered
1 bunch cilantro
½ tsp cumin powder
1 cup chicken broth

Directions

Preheat the oven to 350°F. Set your Instant Pot to Sauté and heat olive oil. Season pork with salt and pepper, and sear until golden brown on both sides, 8 minutes. Arrange the peppers, garlic, tomatillos, and onion on a baking sheet. Roast in the oven for 3 to 5 minutes or until slightly charred. Quickly blend roasted vegetables with cilantro in a blender. Pour the mixture over the pork. Add cumin and broth.

Seal the lid, select Pressure Cook on High, and set the time to 15 minutes. Once done, perform a natural release for 10 minutes; unlock the lid. Stir sauce, adjust the taste, and dish into serving bowls. Serve warm with tortillas.

Pork Ramen with Broccoli & Cabbage

Total Time: 40 minutes | **Servings:** 4

Ingredients

1 lb boneless pork chops, cut in ½ inch strips
3 tsp olive oil, divided
2 (3 oz) packs ramen noodles
¼ cup soy sauce
2 tbsp Worcestershire sauce
2 tbsp ketchup
2 tsp granulated sugar

¼ tsp red chili flakes
1 cup broccoli florets
1 cup shredded red cabbage
1 cup shredded green cabbage
4 garlic cloves, minced
2 cups chicken broth

Directions

To your Instant Pot, add ramen noodles (discard seasoning) and 2 ½ cups of salted water. Seal the lid, select Pressure Cook on High, and set the time to 1 minute. After cooking, do a quick pressure release; unlock the lid. Drain noodles and set them aside. Clean the inner pot. Press Sauté.

In a small bowl, mix soy sauce, Worcestershire sauce, ketchup, sugar, red chili flakes, and 2 teaspoons of olive oil. Pour mixture into the inner pot, let heat for 1 minute, and add pork; cook until no longer pink.

With a slotted spoon, strain the pork, and transfer to a plate. To the pot, add broccoli, cabbages, garlic, and broth. Cook for 2 minutes and return pork to pot. Seal the lid, select Pressure Cook on High, and set to 15 minutes. Allow a natural release for 10 minutes. Stir in ramen. Press Sauté and heat noodles for 2 minutes. Spoon into plates to serve.

Hot Pork Chops

Total Time: 45 minutes + marinating time | **Servings:** 4

Ingredients

2 tbsp sesame oil
2 tbsp olive oil
4 boneless pork chops
2 tbsp hot sauce

1 lemon, juiced
1 tbsp soy sauce
1 ½ tsp sriracha sauce
1 cup chicken broth

Directions

Place pork chops in a plastic zipper bag. In a small bowl, mix hot sauce, sesame oil, lemon juice, soy sauce, and sriracha sauce. Pour mixture over pork, close bag, and massage marinade into the meat. Refrigerate for 1 hour.

Set your Instant Pot to Sauté and heat olive oil. Remove pork from the fridge and marinade, and sear on both sides until brown, 6 minutes. Pour in the chicken broth. Seal the lid, select Pressure Cook on High, and set the time to 20 minutes. After cooking, allow a natural release for 10 minutes, and unlock the lid. Remove pork onto serving plates and baste with a little sauce. Serve and enjoy!

Pork Bean Dip

Total Time: 35 minutes | **Servings:** 4

Ingredients

1 tbsp olive oil
½ lb ground pork
Salt and black pepper to taste
2 cups black beans, soaked

½ cup chicken broth
1 tbsp coriander powder
1 tbsp cumin powder
¼ cup grated cheddar cheese

Directions

Set your Instant Pot to Sauté and heat olive oil. Season pork with salt and pepper, and sear until brown, 10 minutes; set aside. Pour black beans, broth, coriander, and cumin. Seal the lid, select Pressure Cook on High, and set the time to 15 minutes. After cooking, do a quick pressure release and unlock the lid. Using an immersion blender, puree ingredients and stir in pork. Adjust taste with salt and black pepper. Dish, top with cheddar cheese and serve.

Pork Cheeseburger Soup

Total Time: 35 minutes | **Servings:** 4

Ingredients

2 tbsp olive oil
½ lb ground pork
Salt and black pepper to taste
2 russet potatoes, chopped
3 celery stalks, chopped
2 carrots, chopped

1 white onion, chopped
2 tsp dried tarragon
½ tsp garlic powder
4 cups chicken broth
8 oz Velveeta cheese
8 oz cream cheese, softened

Directions

Set your Instant Pot to Sauté. Heat olive oil. Cook pork until brown, 5 minutes; season with salt and pepper. Add potatoes, celery, carrots, onion, tarragon, garlic powder, and broth. Seal the lid, select Pressure Cook on High, and set the time to 20 minutes. After cooking, do a quick pressure release. Select Sauté and stir in Velveeta and cream cheese until melted and well combined. Adjust the taste. Serve.

Saucy Meatballs with Tagliatelle

Total time: 25 minutes | **Servings:** 6

Ingredients

1 (24-oz) can tomato & basil pasta sauce
2 tbsp olive oil
1 lb pork meatballs
1 lb dried tagliatelle

½ cup dry white wine
1 cup shredded Parmesan
2 tbsp fresh parsley, chopped

Directions

Set your Instant Pot to Sauté and heat olive oil. Cook pork meatballs for 5-6 minutes on all sides. Add in the tagliatelle on top and pour in the tomato sauce. Pour 8 cups of water and white wine over. Seal the lid, select Pressure Cook on High, and set to 10 minutes. When done, do a quick release. Add in Parmesan and stir. Serve topped with parsley.

Pork Sausage & Mozzarella Calzone

Total Time: 30 minutes | **Servings:** 4

Ingredients

2 tbsp olive oil
1 green bell pepper, chopped
2 Italian pork sausages, sliced

1 lb bread dough, thawed
¼ cup tomato sauce
1 cup shredded mozzarella

Directions

Set your Instant Pot to Sauté. Heat the olive oil. Sauté bell pepper and sausages for 5 minutes, stirring often. Use your hands to press each bread dough into a circle about 7 inches in diameter. Spread 1 tbsp of the tomato sauce over half of each dough circle. Arrange the sausages in a single layer and sprinkle with ¼ of green peppers. Top with ¼ cup of cheese. Fold the uncovered half of each circle over the filling and pinch the edges together to seal. Brush the calzones with the remaining oil and transfer to a baking dish. Put a trivet in the pot and pour 1 cup of water. Place baking dish on the trivet. Seal the lid, select Pressure Cook on High, and set the time to 6 minutes. After cooking, do a quick pressure release, and unlock the lid. Serve hot.

Bolognese-Style Pizza with Ground Pork

Total Time: 20 minutes | **Servings:** 4

Ingredients

½ lb ground pork, cooked and crumbled
1 pizza crust
½ cup canned crushed tomatoes
1 yellow bell pepper, sliced

1 cup shredded mozzarella
1 tsp red chili flakes, divided
1 tbsp chopped fresh basil

Directions

Grease one side of a pizza crust with cooking spray and lay on a baking pan. Top the crust with crushed tomatoes, bell pepper, ground pork, mozzarella, and chili flakes.

Pour 1 cup of water into your Instant Pot and fit in a trivet. Lay the pan on top. Seal the lid, select Pressure Cook on High, and set the cooking time to 10 minutes. When ready, do a quick release. Top with the basil. Serve and enjoy!

Classic Mississippi Pork

Total Time: 50 minutes | **Servings:** 4

Ingredients

16 oz deli sliced pepperoncini peppers with ½ cup juices
1 lb pork shoulder   Salt and black pepper to taste
1 pack ranch dressing mix

Directions

Combine pork, ranch dressing mix, and pepperoncini with juices in your Instant Pot. Pour in 1 cup of water. Seal the lid, select Pressure Cook on High, and set the cooking time to 30 minutes. After cooking, allow a natural release for 10 minutes. Unlock the lid and, using two forks, shred meat into small strands, adjust the taste, and serve over.

Habanero Bacon & Corn Bundt Casserole

Total Time: 45 minutes | **Servings:** 4

Ingredients

¼ cup salted butter, melted
8 bacon strips, chopped
2 eggs, beaten
1 cup shredded cheddar cheese
3 tbsp minced habanero chilies

1 (15 oz) can corn, drained
1 (8.5 oz) pack corn muffin mix
10.5 oz cream of sweet corn
¾ cup heavy cream

Directions

Set your Instant Pot to Sauté and cook bacon until crispy, 5 minutes. Fetch bacon into a large bowl and clean the inner pot. In the bowl, add eggs, cheddar cheese, habanero chilies, corn, muffin mix, corn cream, butter, and heavy cream.

Pour mixture into a greased bundt pan and cover with aluminum foil. Pour 1 cup water in the pot, fit in a trivet, and sit bundt pan on top. Seal the lid, select Pressure Cook on High, and set the time to 20 minutes.

When done cooking, do a natural pressure release for 10 minutes. Unlock the lid and carefully remove the bundt pan. Take off foil and turn the casserole over onto a plate. Garnish with parsley, slice, and serve.

Thyme Pork with Mushrooms & Shallots

Total Time: 55 minutes | **Servings:** 4

Ingredients

2 tbsp olive oil
2 tbsp butter
4 boneless pork chops
Salt and black pepper to taste
2 shallots, thinly sliced
2 garlic cloves, minced

1 cup sliced cremini mushrooms
½ cup Marsala wine
1 cup chicken stock
1 tsp thyme leaves
¼ cup plain flour
2 tbsp chopped parsley

Directions

Set your Instant Pot to Sauté and heat the olive oil and butter. Season the pork with salt and black pepper, and sear until golden brown on both sides, 8 minutes. Transfer to a plate. Stir in shallots and garlic until softened and fragrant, 2 minutes. Add mushrooms, and cook for 2 minutes. Pour in marsala wine, allow reduction by one-third, and add chicken stock and thyme; return the pork to the pot. Seal the lid, select Pressure Cook on High, and set to 20 minutes.

After cooking, allow a natural release for 10 minutes. Stir in flour and cook sauce further in Sauté until slightly thickened. Spoon pork and sauce onto serving plates and garnish with parsley.

Tropical Pineapple Pork Pot

Total Time: 40 minutes | **Servings:** 4

Ingredients

1 (20 oz) can pineapple chunks in juice
2 tbsp olive oil, separated
1 tbsp cornstarch
3 tbsp maple syrup
2 tbsp coconut aminos
2 tbsp brown sugar
1 tbsp grated ginger
3 garlic cloves, minced

1 lb pork stew meat, cubed
Salt and black pepper to taste
1 onion, chopped
1 red bell pepper, chopped
1 green bell pepper, chopped
1 tsp dried oregano
2 tbsp chopped parsley

Directions

In a bowl, combine 2 tbsp water, cornstarch, maple syrup, coconut aminos, sugar, ginger, and garlic. Stir in pineapples with juice; set aside. Set your Instant Pot to Sauté, heat olive oil, season pork with salt and pepper, and sear until golden brown 5 minutes. Stir in onion, bell peppers, oregano, and cook until softened, 5 minutes.

Add pineapple mixture and 1 cup of water. Seal the lid, select Pressure Cook on High, and set the time to 10 minutes. When done, allow a natural release for 10 minutes. Stir food and adjust the taste. Top with parsley and serve.

Salsa Verde Pork with Velveeta Cheese

Total Time: 30 minutes | **Servings:** 4

Ingredients

2 tbsp olive oil
1 lb ground pork
Salt and black pepper to taste
½ cup milk

2 tbsp white Velveeta cheese
1 (16 oz) jar salsa verde
16 oz sour cream
2 jalapeño peppers, sliced

Directions

Set your Instant Pot to Sauté mode and heat olive oil. Cook pork until brown, 5 minutes. Season with a little salt and black pepper. Add in milk and ½ cup of water and seal the lid. Select Pressure Cook, and set the time to 15 minutes. When ready, do a quick pressure release. Press Sauté, mix in Velveeta cheese, salsa verde, sour cream, and jalapeño peppers. Cook with frequent stirring until cheese melts. Dish into serving bowls and serve warm.

Pork with Pepper Sauce & Potatoes

Total Time: 45 minutes | **Servings:** 4

Ingredients

1 lb pork tenderloin, cut into 2 pieces
1 roasted red bell pepper, cut into strips
2 tsp pickling liquid from the peppers
2 tbsp olive oil
2 tbsp butter
Salt and black pepper to taste
4 potatoes, quartered

½ cup dry white wine
1 cup chicken stock
2 garlic cloves, minced
6 pickled pimientos, quartered

Directions

Season the pork with salt and pepper. On Sauté, heat oil and sear the pork for 6 minutes until browned. Remove to a plate. Pour in the wine and scrape off any browned bits at the bottom. Let the wine reduce by one-third.

Stir in potatoes, stock, and garlic. Return the pork to the pot. Seal the lid, select Pressure Cook on High, and set the time to 20 minutes. After cooking, allow a natural release for 10 minutes. Remove the pork and let it rest. Select Sauté and stir in the roasted pepper, pimientos, and pickling liquid. Taste and adjust the seasoning.

To serve, stir in the butter. Slice the tenderloin and lay the pieces on a plate. Ladle the peppers and potatoes around the pork, and spoon the sauce over.

Oregano Pork Sausage Ragoût

Total Time: 35 minutes | **Servings:** 4

Ingredients

2 tbsp olive oil
1 lb Italian pork sausages, sliced
1 onion, chopped
2 garlic cloves, minced
1 tbsp red wine vinegar
Salt and black pepper to taste

6 oz canned tomatoes
½ tsp dried oregano
1 bay leaf
2 tbsp capers
8 oz spirals pasta

Directions

Set your Instant Pot to Sauté, heat the olive oil, and stir-fry in onion, garlic, salt, and pepper for 5 minutes. Brown sausages on all sides for 6 minutes. Pour in the vinegar, pasta, tomatoes, oregano, bay leaf, and 2 cups of water.

Seal the lid, select Pressure Cook on High, and set the time to 8 minutes. When done cooking, allow a natural release for 6 minutes, then a quick pressure release. Unlock the lid and stir in the capers. Serve hot.

Pulled BBQ Pork

Total Time: 45 minutes | **Servings:** 4

Ingredients

2 tbsp olive oil
1 tsp onion powder
2 tsp garlic powder
¼ tsp cayenne powder
2 tsp chili powder
1 tsp dry mustard
Salt and black pepper to taste
1 tbsp brown sugar
1 tbsp smoked paprika
1 ½ tsp cumin powder
1 lb pork shoulder, cubed
1 cup bbq sauce
1 cup ketchup
2 tbsp Worcestershire sauce
1 ½ cups chicken broth
½ cup grated cheddar cheese

Directions

In a bowl, mix onion and garlic powders, cayenne, chili, mustard, salt, pepper, sugar, paprika, and cumin. Set your Instant Pot to Sauté and heat olive. Season pork with dry rub on all sides and sear it until golden brown, 10 minutes.

Pour in bbq sauce, ketchup, Worcestershire sauce, and broth. Seal the lid, select Pressure Cook on High, and set the time to 15 minutes. After cooking, allow a natural release for 10 minutes. Using two forks, shred pork into strands. Select Sauté, mix in cheddar cheese, and cook until cheese melts and is evenly combined onto the meat. Serve.

Chinese-Style Pork Chili

Total Time: 35 minutes | **Servings:** 4

Ingredients

1 tbsp Sichuan peppercorns, crushed
1 tbsp olive oil
1 lb ground pork
2 brown onions, chopped
4 jalapeños, minced
1 green bell pepper, chopped
1 tbsp grated ginger
4 garlic cloves, minced
1 tbsp five-spice powder
¼ cup hoisin sauce
¼ cup soy sauce
2 cups chicken broth
12 oz amber colored beer
1 cup chopped tomatoes
1 tbsp rice wine vinegar
2 tsp Sriracha sauce
3 tbsp chopped cilantro

Directions

Add pork, onions, jalapeños, bell pepper, and olive oil. Set on Sauté and brown pork for 5 minutes. Stir in ginger, garlic, five-spice powder, peppercorns, hoisin sauce, soy sauce, broth, beer, tomatoes, vinegar, and Sriracha sauce.

Seal the lid, set on Pressure Cook mode on High, and set the cooking time to 10 minutes. After cooking, do a natural pressure release for 10 minutes. Stir in cilantro, adjust taste with salt, pepper, and dish chili into bowls. Serve.

Pulled Pork Burritos

Total Time: 70 minutes | **Servings:** 4

Ingredients

1 lb pork shoulder
1 cup beef stock
1 tsp ground coriander
4 garlic cloves, crushed
1 onion, chopped
2 bay leaves
Salt and black pepper to taste
1 tbsp soy sauce
½ cup enchilada sauce
12 corn tortilla wraps, warm
1 lime, juiced
Spicy pico de gallo for garnish

Directions

Mix pork, garlic, onion, ground coriander, bay leaves, soy sauce, enchilada sauce, salt, and pepper in a bowl and marinate for 20 minutes, covered. Then, place the mixture in the inner pot along with the beef stock. Seal the lid, select Pressure Cook on High, and set the time to 30 minutes. When done cooking, allow a natural pressure release for 10 minutes. Unlock the lid and transfer the meat to a cutting board to cool. Shred with a fork and return to the pot. To serve, fill the tortillas with the pork and top with pico de gallo and lime juice.

Pork Chops in Berry Gravy

Total Time: 45 minutes | **Servings:** 4

Ingredients

½ tbsp cornstarch mixed with 1 tbsp of water
1 tbsp butter
4 pork chops
Salt and black pepper to taste
¼ tsp dried thyme
1 tsp garlic powder
1 tsp onion powder
2 cups frozen mixed berries
4 tbsp granulated sugar
½ lemon, juiced
2 tbsp rosemary, chopped
¾ cup water
¼ cup red wine

Directions

Set the Instant Pot to Sauté and melt butter. Season pork with salt, pepper, thyme, garlic powder, and onion powder. Fry in butter until brown on both sides and almost cooked, 8 minutes. Transfer meat to plate and set aside.

Discard fat from inner pot, wipe clean with paper towels, and select Sauté. Pour in berries, sugar, lemon juice, and 3 tbsp water. Stir until sugar dissolves. Add red wine, remaining water, and meat; baste the meat with sauce. Seal the lid, select Pressure Cook on High, and set the time to 15 minutes.

After cooking, allow a natural release for 10 minutes. Unlock the lid and plate the meat. Set to Sauté and stir cornstarch into the sauce for 2 minutes until it thickens. Spoon sauce all over the meat, garnish with rosemary and serve.

Thyme Hot Pork with Zucchini

Total Time: 45 minutes | **Servings:** 4

Ingredients

2 tbsp olive oil
1 lb ground pork
1 yellow onion, chopped
3 cloves garlic, chopped
Salt and black pepper to taste
½ tsp dried thyme
2 zucchinis, sliced into coins
1 tsp red chili powder
1 handful parsley, chopped

Directions

Set your Instant Pot to Sauté, heat olive oil, and brown pork for 10 minutes. Stir-fry onion and garlic for 3 minutes. Season with salt, pepper, chili, thyme, and stir in 1 cup of water. Seal the lid, select Pressure Cook, and set to 15 minutes on High. When done, perform a quick pressure release until steam is out. Unlock the lid and stir in zucchinis. Press Sauté and cook until zucchinis soften, 7-10 minutes. Garnish with parsley and serve warm.

Marinated Pork Chops with Red Sauce

Total Time: 40 minutes + marinating time | **Servings:** 4

Ingredients

1 ½ tbsp cornstarch mixed with 2 tbsp water

¼ tsp sesame oil

1 tbsp peanut oil

4 boneless pork loin chops

1 onion, sliced

4 garlic cloves, minced

8 mushrooms, sliced

¼ cup tomato paste

2 tbsp ketchup

1 tsp tabasco sauce

1 cup water

Salt and black pepper to taste

2 tbsp sambal oelek chili paste

½ tsp brown sugar

2 tbsp light soy sauce

Directions

Using a meat mallet, flatten the pork chops. In a bowl, combine sugar, salt, soy sauce, sesame oil, and chili paste. Stir in chops, cover, and marinate for 30 minutes. Set the Instant Pot to Sauté and heat peanut oil. Place in marinated pork chops and cook for 2 minutes per side. Remove to a plate. Add in onion, garlic, mushrooms, salt, and pepper.

Cook for 2-3 minutes until tender. Pour in water to scrape off any browned bits from the bottom. Place in ketchup, tabasco sauce, and tomato paste and stir. Return the chops to the pot along with the meat juice. Seal the lid, select Pressure Cook on High, and set the time to 15 minutes. Allow a natural release for 10 minutes. Remove the chops. Select Sauté and stir in the cornstarch slurry. Cook until you have a thick sauce. Adjust the taste and serve.

Pork & Cucumber Salad

Total Time: 35 minutes | **Servings:** 4

Ingredients

2 tbsp olive oil

1 lb ground pork

1 small red chili, minced

2 ½ tbsp grated ginger

2 garlic cloves, minced

2 tbsp soy sauce

2 limes, juiced

1 tsp brown sugar

1 cup chicken broth

1 cucumber, thinly sliced

2 scallions, thinly sliced

1 cup chopped cilantro

Directions

Set your Instant Pot to Sauté, heat oil, and cook pork until brown, 5 minutes. Add red chili, ginger, garlic, and cook until softened, 3 minutes. In a bowl, mix soy sauce, lime juice, sugar, and broth. Pour mixture onto pork and stir.

Seal the lid, set on Pressure Cook on High, and set the time to 10 minutes. After cooking, allow a natural release for 10 minutes; unlock the lid. Stir and spoon pork into a bowl. Top with cucumber, scallions, and cilantro to serve.

Dijon Pork with Rosemary & Lemon

Total Time: 55 minutes | **Servings:** 4

Ingredients

1 tbsp olive oil

4 bone-in pork chops

Salt and black pepper to taste

2 tsp garlic powder

1 cup chicken broth

1 lemon, zested and juiced

4 rosemary sprigs

½ tsp Dijon mustard

Directions

Set your Instant Pot to Sauté, heat olive oil, season pork with salt, pepper, garlic powder, and sear on both sides until golden brown, 6 minutes. Pour in broth, lemon zest and juice, rosemary sprigs, and mix in Dijon mustard.

Seal the lid, select Pressure Cook on High, and set the time to 25 minutes. After cooking, perform a natural pressure release for 10 minutes. Unlock the lid. Remove pork onto serving plates, allow sitting for 2 minutes, and serve warm.

Spanish Carcamusa (Spanish-Style Chili)

Total time: 40 minutes | **Servings:** 6

Ingredients

1 tbsp olive oil

1 ½ lb ground pork

1 cup frozen green peas

2 yellow onions, chopped

2 garlic cloves, minced

2 (14-oz) cans tomatoes, drained

2 tbsp chili powder

½ tsp salt

2 tbsp parsley, chopped

Directions

Set your Instant Pot to Sauté, heat the olive oil, and brown the ground pork for 5-6 minutes, crumbling with a spatula. Add in peas, onions, and garlic and cook for 5 minutes. Add in tomatoes, chili powder, salt, and 2 cups of water.

Stir and allow simmering for 2 minutes. Seal the lid, select Pressure Cook on High, and set the time to 15 minutes. When done, perform a quick pressure release and unlock the lid. Serve garnished with parsley.

Easy Baby Back Ribs

Total Time: 55 minutes | **Servings:** 4

Ingredients

2 tbsp brown sugar

¼ tsp onion powder

½ tsp garlic powder

Salt and black pepper to taste

½ tsp smoked paprika

1 rack baby back ribs

1 cup chicken broth

½ cup bbq sauce + for serving

2 tsp hickory liquid smoke

Directions

In a bowl, combine sugar, onion powder, garlic powder, salt, pepper, and paprika. Cut ribs into four pieces each and rub generously with spice mixture. Place in your Instant Pot. Top with chicken broth, bbq sauce, and liquid smoke.

Seal the lid, select Pressure Cook on High, and set the time to 35 minutes. Once done, allow a natural release for 10 minutes, and unlock the lid. Using tongs, remove ribs into serving plates, brush with bbq sauce, and serve warm.

Sticky Barbecue Pork Ribs

Total Time: 60 minutes | **Servings:** 4

Ingredients

1 rack pork baby back ribs

1 tbsp garlic powder

1 tsp New Mexico chili powder

1 tsp mustard powder

4 tbsp BBQ sauce

Salt and black pepper to taste

Directions

Rub the back ribs with garlic powder, chili, mustard, salt, and pepper. Pour 1 cup of water into the pot and fit in a trivet. Place the ribs on the trivet. Seal the lid, select Pressure Cook on High, and set the time to 25 minutes.

When done cooking, allow a natural release for 10 minutes. Unlock the lid and remove the ribs to a lined baking sheet.

Brush with BBQ sauce and set under the broiler for 10-15 minutes until the ribs are sticky and charred. Serve warm.

Primavera Risotto with Crispy Bacon

Total Time: 30 minutes | **Servings:** 4

Ingredients

1 cup Pecorino Romano cheese, grated
2 tbsp butter
4 spring onions, sliced
1 cup Arborio rice
1 ½ cups mushrooms, sliced
¼ cup white wine

2 cups chicken broth
1 cup capers
¼ cup bacon, chopped
Salt and black pepper to taste

Directions

On Sauté, melt butter and stir-fry bacon and capers for 5 minutes, until the bacon is crispy; set aside. Add in spring onions and mushrooms and cook for 5 minutes, stirring often. Place in rice and cook for 2 minutes. Pour in the wine and broth, and stir. Season with salt and pepper. Seal the lid, select Pressure Cook, and cook for 7 minutes on High.

When done, perform a quick pressure release to let out the remaining steam. Unlock the lid and stir in the Pecorino Romano cheese until melted. Serve risotto topped with the capers and bacon.

Sweet & Sour Pork Stew

Total Time: 50 minutes | **Servings:** 4

Ingredients

3 tbsp olive oil
¼ cup cornstarch
1 lb pork shoulder, cubed
Salt and black pepper to taste
1 red bell pepper, cut into strips
1 white onion, thinly sliced

¼ cup white vinegar
¼ cup granulated sugar
¼ cup ketchup
1 tsp freshly grated ginger
1 cup chopped pineapples
1 cup chicken broth

Directions

Reserve 1 tbsp of cornstarch and pour the remaining onto a plate. Season pork with salt, pepper, and dredge lightly in cornstarch. Set your Instant Pot to Sauté and heat olive oil. Fry pork until golden brown on the outside, 8 minutes. Remove onto a plate and set aside. Add and sauté bell pepper and onion until softened, 5 minutes.

In a bowl, mix vinegar, sugar, ketchup, and ginger. Pour mixture onto vegetables and cook for 2 minutes. Return pork to inner pot and top with pineapples and chicken broth. Seal the lid, set on Pressure Cook on High, and set to 15 minutes. After cooking, allow a natural release for 10 minutes. Serve and enjoy!

Tuscan Pork Chops

Total Time: 45 minutes | **Servings:** 4

Ingredients

1 tbsp olive oil
4 pork chops, fat trimmed
Salt and black pepper to taste
1 large red onion, chopped
3 garlic cloves, minced

1 ½ chopped tomatoes
1 tsp dried oregano
1 tsp dried basil
2 cup chicken broth

Directions

Set your Instant Pot to Sauté, heat olive oil, season pork with salt, pepper, and sear until golden, 8 minutes. Stir in onion and garlic until softened and fragrant, 2 minutes.

Add tomatoes, oregano, and basil and cook for 2 minutes, turning the meat halfway. Pour in chicken broth and season with salt and pepper.

Seal the lid, select Pressure Cook on High, and set the cooking time to 15 minutes. After cooking, allow a natural release for 10 minutes. Unlock the lid. Stir and plate. Serve.

Saucy Red Chili Pork

Total Time: 35 minutes | **Servings:** 4

Ingredients

1 lb pork loin
¼ cup red chili puree
1 cup chicken broth

Salt and black pepper to taste
1 tsp dried rosemary

Directions

In the inner pot of your Instant Pot, combine pork, red chili puree, broth, salt, pepper, and rosemary. Seal the lid, select Pressure Cook on High, and set the time to 15 minutes.

Once done, allow a natural release for 10 minutes. Shred pork with two forks, stir and adjust taste with salt and pepper. Serve with rice and bread dishes.

Pork Chops with Barbecue Sauce

Total Time: 30 minutes | **Servings:** 4

Ingredients

1 tbsp olive oil
3 tbsp brown sugar
1 ½ tbsp smoked paprika
2 tsp garlic powder

Salt and black pepper to taste
4 bone-in pork chops
1 ½ cups chicken broth
4 tbsp barbecue sauce

Directions

In a bowl, mix sugar, salt, paprika, garlic powder, and pepper. Season the pork with the rub.

Select Sauté and heat the oil. Sear the pork chops on both sides for about 5 minutes. Pour in the chicken broth and barbecue sauce.

Seal the lid, select Pressure Cook on High, and set the time to 5 minutes. When done, allow a natural release for 10 minutes. Carefully unlock the lid. Serve warm.

BEEF & LAMB RECIPES

Yummy Beef with Snap Peas

Total Time: 25 minutes | **Servings:** 4

Ingredients

1 lb beef sirloin, sliced against the grain
2 tbsp sesame oil
¼ cup soy sauce
2 tbsp maple syrup
½ tsp hot sauce
1 tsp balsamic vinegar

1 cup chicken. stock
½ cup + 2 tsp cornstarch
2 cups snap peas
3 garlic cloves, minced
3 scallions, thinly sliced

Directions

In a bowl, combine soy sauce, 1 tbsp of sesame oil, maple syrup, hot sauce, vinegar, stock, and 2 tbsp of cornstarch; set aside. Pour remaining cornstarch on a plate. Toss the beef lightly in cornstarch.

Set your Instant Pot to Sauté, heat the remaining sesame oil in the pot, and fry the beef until brown, 5 minutes. Plate and set aside. Discard the fat, wipe the pot clean with a paper towel, and pour in soy sauce mixture. Return meat to sauce; add snow peas and garlic. Seal the lid, select Pressure Cook on High, and set the time to 3 minutes.

When done cooking, perform natural pressure release for 10 minutes, then quickly release the remaining steam. Unlock the lid, stir and adjust the taste with salt and black pepper. Garnish with scallions and serve warm.

Irish Beef Shepherd's Pie

Total Time: 50 minutes | **Servings:** 4

Ingredients

2 tbsp butter
3 russet potatoes, cubed
1 egg, cracked into a bowl
Salt and black pepper to taste
1 lb ground beef
1 tsp garlic powder
1 tbsp Worcestershire sauce

2 medium white onion
1 cup mushrooms, chopped
3 carrots, chopped
¼ cup Guinness stout
1 cup beef broth
2 tbsp all-purpose flour
1 cup grated cheddar cheese

Directions

Pour potatoes, 1 cup of water, and salt into your Instant Pot. Seal the lid, select Pressure Cook on High, and set the time to 8 minutes. After cooking, allow a natural release for 10 minutes. Unlock the lid and drain potatoes. Transfer to a bowl and add butter, egg, salt, and black pepper. Mash using a masher until smooth; set aside.

Wipe the inner pot clean with paper towels and select Sauté. Add beef to the pot and brown for 6 minutes. Add garlic powder, Worcestershire sauce, onion, mushrooms, carrots, and stout. Cook until vegetables soften, 4 minutes. In a bowl, mix broth with flour and pour into beef mixture. Cook until the sauce thickens, 3 minutes. Spoon beef filling into four ramekins, spread potato mixture on top, and cover with aluminum foil. Clean the pot.

Pour in 1 cup water. Fit in a trivet and place ramekins on top. Seal the lid, select Pressure Cook, and set to 10 minutes. After cooking, do a quick pressure release. Remove ramekins, take off the aluminum foil, and top with cheese.

Barbecue Beef Sloppy Joes

Total time: 25 minutes | **Servings:** 4

Ingredients

2 tbsp olive oil
1 onion, chopped
1 lb ground beef
1 red pepper, chopped
1 celery stick, chopped
1 cup beef broth
1 garlic clove, minced
¾ cup tomato purée

1 tbsp yellow mustard
2 tsp brown sugar
2 tsp BBQ sauce
Salt to taste
½ tsp hot sauce
4 seeded burger buns, halved
4 lettuce leaves

Directions

Set your Instant Pot to Sauté and warm olive oil. Brown the beef for 4 minutes, breaking the meat with a spatula. Stir in onion, red pepper, and celery. Pour in broth, garlic, tomato puree, mustard, sugar, BBQ sauce, and salt and stir.

Seal the lid, select Pressure Cook on High, and set to 12 minutes. Do a quick pressure release. Stir in hot sauce. Arrange the lettuce leaves on the bottom bun halves, top with meat and sauce, and finish with the other bun halves.

Beef Casserole with Macaroni & Onion

Total Time: 35 minutes | **Servings:** 4

Ingredients

1 tbsp olive oil
1 lb ground beef
Salt and black pepper to taste
2 large celery stalks, chopped
1 brown onion, chopped

8 oz raw macaroni
6 cups chicken broth
2 cups chopped tomatoes
3 cups grated cheddar cheese

Directions

Set your Instant Pot to Sauté, heat olive oil, and brown beef, for 5 minutes. Season with salt and pepper. Mix in celery, onion, and cook until softened, 3 minutes. Pour in chicken broth and tomatoes. Seal the lid, select Pressure Cook on High, and set to 15 minutes. After cooking, do a quick release. Stir in macaroni, seal the lid again and cook on Pressure Cook for 4 minutes. Do a quick pressure release. Spoon into bowls and serve sprinkled with cheddar cheese.

Easy Beef & Lentil Chili

Total Time: 30 minutes | **Servings:** 4

Ingredients

1 tbsp oil
1 lb ground beef
¼ tsp lemon pepper seasoning
1 onion, chopped
2 garlic cloves, minced
1 can (14.5 oz) diced tomatoes
1 tbsp chili powder

1 tbsp ground cumin
1 tsp dried oregano
¼ tsp crushed red pepper
1 cup beef broth
1 cup canned lentils
Salt and black pepper to taste
Chives, chopped for garnish

Directions

Set your Instant Pot to Sauté and heat the oil. Add the beef, salt, and lemon pepper. Stir-fry for 8 minutes until the meat is brown. Add onion and garlic and cook for 2 minutes. Stir in tomatoes, remaining spices, broth, and lentils.

Seal the lid, select Pressure Cook, and set the time to 10 minutes on High. When done, perform a quick pressure release. Adjust the seasoning with salt and black pepper, top with chopped chives, and serve.

Paprika Ground Beef Stuffed Empanadas

Total Time: 35 minutes | **Servings:** 2

Ingredients

6 green olives, pitted and chopped
1 cup olive oil
1 garlic clove, minced
½ white onion, chopped
¼ lb ground beef
¼ tsp cumin powder

¼ tsp paprika
¼ tsp cinnamon powder
2 small tomatoes, chopped
8 square wonton wrappers
1 egg, beaten

Directions

Select Sauté and heat 1 tbsp of olive oil. Cook the garlic, onion, and ground beef for 5 minutes, stirring occasionally until fragrant and the meat is no longer pink. Stir in olives, cumin, paprika, and cinnamon, and cook for 3 minutes.

Add the tomatoes and 1 cup of water, and cook for 1 minute. Seal the lid, select Pressure Cook on High, and set the time to 8 minutes. Allow a natural release for 10 minutes. Spoon the beef mixture onto a plate and let cool for a few minutes. Lay the wonton wrappers on a flat surface.

Place 2 tbsp of the beef mixture in the middle of each wrapper. Brush the edges of the wrapper with egg and fold in half to form a triangle. Pinch the edges together to seal. Wipe the pot clean. Press Sauté. Heat the remaining oil. Fry the empanadas in a single layer, about 20 seconds per side. Remove to paper towels to soak up excess fat. Serve.

Beef Meatballs in Orange-Honey Sauce

Total Time: 40 minutes | **Servings:** 4

Ingredients

2 tbsp olive oil
1 cup quick-cooking oats
½ cup crushed graham crackers
2 large eggs, lightly beaten
1 (5 oz) can evaporated milk
1 tbsp dried minced onion
Salt and black pepper to taste
1 tsp garlic powder
1 tsp cumin powder

1 tsp honey
1 ½ lb ground beef
3 tbsp brown sugar
¼ cup orange marmalade
2 tbsp cornstarch
2 tbsp soy sauce
2 tbsp hot sauce
1 tbsp Worcestershire sauce
1 cup chicken broth

Directions

In a bowl, combine oats, graham crackers, eggs, milk, onion, salt, pepper, garlic, cumin, honey, and beef. Mix and form mixture into 2-inch balls. Set the pot to Sauté, heat oil, and fry meatballs until golden, 5 minutes; set aside.

In the pot, mix sugar, marmalade, cornstarch, soy and hot sauces, Worcestershire sauce, and broth. Let simmer for 5 minutes. Return meatballs to the pot and coat with sauce. Seal the lid, select Pressure Cook on High, and set the time to 10 minutes. After cooking, allow a natural release for 10 minutes. Dish meatballs and spoon sauce over meatballs.

French Onion Beef Soup

Total Time: 80 minutes | **Servings:** 4

Ingredients

2 tbsp olive oil
2 tbsp butter
1 ½ lb short ribs
Salt and black pepper to taste
1 tsp dried rosemary
1 tsp dried tarragon

6 medium onions, thinly sliced
½ tsp dried thyme
¼ cup dry white wine
4 cups hot beef stock
4 cups grated Gruyere cheese
8 slices toasted baguettes

Directions

Set your Instant Pot to Sauté, heat olive oil, season meat with salt, pepper, rosemary, and tarragon and sear in oil until brown on both sides, 8 minutes. Plate and set aside. Melt butter in the inner pot and cook onions with frequent stirring until caramelized, 30 minutes. Pour in thyme, wine, and stock. Once boiling, place in beef.

Seal the lid, select Pressure Cook on High, and set the time to 15 minutes. After cooking, allow a natural release for 10 minutes. Unlock the lid, stir and adjust the taste. Spoon soup into 4 serving bowls, place two baguette slices in each bowl and cover with Gruyere cheese. Place soup bowls under a broiler to melt cheese, 4 minutes. Serve.

Spiced Beef Hot Pot

Total Time: 25 min + marinating time | **Servings:** 4

Ingredients

½ tsp sesame oil
2 tbsp olive oil
1 lb beef stew meat, cubed
1 tbsp soy sauce
½ tsp miso paste
1 tsp garlic puree
1 tsp cumin powder
1 tsp chili powder
1 tsp ginger paste
A pinch of five-spice

Salt and black pepper to taste
1 tbsp rice wine
1 onion, chopped
1 red bell pepper, chopped
1 green bell pepper, chopped
1 lemongrass stalk, thinly sliced
2 garlic cloves, minced
1 cup jasmine rice
2 cups chicken broth
2 tbsp chopped parsley

Directions

In a bowl, add beef and top with soy sauce, miso paste, garlic puree, cumin, chili, ginger paste, five-spice, salt, pepper, rice wine, and sesame oil. Mix and marinate meat for 30 minutes.

Set the pot to Sauté, heat oil, drain beef from marinade, and brown for 5 minutes. Stir in onion, bell peppers, lemongrass, and garlic. Cook for 3 minutes. Mix in rice and add in the broth. Seal the lid, select Pressure Cook on High, and set the time to 5 minutes. Perform a quick release. Stir and adjust the taste. Garnish with parsley. Serve.

Paleo Thai Basil Beef

Total Time: 20 minutes | **Servings**: 4

Ingredients

1 tbsp sesame oil	1 yellow onion, thinly sliced
¼ cup soy sauce	1 green pepper, thinly sliced
1 tsp honey	1 large red pepper, thinly sliced
1 tbsp fish sauce	3 garlic cloves, minced
1 tsp chili paste	1 tsp freshly grated ginger
1 tbsp oyster sauce	1 cup Thai basil
1 tsp fresh garlic puree	1 tsp sesame seeds
1 tsp cornstarch	Salt and black pepper to taste
1 lb thinly sliced beef steaks	

Directions

In a medium bowl, whisk soy sauce, honey, fish sauce, chili paste, oyster sauce, garlic paste, and cornstarch; set aside. Set your Instant Pot to Sauté. Heat the sesame oil and cook the beef on both sides until brown, 5-6 minutes. Top with onion, bell peppers, and allow softening for 3 minutes. Add garlic and ginger; cook until fragrant, 1 minute. Pour sauce mixture all over, stir and cook until sauce is syrupy, 1 minute. Stir in Thai basil and allow slight wilting, 45 seconds. Adjust the taste. Spoon stir-fry into bowls, garnish with sesame seeds, and serve.

Honey Short Ribs

Total Time: 60 minutes | **Servings**: 4

Ingredients

2 tbsp olive oil	1 cup beef broth
1 ½ lb large beef short ribs	1 tbsp honey
1 onion, finely chopped	2 tbsp tomato paste
3 garlic cloves, minced	1 tbsp cornstarch
½ cup apple cider vinegar	

Directions

Select Sauté, heat olive oil, fry the ribs until brown, about 8 minutes. Plate and set aside. Sauté onion, garlic, and cook until soft and fragrant, 4 minutes. Stir in apple cider vinegar, broth, honey, tomato paste, and once simmering, add ribs. Seal the lid, select Pressure Cook on High, and set the time to 25 minutes.

Once done cooking, allow a natural release for 10 minutes. Unlock the lid, transfer ribs to serving plates. Stir cornstarch into sauce until thickened, 1 minute, on Sauté. Spoon sauce over ribs and serve.

Beef with Cabbage & Bell Pepper

Total Time: 40 minutes | **Servings**: 4

Ingredients

1 tbsp olive oil	1 green cabbage, shredded
1 tbsp sesame oil	1 red bell pepper, chopped
1 lb ground beef	2 tbsp tamarind sauce
Salt and black pepper to taste	1 tbsp hot sauce
1 tbsp grated ginger	½ tbsp honey
3 garlic cloves, minced	2 tbsp walnuts
1 red cabbage, shredded	1 tsp toasted sesame seeds

Directions

Set your Instant Pot to Sauté and heat olive oil. Add beef, season with salt, pepper, ginger, and garlic and cook for 5 minutes. Add in cabbage, bell pepper, and stir-fry for 5 minutes. Pour in 1 cup of water and seal the lid. Select Pressure Cook and set the time to 10 minutes on High.

When done, allow a natural release for 10 minutes. In a bowl, combine tamarind sauce, hot sauce, honey, and sesame oil. Stir in the pot, add walnuts, and cook for 1 to 2 minutes on Sauté. Garnish with sesame seeds and serve.

Fall Beef Pot Roast with Pearl Onions

Total Time: 50 minutes | **Servings**: 6

Ingredients

2 tbsp olive oil	Salt and black pepper to taste
1 (3-lb) chuck roast	1 small red onion, quartered
½ cup dry red wine	1-lb butternut squash, chopped
1 ½ cups beef broth	2 carrots, chopped
1 tsp dried oregano leaves	¾ cup pearl onions
1 bay leaf	

Directions

On your Instant Pot, select Sauté and heat the oil. Season the beef with salt and cook in the pot for 3 minutes per side or until deeply browned. Add the wine to the pot and stir with a wooden spoon, scraping the bottom of the pot to let off any browned bits. Bring to a boil and cook for 2 minutes or until the wine has reduced by half. Mix in broth, butternut squash, pearl onions, oregano, bay leaf, carrots, black pepper, and red onion. Stir to combine and add the beef with its juices. Seal the lid, select Pressure Cook on High, and set the time to 35 minutes. After cooking, do a quick pressure release. Remove the beef and slice. Spoon over the sauce and vegetables to serve.

South Indian Spicy Beef

Total Time: 30 minutes | **Servings**: 4

Ingredients

1 tbsp olive oil	½ tsp garam masala powder
1 lb beef stew meat, cubed	½ tsp red chili powder
Salt and black pepper to taste	¼ tsp turmeric powder
1 cup grated carrots	1 tsp cumin powder
2 white onions, sliced	1 cup basmati rice
2 garlic cloves, minced	2 cups beef broth
½ tsp ginger puree	¼ cup cashew nuts
1 tbsp cilantro leaves	

Directions

Set your Instant Pot to Sauté, heat olive oil, season beef with salt and pepper, and brown on both sides, 5 minutes; plate and set aside. In the pot, stir-fry onions, garlic, ginger, cilantro, garam masala, red chili, turmeric, cumin, salt, and pepper, for 2 minutes. Stir in rice, carrots, beef, and broth all over. Seal the lid, select Pressure Cook, and set the time to 6 minutes. When done, let sit for 10 minutes. Fluff the rice and stir in cashews. Serve rice with coconut yogurt.

Hoisin Beef with Vegetables

Total Time: 25 minutes | **Servings:** 4

Ingredients

1 tbsp sesame oil
6 cups boiled water
8 oz rice noodles
¼ cup tamarind sauce
1 tbsp hoisin sauce
1 tsp maple syrup
1 tsp grated ginger
3 garlic cloves, minced

1 lb ground beef
2 cups sliced shitake mushrooms
1 yellow onion, thinly sliced
½ cup julienned carrots
1 cup shredded green cabbage
¼ cup sliced scallions
Sesame seeds for garnish

Directions

In a bowl, whisk tamarind sauce, hoisin sauce, maple syrup, ginger, and garlic. Set aside. Pour boiling water into a bowl and add rice noodles. Cover the bowl with a napkin and allow softening for 5 minutes. Drain and set aside.

Set your Instant Pot to Sauté and heat sesame oil. Cook beef until brown, 5 minutes. Stir in mushrooms, onion, carrots, and cabbage; cook until softened, 3 to 5 minutes. Add in noodles. Top with sauce and mix well. Cook further for 1 minute to allow the flavors to incorporate. Garnish with scallions and sesame seeds and serve immediately.

Korean-Style Beef & Tofu Soup

Total Time: 35 minutes | **Servings:** 4

Ingredients

2 tbsp coconut oil
½ lb ground beef
Salt and black pepper to taste
1 medium onion, diced
1 green bell pepper, diced
1 cup sliced shiitake mushrooms

½ cup kimchi
1 lb extra-firm tofu, cubed
4 cups beef broth
2 tbsp coconut aminos
1 tbsp mirin
2 tsp lemon juice

Directions

Set your Instant Pot to Sauté, heat coconut oil, add beef, season with salt and pepper, and cook until brown, 5 minutes. Add onion, bell pepper, and mushrooms; cook until softened, 3 minutes. Stir in kimchi and tofu and cook for 1 minute. Pour in broth, coconut aminos, mirin, and lemon juice. Seal the lid, select Pressure Cook on High, and set to 5 minutes. Allow a natural release for 10 minutes. Adjust the taste with salt and pepper and serve warm.

Beef Steaks with Mushroom Sauce

Total Time: 35 minutes | **Servings:** 2

Ingredients

2 tbsp olive oil
2 beef steaks, boneless
Salt and black pepper to taste
4 oz mushrooms, sliced
½ onion, chopped

1 garlic clove, minced
1 cup vegetable stock
1 ½ tbsp cornstarch
1 tbsp half and half

Directions

Rub the beef steaks with salt and pepper. Select Sauté on your Instant Pot and warm the oil. Sear the beef for 2 minutes per side; reserve. Add in mushrooms, onion, and garlic and cook for 5 minutes, until fragrant and aromatic. Return the steaks to the pot and pour in the stock. Seal the lid, select Pressure Cook, and set the time to 15 minutes on High. When done, do a quick release and unlock the lid and transfer the chops to a plate. Press Sauté.

In a bowl, combine the cornstarch and half and half and mix well. Pour the slurry into the pot and cook until the sauce reaches the desired consistency. Serve warm.

Beef Niçoise Sandwiches

Total time: 1 hour 45 minutes | **Servings:** 6

Ingredients

6 small French baguettes, halved lengthwise
1 (10-oz) can condensed onion soup
1 tbsp olive oil
1 onion, chopped
1 garlic clove, minced
3 lb beef chuck roast
Salt and black pepper to taste

1 tbsp soy sauce
1 ½ cups beef broth
2 bay leaves
6 Fontina cheese slices
2 tbsp Dijon mustard

Directions

Set your Instant Pot to Sauté and warm the olive oil. Rub the roast with salt and pepper and put it in the pot. Brown for 5 minutes per side. Add in garlic, onion, soy sauce, onion soup, broth, and bay leaves.

Seal the lid, select Pressure Cook and cook for 80 minutes on High. When done, allow a natural release for 10 minutes. Unlock the lid and transfer the roast to a plate. Let it cool slightly before shredding with a fork. Divide the cheese and mustard among the baguettes, top with shredded meat, and serve with the cooking sauce.

Tex-Mex Chili

Total time: 35 minutes | **Servings:** 6

Ingredients

1 (14.5-oz) can fire-roasted tomatoes
2 tbsp olive oil
1 ½ lb lean ground beef
3 garlic cloves, minced
2 onions, chopped
1 red bell pepper, chopped
1 tsp ground cumin
Salt and black pepper to taste

1 tbsp chili powder
2 jalapeño peppers, minced
2 cups beef broth
1 (15-oz) can pinto beans
2 tbsp cornmeal
½ cup shredded cheddar
¼ cup cilantro, chopped

Directions

Set your Instant Pot to Sauté and heat olive oil. Cook the ground beef for 5 minutes until slightly browned. Add in garlic, onions, cumin, bell pepper, chili powder, and jalapeño peppers; sauté for 5 minutes, until everything is thoroughly cooked. Stir in broth and tomatoes. Seal the lid, select Pressure Cook on High, and set to 15 minutes.

When done, perform a quick pressure. Unlock the lid and press Sauté. Put in pinto beans and cornmeal. Stir and cook for another 3 minutes until the chili is thickened. Adjust the taste with salt and pepper. Top with cheddar and cilantro.

Cuban Beef Picadillo

Total Time: 45 minutes | **Servings:** 4

Ingredients

½ cup green olives with pimento stuffing

2 tbsp olive oil	1 sweet potato, chopped
1 lb ground beef	Salt and black pepper to taste
1 tbsp cumin powder	½ cup Marsala wine
¼ tsp chili powder	1 ½ cups tomatoes, chopped
1 large yellow onion, chopped	3 tbsp raisins
1 red bell pepper, chopped	¼ cup capers, drained
6 garlic cloves, minced	1 tbsp chopped cilantro

Directions

On Sauté, heat oil and brown beef, for 5 minutes. Season with half tbsp of cumin and chili powder. Place on a plate and set aside. Add in onion, garlic, and bell pepper and sauté until softened, 5 minutes. Mix in potatoes, remaining cumin, salt, pepper, and 1 cup of water; cook for 5 minutes. Return beef, wine, tomatoes, and raisins; stir. Seal the lid, select Pressure Cook on High, and set the time to 10 minutes. After cooking, allow a natural release for 10 minutes. Stir in capers and olives. Garnish with cilantro and serve warm.

Tasty Beef & Cheese Quiche

Total time: 45 minutes | **Servings:** 6

Ingredients

2 ½ cups grated Monterrey Jack cheese

3 tbsp olive oil	½ cup salsa
1 lb ground beef	4 flour tortillas
3 tbsp taco seasoning	¼ cup habanero hot sauce
1 ½ cups canned refried beans	1 large tomato, sliced

Directions

Set your Instant Pot to Sauté and warm the olive oil. Brown the beef for 7 minutes; scatter with the taco seasoning and stir. Remove to a plate. Wipe the inner pot clean with a paper towel, pour in 1 ½ cups water, and fit in a trivet.

In a bowl, mix together refried beans and salsa. In a greased baking pan, lay one flour tortilla, ½ cup of the bean mixture, 1 cup of ground beef, a little bit of habanero sauce, and ¼ cup of cheese. Repeat these steps for the 3 layers. Top with the fourth tortilla and cover with foil. Place the pan on the trivet. Seal the lid, select Pressure Cook on High, and set to 15 minutes. Allow a natural release for 10 minutes; remove the foil. Top with cheese and tomato to serve.

Wine Short Ribs in Fig-Tomato Chutney

Total Time: 50 minutes | **Servings:** 4

Ingredients

1 tsp olive oil	3 garlic cloves, minced
3 bacon slices, chopped	2 cups beef broth
4 lb beef short ribs	1 cup Marsala wine
Salt and black pepper to taste	¼ cup fig preserves
1 lb cherry tomatoes, halved	3 tbsp thyme leaves
1 white onion, chopped	

Directions

Set your Instant Pot to Sauté and brown bacon until crispy, 5 minutes. Remove to a paper towel-lined plate. Heat olive oil, season beef ribs with salt and pepper, and cook on both sides until brown. Transfer next to the bacon.

Add tomatoes, onion, and garlic to the inner pot and cook until softened, 5 minutes. Stir in beef broth, Marsala wine, fig preserves, and thyme. Return beef and bacon to the pot. Seal the lid, select Pressure Cook on High, and set the time to 20 minutes. After cooking, allow a natural release for 10 minutes. Unlock the lid. Stir and serve.

Ketchup-Glazed Beef Meatloaf

Total time: 45 minutes | **Servings:** 6

Ingredients

2 lb ground beef	1 tsp allspice
1 ½ cups breadcrumbs	Salt and black pepper to taste
1 tsp fennel seeds	A bunch of parsley, chopped
½ tsp chili flakes	1 cup ketchup
2 eggs	2 tsp Worcestershire sauce
1 onion, minced	2 tsp brown sugar
1 garlic clove, minced	1 tbsp Wasabi powder

Directions

Mix the beef, breadcrumbs, fennel seeds, chili flakes, eggs, onion, garlic, all spices, salt, pepper, and parsley in a bowl. Shape the mixture into a greased round loaf. Combine ketchup, Worcestershire sauce, brown sugar, and wasabi powder in another bowl, and mix until the sugar is dissolved. Spread the mixture over the top of the meatloaf.

Pour 1 cup water into the pot and fit in a trivet. Lower the meatloaf onto the trivet. Seal the lid, Pressure Cook on High, and cook for 30 minutes. Perform a quick pressure release. Let rest the meatloaf for 5 minutes before slicing.

Beef & Rice with Veggie Mix

Total Time: 40 minutes | **Servings:** 4

Ingredients

2 tbsp olive oil	½ tsp cumin powder
1 medium onion, chopped	1 tsp onion powder
1 red bell pepper, chopped	1 tsp Italian seasoning
1 cup sliced cremini mushrooms	¼ tsp chili powder
2 garlic cloves, minced	1 cup basmati rice
1 lb ground beef	2 cups chicken broth
2 ½ tbsp tomato paste	2 cups frozen mixed veggies
Salt and black pepper to taste	

Directions

Set your Instant Pot to Sauté, heat olive oil and sauté onion, bell pepper, garlic, and mushrooms until softened, 5 minutes. Mix in beef and cook until brown, 5 minutes. Stir in tomato paste, salt, pepper, cumin, onion powder, Italian seasoning, and chili. Allow releasing of fragrance for 1 minute and stir in rice. Cook further for 1 minute. Pour in broth and stir. Seal the lid, select Pressure Cook mode on High, and set the cooking time to 5 minutes.

Allow sitting (covered) for 10 minutes and then perform quick pressure release. Unlock the lid and select to Sauté mode. Stir in mixed veggies and cook until warmed, 3 minutes. Dish food into serving bowls and serve warm.

Ground Beef Chili with Tomatoes

Total Time: 35 minutes | **Servings**: 4

Ingredients

2 tbsp butter
1 lb ground beef
1 white onion, chopped
1 red bell pepper, chopped
2 garlic cloves, minced

2 cups canned black beans
1 ½ cups chopped tomatoes
2 cups chicken broth
2 tbsp chili powder

Directions

Set your Instant Pot to Sauté and melt butter. Add in beef, onion, bell pepper, and garlic and cook for 5 minutes. Stir in black beans, tomatoes, chicken broth, and chili powder. Seal the lid, select Pressure Cook on High, and set the time to 10 minutes. After cooking, allow a natural release for 10 minutes. Serve warm with rice or bread.

Greek-Style Beef Gyros

Total Time: 35 minutes | **Servings**: 4

Ingredients

1 tbsp olive oil
1 lb beef meat, cut into strips
Salt and black pepper to taste
1 small white onion, chopped
3 garlic cloves, minced
2 tsp hot sauce

1 cup beef broth
1 medium tomato, chopped
1 cucumber, chopped
4 whole pita bread, warmed
1 cup Greek yogurt
1 tsp chopped dill

Directions

Heat olive oil in your Instant Pot on Sauté. Season the beef with salt and pepper and brown it for 5 minutes, stirring occasionally. Add the onion and garlic and sauté until softened, 3 minutes. Stir in hot sauce and broth.

Seal the lid, select Pressure Cook mode on High, and set the time to 20 minutes. After cooking, allow a natural release, and unlock the lid. Stir beef and spoon into a bowl. Mix in tomatoes, cucumber, and spoon beef mixture into pita bread. In a medium bowl, mix yogurt and dill. Top beef with yogurt mixture and serve immediately.

Gourmet Carbonade à la Flamande

Total Time: 65 minutes | **Servings**: 4

Ingredients

1 tbsp olive oil
2 lb brisket, cut into 3 pieces
Salt to taste
1 large onion, sliced
8 oz Ale beer

¼ tsp dried rosemary leaves
1 cup beef broth
½ tsp Dijon mustard
2 tbsp chopped fresh chervil

Directions

Season the brisket with salt. On your Instant Pot, select Sauté and heat olive oil. Sear the brisket for 4 minutes.

Move the beef to the side. Add onion on the other side. Cook, stirring, for 2 minutes. Pour in beer, scraping off any browned bits from the bottom of the pot. Cook until the beer has reduced by half. Stir in the rosemary and broth.

Seal the lid, select Pressure Cook on High, and set the time to 35 minutes. After cooking, allow a natural release for 10 minutes. Remove beef onto a cutting board. Stir in the mustard. Select Sauté and cook for 5 minutes to reduce the liquid. Slice beef and return to the sauce to reheat. Serve garnished with chervil.

Beefy Mushroom Soup

Total Time: 40 minutes | **Servings**: 4

Ingredients

1 lb sliced baby Portobello mushrooms
1 tbsp coconut oil
½ lb ground beef
½ lb oyster mushrooms, sliced
1 oz dried shiitake mushrooms
2 medium carrots, halved
1 celery ribs, halved

1 medium onion, quartered
2 tbsp soy sauce
5 cups chicken broth
2 bay leaves
1 tbsp lemon juice
¼ tsp cayenne pepper

Directions

Set your Instant Pot to Sauté, heat oil, and brown beef for 5 minutes. Add oyster and dried mushrooms, carrots, celery, and onion. Stir and cook until softened, 5 minutes. Mix in soy sauce, broth, bay leaves, lemon juice, and cayenne pepper. Seal the lid, select Pressure Cook on High, and set the time to 10 minutes. After cooking, do a natural pressure release for 10 minutes. Stir soup and adjust taste with salt and black pepper. Dish into bowls and serve.

Classic Beef Spaghetti Bolognese

Total Time: 35 minutes | **Servings**: 4

Ingredients

2 tbsp olive oil
½ lb ground beef
1 lb spaghetti
1 carrot, grated
3 cloves garlic, minced
1 celery, chopped
1 onion, chopped
¼ cup red wine

1 tsp dried oregano
2 tbsp fresh basil, chopped
Salt and black pepper to taste
Parmesan cheese, grated to serve
1 cup beef stock
½ cup canned tomato sauce
2 tbsp Worcestershire sauce

Directions

Set your Instant Pot to Sauté and warm olive oil. Place in the ground beef, salt, and pepper. Cook until browned, about 5-6 minutes. Set aside. Add in garlic, onion, carrot, celery, oregano, basil, salt, and pepper and sauté for 5 minutes. Add in red wine to scrape up any browned bits from the bottom of the pot. Pour in the stock, 2 cups of water, and Worcestershire sauce and return the beef; stir.

Mix in spaghetti and tomato sauce. Seal the lid, select Pressure Cook on High, and set the time to 4 minutes. Allow a natural release for 10 minutes. Serve garnished with grated Parmesan cheese. Enjoy!

One-Pot Spinach Beef Tagliatelle

Total Time: 25 minutes | **Servings**: 4

Ingredients

1 tbsp olive oil
1 lb ground beef
1 small yellow onion, chopped
1 cup sliced cremini mushrooms
2 garlic cloves, minced
2 (26-oz) jars tomato pasta sauce

6 cups water
8 oz tagliatelle
1 tbsp Italian seasoning
1 tsp dried basil
Salt and black pepper to taste
1 cup baby spinach

Directions

Set your Instant Pot to Sauté and heat oil. Brown the beef for 5 minutes. Add onion, mushrooms, garlic, and cook until vegetables soften, 3 minutes. Stir in tomato sauce, water, tagliatelle, Italian seasoning, basil, salt, and pepper. Seal the lid, select Pressure Cook on High, and set the time to 5 minutes. After cooking, do a quick release, and unlock the lid. Select Sauté and mix in spinach. Allow wilting for 5 minutes and adjust the taste. Dish food and serve.

The Best Homemade Sloppy Joes

Total Time: 35 minutes | **Servings**: 4

Ingredients

1 tbsp olive oil
1 lb ground beef
1 medium onion, chopped
1 red bell pepper, chopped
3 garlic cloves, minced
1 tbsp light soy sauce
1 tbsp Worcestershire sauce
¾ cup ketchup

1 tbsp tomato paste
1 tbsp brown sugar
1 tsp Dijon mustard
1 cup chicken broth
Salt and black pepper to taste
2 drops liquid smoke
4 burger buns, halved

Directions

Set your Instant Pot to Sauté and heat olive oil. Brown the beef, while breaking the lumps that form, 5 minutes. Add onion, bell pepper, and garlic. Cook for 3 minutes. In a bowl, whisk soy and Worcestershire sauces, ketchup, tomato paste, sugar, and mustard. Stir the mixture into the beef. Top with broth, salt, pepper, and liquid smoke. Seal the lid, select Pressure Cook, and cook for 15 minutes. Perform a quick pressure release. Spoon into buns and serve.

Cilantro Beef the Malaysian Way

Total Time: 50 minutes | **Servings**: 4

Ingredients

1 tbsp olive oil
1 ½ lb beef shanks, cross-cut
½ tsp ginger, grated
1 garlic clove, minced
1 cup water
½ cup coconut milk

¾ cup brown sugar
1 tbsp cornstarch
1 ½ tbsp cold water
Cilantro, chopped for garnish
1 red chili, finely sliced

Directions

Set your Instant Pot to Sauté, heat olive oil, and brown meat for 5 minutes on all sides. Stir in ginger, garlic, water, and coconut milk. Seal the lid, select Meat/Stew, and cook for 35 minutes. When done, do a quick pressure release.

Unlock the lid and select Sauté. Add in brown sugar and stir. In a bowl, mix the cornstarch with cold water and stir until obtaining a slurry. Pour in the pot and mix well. Cook until the sauce thickens. Top with cilantro and red chili.

Coconut-Saffron Beef with Basmati Rice

Total Time: 36 minutes | **Servings**: 4

Ingredients

1 tbsp olive oil
1 lb ground beef
Salt and black pepper to taste
3 garlic cloves, minced
1 cup basmati rice

½ cup coconut milk
2 cups chicken broth
20 saffron threads
2 scallions, thinly sliced

Directions

Set your Instant Pot to Sauté, heat olive oil, add beef, season with salt and pepper, and cook until brown, 5 minutes. Add garlic and cook until fragrant, 30 seconds. Stir in rice for 2 minutes and pour in coconut milk, broth, and saffron.

Seal the lid, select Pressure Cook, and set the time to 6 minutes. When done cooking, allow a natural release for 10 minutes. Unlock the lid, fluff rice, and plate. Garnish with scallions and serve warm with curry sauce.

Herby Beef & Ripe Plantain Chili

Total Time: 30 minutes | **Servings**: 4

Ingredients

1 scotch bonnet pepper, chopped
3 tbsp palm oil
1 lb ground beef
1 medium red onion, chopped
2 garlic cloves, minced
2 tbsp chopped parsley
1 ½ cups tomato sauce

1 cup chicken stock
2 ripe plantains, peeled and diced
1 tbsp mixed herbs
Salt and black pepper to taste
2 cups baby spinach

Directions

Set your Instant Pot to Sauté, heat 1 tbsp of palm oil, and brown beef for 5 minutes. Add onion, garlic, parsley, and cook until fragrant, 3 minutes. Mix in tomato sauce, stock, plantains, bonnet pepper, mixed herbs, salt, and pepper.

Seal the lid, select Pressure Cook on High, and set the time to 10 minutes. After cooking, do a quick pressure release. Select Sauté and stir in spinach. Cook until wilted, 3 minutes. Adjust the taste and dish into serving bowls.

Beef & Veggie Pot

Total Time: 30 minutes | **Servings**: 4

Ingredients

¾ cup chopped baby Bella mushrooms
2 tbsp olive oil
1 lb ground beef
1 small onion, finely chopped
1 carrot, peeled and chopped
1 celery stick, chopped
1 garlic clove, minced

2 tbsp tomato paste
1 tbsp Worcestershire Sauce
1 tsp cinnamon powder
2 cups beef stock
2 sweet potatoes, chopped

Directions

Set your Instant Pot to Sauté. Heat olive oil and brown beef for 5 minutes. Mix in onion, carrot, celery, mushrooms, and garlic. Cook until veggies soften, 5 minutes. Mix in tomato paste, Worcestershire sauce, and cinnamon.

Cook for 1 minute. Pour in beef stock and potatoes; stir. Seal the lid, select Pressure Cook on High, and set to 10 minutes. After cooking, allow a natural release. Stir and adjust the taste with salt and pepper. Dish food and serve.

Colby Cheese & Beef Carnitas

Total Time: 45 minutes | **Servings**: 4

Ingredients

2 ½ lb bone-in country ribs
Salt to taste
¼ cup orange juice
1 ½ cups beef stock
1 onion, cut into wedges
2 garlic cloves, minced
1 tsp chili powder
4 flour tortillas, warmed
1 cup shredded colby cheese

Directions

Season the ribs with salt. In your Instant Pot, combine the orange juice and stock. Drop in the onion and garlic; stir. Put the ribs in the pot, seal the lid, select Pressure Cook on High, and cook for 25 minutes. After cooking, do a natural pressure release for 10 minutes. Transfer beef to a plate to cool. Remove and discard the bones. Shred the meat with two forks. Stir into the sauce and sprinkle with chili powder. Serve the carnitas on tortillas sprinkled with cheese.

Garlic & Rosemary Sweet Short Ribs

Total Time: 55 minutes | **Servings**: 4

Ingredients

2 tbsp olive oil
1 ½ lb beef short ribs, silver skin
Salt and black pepper to taste
1 onion, chopped
2 tbsp honey
1 cup beef broth
2 tbsp minced fresh rosemary
3 garlic cloves, minced
½ cup red wine

Directions

Season the ribs on all sides with salt and pepper. Select Sauté and heat 1 tbsp of olive oil. Brown the ribs on all sides, about 6 minutes in total. Stir in onion, honey, broth, red wine, and garlic. Seal the lid, select Pressure Cook on High, and set the time to 40 minutes. When ready, do a quick release. Serve the ribs sprinkled with rosemary.

Asian-Style Beef with Rice & Scallions

Total Time: 35 minutes | **Servings**: 4

Ingredients

2 tbsp olive oil
2 tsp sesame oil
1 lb ground beef
3 garlic cloves, minced
¼ cup tamarind sauce
¼ cup packed brown sugar
¼ tsp ground ginger
¼ tsp red chili flakes
1 cup brown rice
2 cups beef broth
2 scallions, thinly sliced
½ tsp sesame seeds

Directions

Set your Instant Pot to Sauté, heat oil, and fry beef for 5 minutes. Add garlic and cook until fragrant, 30 seconds. In a bowl, whisk tamarind sauce, sugar, sesame oil, ginger, and red chili flakes. Pour mixture over beef, stir in rice and broth. Seal the lid, select Pressure Cook, and set the time to 10 minutes. When done, allow a natural release for 10 minutes. Unlock the lid, fluff rice, and plate. Garnish with scallions and sesame seeds. Serve.

Braised Lamb Shanks

Total Time: 80 minutes | **Servings**: 4

Ingredients

2 tbsp olive oil
2 lb lamb shanks
Salt and black pepper to taste
6 garlic cloves, minced
¾ cup red wine
1 cup chicken broth
2 cups crushed tomatoes
1 tsp dried oregano
¼ cup chopped parsley

Directions

Set your Instant Pot to Sauté, heat olive oil, season with lamb with salt and pepper, and sear until brown, 3 minutes per side. Transfer to a plate. Stir in garlic and sauté until fragrant, 30 seconds.

Mix in red wine and cook for 2 minutes while stirring and scraping the bottom of any attached bits. Add broth, tomatoes, and oregano. Stir and cook for 2 minutes.

Return lamb to pot and baste with sauce. Seal the lid, select Pressure Cook on High, and set the time to 45 minutes. After cooking, allow a natural release for 15 minutes, then a quick pressure release to let out the remaining steam. Unlock the lid, stir in parsley, and adjust the taste with salt and pepper. Divide between plates and serve.

Fusilli with Beef & Mustard Greens

Total Time: 30 minutes | **Servings**: 4

Ingredients

1 tbsp olive oil
Salt and black pepper to taste
8 oz fusilli pasta
1 lb ground beef
½ medium brown onion, diced
2 garlic cloves, minced
1 ½ tsp dried mixed herbs
2 cups beef stock
1 (15-oz) can tomato sauce
¾ cup heavy cream
1 cup mustard greens, chopped
6 oz Monterey Jack, shredded

Directions

Cover the pasta with salted water in the pot. Seal the lid, select Pressure Cook on High, and set the time to 4 minutes. Do a quick pressure release, and drain pasta; set aside. Set your Instant Pot to Sauté. Heat oil and brown beef for 5 minutes. Add onion, garlic, and mixed herbs and cook for 3 minutes. Mix in stock and tomato sauce.

Seal the lid, select Pressure Cook on High, and set to 5 minutes. Do a quick pressure release. Select Sauté. Stir in pasta, heavy cream, greens, salt, pepper, and cheese. Cook until cheese melts and greens wilt. Serve.

Savory Beef Steak with Broccoli

Total Time: 40 minutes | **Servings**: 4

Ingredients

1 tbsp olive oil
2 lb skirt steak, cut into strips
4 garlic cloves, minced
½ cup coconut aminos
½ cup dark brown sugar
½ tsp ginger puree
2 tbsp cornstarch
1 head broccoli, cut into florets
3 scallions, thinly sliced

Directions

On Sauté, heat olive oil and brown the steak on both sides, about 5 minutes in total; set aside. Add in garlic and cook for 1 minute or until fragrant. Stir in the coconut aminos, 2 cups of water, brown sugar, and ginger.

Mix and return the beef. Seal the lid, select Pressure Cook on High, and set to 20 minutes. In a bowl, whisk cornstarch and 3 tbsp of water. Do a quick release. Open the lid and stir in the cornstarch mixture until the sauce becomes syrupy on Sauté. Add the broccoli, stir to coat in the sauce, and cook for 5 minutes. Garnish with scallions and serve.

Beef & Rigatoni with Tomato Sauce

Total Time: 35 minutes | **Servings**: 4

Ingredients

1 tbsp butter
1 lb ground beef
2 (24-oz) cans tomato sauce
1 cup dry red wine
16 oz dry rigatoni
½ tsp garlic powder
Salt to taste
1 cup cottage cheese
1 cup shredded mozzarella

Directions

Select Sauté on your Instant Pot and melt the butter. Add the ground beef and cook for 5 minutes or until browned and cooked well. Stir in the tomato sauce, wine, 4 cups water, and rigatoni; season with garlic powder and salt. Seal the lid, select Pressure Cook on High, and set the cooking time to 10 minutes. When done, allow a natural release for 10 minutes. Stir in the cottage cheese and sprinkle the top of the pasta with mozzarella. Serve.

Chipotle Shredded Beef

Total Time: 50 minutes | **Servings**: 4

Ingredients

1 tbsp olive oil
1 lb tender chuck roast, halved
1 (8 oz) can tomato sauce
3 tbsp chipotle sauce
1 cup beef broth
½ cup chopped cilantro
1 lime, zested and juiced
1 tsp cayenne pepper
2 tsp cumin powder
Salt and black pepper to taste
½ tsp garlic powder

Directions

In the inner pot, add beef, tomato sauce, chipotle sauce, beef broth, cilantro, lime zest, lime juice, cayenne pepper, cumin powder, salt, pepper, and garlic powder. Seal the lid, select Pressure Cook on High, and cook for 30 minutes.

After cooking, allow a natural release for 10 minutes. Unlock the lid. Using two forks, shred beef into strands. Adjust taste with salt, black pepper, and stir in olive oil. Dish and serve warm with tortilla bread.

Savory Beef Gumbo

Total Time: 30 minutes | **Servings**: 4

Ingredients

1 tbsp butter
1 lb beef stew meat, cubed
Salt and black pepper to taste
2 bell peppers, diced
1 large onion, chopped
2 garlic cloves, minced
1 tbsp all-purpose flour
4 cups beef broth
1 cup canned whole tomatoes
1 cup sliced okras
¼ cup short-grain rice
¼ tsp dried rosemary
1 bay leaf
½ tsp hot sauce

Directions

Set your Instant Pot to Sauté, melt butter, season beef with salt and pepper, and brown on both sides, 5 minutes. Pour in bell peppers, onion, garlic, flour, beef broth, tomatoes, okras, rice, rosemary, bay leaf, hot sauce, and 2 cups of water. Seal the lid, select Pressure Cook, and set the time to 15 minutes. Do a quick release, adjust the taste, and serve.

Veggie & Beef Stew

Total Time: 45 minutes | **Servings**: 4

Ingredients

2 tbsp olive oil
1 ½ lb beef stew meat
¼ cup flour
3 cups beef broth
1 onion, cut into wedges
2 carrots, chopped
2 tomatoes, chopped
5 cloves garlic, minced
1 tbsp oregano
4 potatoes, cubed
3 celery stalks, chopped
Salt and black pepper to taste

Directions

Coat beef with flour. Set your Instant Pot to Sauté and heat oil. Brown the beef for 5 minutes. Add in onion and cook for 3 minutes. Pour in broth, carrots, tomatoes, garlic, oregano, potatoes, celery, salt, and pepper. Seal the lid, select Pressure Cook on High, and set to 30 minutes. When done, do a quick pressure release. Serve warm.

Authentic Mongolian Beef

Total Time: 55 minutes | **Servings**: 4

Ingredients

¼ cup olive oil
1 lb flank steak, cut into strips
¼ cup cornstarch
1 broccoli, cut into florets
2 tsp grated ginger
1 tbsp garlic cloves, minced
½ cup soy sauce
½ cup dark brown sugar
4 scallions, thinly sliced

Directions

Dredge the flank steak in cornstarch. Set your Instant Pot to Sauté, heat olive oil, and brown beef for 5 minutes. Stir in ginger and garlic and cook until softened, 5 minutes. Pour in soy sauce, 1 cup of water, and sugar.

Seal the lid, select Pressure Cook on High, and set the time to 20 minutes. After cooking, allow a natural release for 10 minutes. Stir in broccoli and cook for 5 minutes on Sauté. Top with scallions and serve.

Cannellini Bean & Beef Soup

Total Time: 35 minutes | **Servings:** 4

Ingredients

2 tbsp olive oil
1 cup kale, chopped
½ lb ground beef
1 carrot, chopped
1 celery stalk, chopped
1 red onion, chopped
1 garlic clove, minced
1 can (14 oz) crushed tomatoes

4 cups beef broth
1 bay leaf
½ tsp dried oregano
½ tsp dried basil
¼ tsp dried thyme
1 can (8-oz) cannellini beans
½ cup penne pasta

Directions

Set your Instant Pot to Sauté and warm olive oil. Add in beef, carrot, celery, onion, and garlic. Cook for 8 minutes until the meat browns. Stir in spices, broth, and tomatoes. Seal the lid, select Pressure Cook, and set to 15 minutes.

After cooking, perform a quick pressure release. Unlock the lid. Stir in the pasta, kale, and beans. Seal the lid and cook for 4 minutes on Pressure Cook. Do a quick pressure release. Discard bay leaf and serve in bowls.

Beef-Butternut Squash Stew

Total Time: 40 minutes | **Servings:** 4

Ingredients

1 (1 lb) butternut squash, chopped
2 tbsp olive oil
1 lb beef stew meat, cubed
Salt and black pepper to taste
1 cup beef broth

1 tsp onion powder
1 tsp garlic powder
2 thyme sprigs, chopped
1 tsp cornstarch

Directions

Set your Instant Pot to Sauté, heat olive oil, season beef with salt and pepper, and fry in oil until brown on all sides, 4 minutes. Pour in beef broth; add onion powder, garlic powder, butternut squash, and thyme.

Seal the lid, select Pressure Cook on High, and set the time to 15 minutes. Allow a natural release for 10 minutes. Unlock the lid and stir in cornstarch, adjust the taste, and cook for 1 minute on Sauté. Serve with freshly baked bread.

Lamb & Bella Mushroom Stew

Total Time: 45 minutes | **Servings:** 4

Ingredients

1 tbsp olive oil
½ lb baby Bella mushrooms, chopped
1 ½ lb lamb shoulder, cubed
Salt and black pepper to taste
1 small onion, chopped
1 garlic cloves minced

½ tbsp tomato paste
1 cup cherry tomatoes, halved
1 cup chicken broth
½ cup chopped parsley

Directions

Set your Instant Pot to Sauté, heat olive oil, season lamb with salt and pepper, and sear meat until brown on the outside, 6-7 minutes. Stir in onion, garlic, and mushrooms and cook until softened, 5 minutes. Mix in tomato paste, cherry tomatoes, broth, and season with salt and pepper. Seal the lid, select Pressure Cook on High, and set the time to 15 minutes. After cooking, allow a natural release for 10 minutes. Sprinkle with parsley to serve.

Chili Pulled Lamb

Total Time: 90 minutes | **Servings:** 4

Ingredients

2 lb boneless lamb shoulder, cut into 4 pieces
2 tbsp olive oil
2 cups chicken stock
6 tinned anchovies, chopped
1 tsp garlic puree

1 sprig rosemary
1 tsp dried oregano
3 green chilies, minced
Salt to taste

Directions

Set your Instant Pot to Sauté, heat olive oil, and sear lamb on both sides until brown, 5 minutes. Transfer to a plate and set aside. Pour the stock into the inner pot, scrape the bottom to deglaze, and mix in anchovies and garlic. Return lamb to pot and top with rosemary, oregano, green chilies, and salt. Seal the lid, select Pressure Cook, and set the time to 60 minutes. Do a natural release for 15 minutes. Shred lamb with two forks, adjust the taste and serve.

Lamb Rogan Josh

Total Time: 60 minutes | **Servings:** 4

Ingredients

2 tbsp ghee
2 lb boneless lamb shoulder, cubed
1 large onion, chopped
10 garlic cloves, minced
2 tsp minced ginger
1 bay leaf
4 tsp chili powder
3 tsp coriander powder
Salt and black pepper to taste
1 tsp garam masala

1 tsp turmeric
¼ tsp cumin powder
¼ tsp ground cloves
½ tsp cinnamon powder
½ tsp cardamom powder
1 (15 oz) can tomato sauce
8 tbsp plain yogurt
3 tbsp chopped cilantro

Directions

Set your Instant Pot to Sauté, melt ghee, and cook onion and lamb until lamb is no longer pink on the outside, 6 to 7 minutes. Stir in garlic, ginger, bay leaf, chili, coriander, salt, garam masala, turmeric, pepper, cumin, cloves, cinnamon, and cardamom. Cook until fragrant, 3 minutes. Mix in tomato sauce, cook for 2 to 3 minutes, and stir in yogurt one tbsp at a time. Pour in 1 cup of water. Seal the lid, select Pressure Cook on High, and set the time to 20 minutes. After cooking, allow a natural release for 10 minutes. Unlock the lid and press Sauté. Cook further for 4 minutes to boil off some liquid until the consistency is stew-like. Spoon food into bowls, garnish with cilantro, and serve.

Croatian Lamb in Milk

Total Time: 80 minutes | **Servings:** 4

Ingredients

2 lb boneless lamb shoulder, cubed
3 carrots, cubed
1 lb potatoes, cubed
5 garlic cloves
2 rosemary sprigs
4 cups milk
Salt and black pepper to taste
1 tbsp Vegeta seasoning

Directions

Add the cubed lamb shoulder, carrots, potatoes, garlic, rosemary springs, Vegeta seasoning, milk, 2 cups of water, salt, and pepper to your Instant pot. Lock the lid, select Pressure Cook, and set the cooking time to 60 minutes. Once ready, allow a natural release for 10 minutes. Unlock the lid, remove and discard the rosemary spring and serve.

Saffron Lamb & Raisin Biryani

Total Time: 35 minutes + marinating time | **Servings:** 4

Ingredients

½ tsp saffron, soaked in 3 tbsp of hot water
4 tbsp ghee, divided
1 lb lamb leg steak, cubed
1 brown onion, thinly sliced
1 green bell pepper, sliced
½ lime, juiced
½ cup Greek yogurt
1 tbsp garlic paste
Salt to taste
1 tsp paprika
½ tsp turmeric
3 tsp garam masala
¼ tsp cayenne pepper
½ tsp cardamom powder
1 cup basmati rice, rinsed
½ cup chopped cilantro
2 cups warm water
2 tbsp red raisins

Directions

In a bowl, add lamb, onion, and bell pepper. In another bowl, mix lime juice, yogurt, 2 tbsp of ghee, ginger, garlic paste, salt, paprika, turmeric, garam masala, cayenne pepper, and cardamom. Pour mixture over meat and vegetables, mix, and cover with a plastic wrap. Marinate in the refrigerator for 30 minutes.

Remove meat after and drain marinade. On Sauté, melt the remaining ghee and brown lamb, 6-7 minutes. Add basmati rice, cilantro, warm water, and saffron liquid. Do not mix.

Seal the lid, select Pressure Cook on High, and set the time to 10 minutes. After cooking, allow a natural release for 10 minutes. Unlock the lid, stir in raisins, and adjust the taste. Share between bowls and serve.

Cilantro Lamb Shorba

Total Time: 45 minutes | **Servings:** 4

Ingredients

3 tbsp olive oil
1 white onion, chopped
6 garlic cloves, minced
1 cup chopped tomatoes
1 tsp cumin powder
1 tsp coriander powder
1 tsp red chili powder
¼ tsp turmeric
4 cups chicken broth
1 lb lamb shoulder, cubed
1 cup frozen peas
1 cup chopped cilantro

Directions

Set your instant pot to Sauté and heat olive oil. Sauté onion and garlic for 3 minutes. Add tomatoes, cumin, coriander, chili powder, and turmeric. Cook until the sauce reduces by half, 6 minutes. Add broth, allow boiling for 2 minutes, and add the lamb. Seal the lid, select Pressure Cook, and set the time to 20 minutes. After cooking, allow a quick release. Stir in frozen peas and cilantro. Cook on Sauté until peas heat through, 1-2 minutes. Spoon shorba into bowls to serve.

Moroccan-Style Lamb Tagine

Total Time: 50 minutes | **Servings:** 4

Ingredients

2 tbsp ghee
1 ½ lb lamb stew meat, cubed
1 large red onion, chopped
4 carrots, peeled and chopped
6 cloves garlic, minced
1 lemon, zested
2 bay leaves
Salt and black pepper to taste
2 tsp cumin powder
2 tsp coriander powder
2 tsp ginger powder
½ tsp turmeric
¼ tsp cinnamon powder
¼ tsp clove powder
¼ tsp red chili flakes
2 cups vegetable stock
2 cups green olives, pitted
3 tbsp chopped parsley

Directions

Set your Instant Pot to Sauté, melt ghee, and cook lamb until brown, 6 to 7 minutes. Add onion, carrots, and garlic; cook until vegetables soften, 5 minutes. Stir in lemon zest, bay leaves, salt, pepper, cumin, coriander, ginger, turmeric, cinnamon, clove powder, and red chili flakes. Cook until fragrant, 1 to 2 minutes.

Mix in vegetable stock. Seal the lid, select Pressure Cook on High, and set the time to 20 minutes. After cooking, allow a natural release for 10 minutes. Discard bay leaves and stir in green olives and parsley. Serve into bowls.

Indian Lamb Curry

Total Time: 75 minutes | **Servings:** 4

Ingredients

2 tbsp oil
1 lb lamb meat, cubed
2 garlic cloves, minced
1 onion, chopped
2 tomatoes, chopped
1-inch piece of ginger, grated
½ tsp garam masala
½ tbsp ground turmeric
½ tbsp ground cumin
½ tbsp chili flakes
1 tbsp fish sauce
¼ cup cilantro, chopped
¼ cup rice, rinsed
½ cup coconut milk
1 cup chicken stock

Directions

Set your Instant Pot to Sauté, heat the oil, and brown the meat for 3-5 minutes per side; reserve. Add in garlic, onion, tomatoes, and ginger. Stir-fry for 5 minutes. Mix in spices and cook for 10 minutes until they form a paste. Pour in coconut milk, stock, fish sauce, and rice, and return the lamb. Seal the lid, select Meat/Stew, and set to 35 minutes on High. When done, allow a natural release for 10 minutes. Select Sauté and cook the curry until thickened. Serve.

Pea & Cod Paella

Total Time: 35 minutes | **Servings:** 4

Ingredients

A pinch of saffron threads, soaked in 2 tbsp hot water
2 tbsp olive oil
1 yellow onion, chopped
1 red bell pepper, chopped
1 cup basmati rice, rinsed
1 cup fish stock
Salt and black pepper to taste
¼ cup frozen peas
4 cod fillets, cut into cubes
2 tbsp chopped parsley

Directions

Set your Instant Pot to Sauté. Heat olive oil and sauté the onion and bell pepper until softened, 3 minutes. Mix in basmati rice, fish stock, saffron liquid, salt, black pepper, and 1 cup of water. Seal the lid, select Pressure Cook on High, and set the cooking time to 6 minutes. Allow sitting (covered) for 10 minutes. Press Sauté. Mix in frozen peas and cod, cook until softened, 5 minutes. Carefully stir in parsley and serve paella.

Rich Cod in Lettuce Wraps

Total Time: 15 minutes | **Servings:** 4

Ingredients

1 head iceberg lettuce, four big leaves extracted
1 tbsp olive oil
2 garlic cloves, minced
½ cup tomato salsa
1 cup chicken broth
Salt and black pepper to taste
½ lime, juiced
4 cod fillets, cut into cubes
2 scallions, chopped to garnish

Directions

On Sauté, heat olive oil and sauté garlic until fragrant, 30 seconds. Stir in salsa, broth, salt, pepper, lime juice, and fish. Seal the lid, select Pressure Cook on High, and set the time to 3 minutes. After cooking, do a quick release and unlock the lid. Stir and adjust the taste with salt and pepper. On lettuce leaves, spoon food, and garnish with scallions.

Tangy Salmon with Wild Rice

Total Time: 40 minutes | **Servings:** 4

Ingredients

A bunch of asparagus, trimmed and cut diagonally
3 tbsp olive oil, divided
1 cup wild rice
2 cups vegetable stock
4 skinless salmon fillets
Salt and black pepper to taste
2 limes, juiced
2 tbsp honey
1 tsp sweet paprika
2 jalapeño peppers, chopped
4 garlic cloves, minced
2 tbsp chopped fresh parsley

Directions

Pour wild rice and vegetable stock your Instant Pot; stir to combine. Seal the lid, select Pressure Cook on High, and set the time to 20 minutes. In a bowl, toss the asparagus with 1 tbsp of olive oil and season with salt and black pepper.

In another bowl, combine the remaining oil, lime juice, honey, paprika, jalapeño, garlic, and parsley. When ready, do a quick pressure release. Unlock the lid. Fit in a trivet. Lay the salmon fillets into a baking pan and brush it with the honey sauce; reserve a little of the sauce for garnish.

Arrange the asparagus around the salmon. Place the pan on top of the trivet, seal the lid, select Pressure Cook on High, and set the time to 6 minutes. When ready, allow a natural release for 5 minutes. Dish salmon with asparagus and rice, top with parsley and the reserved sauce. Serve.

Catalan Haddock with Samfaina

Total Time: 20 minutes | **Servings:** 4

Ingredients

3 tbsp olive oil
1 (14.5-oz) can diced tomatoes
4 haddock fillets
Salt to taste
½ small onion, sliced
1 jalapeño, seeded and minced
2 large garlic cloves, minced
1 eggplant, cubed
1 bell pepper, chopped
1 bay leaf
½ tsp dried basil
¼ cup sliced green olives
¼ cup chopped fresh chervil
3 tbsp capers

Directions

Season the fish on both sides with salt, and refrigerate. Press Sauté, heat olive oil and stir-fry onion, eggplant, bell pepper, jalapeño, and garlic for 5 minutes. Stir in tomatoes, bay leaf, basil, and olives. Remove the fish from the fridge and lay on top of vegetables. Add 1 cup of water, seal the lid, select Pressure Cook on High, and set to 5 minutes.

After cooking, do a quick pressure release; discard the bay leaf. Transfer the fish to a serving platter and spoon the sauce over. Sprinkle with the chervil and capers to serve.

Traditional Tuscan Seafood Stew

Total Time: 20 minutes | **Servings:** 4

Ingredients

1 tbsp olive oil
1 white onion, chopped
½ tsp red pepper flakes
5 garlic cloves, whole
1 tbsp tomato paste
1 ½ cups white wine
1 cup diced tomatoes
2 cups chicken broth
Salt and black pepper to taste
1 lb clams, scrubbed
1 lb white fish, cut into pieces
½ lb shrimp, deveined
¼ lb scallops
1 lemon, juiced
Parsley to garnish

Directions

In a blender, add onion, flakes, garlic, and process until smooth. On Sauté, heat olive oil, pour in onion mixture and stir-fry until fragrant, 4 minutes. Stir in tomato paste and cook for 1 minute. Pour in wine, tomatoes, and broth.

Season with salt and pepper. Cook for 2 minutes. Stir in clams, fish, shrimp, scallops, and lemon juice.

Seal the lid, select Pressure Cook on High, and set to 3 minutes. Do a quick pressure release, and unlock the lid. Remove any closed clams. Season stew with salt and black pepper. Spoon into bowls, garnish with parsley, and serve.

Crispy Cod on Quinoa

Total Time: 15 minutes | **Servings:** 4

Ingredients

1 tbsp olive oil	1 cup panko breadcrumbs
4 tbsp melted butter	¼ cup minced fresh cilantro
1 cup quinoa	1 tsp lemon zest
1 yellow bell pepper, chopped	1 lemon, juiced
1 red bell pepper, chopped	Salt to taste
2 cups vegetable broth	4 cod fillets

Directions

Combine olive oil, quinoa, bell peppers, and broth in your Instant Pot. Seal the lid, select Pressure Cook on High, and set the time to 6 minutes. In a bowl, whisk the breadcrumbs, half of the butter, cilantro, lemon zest, lemon juice, and salt. Spoon the breadcrumb mixture evenly on the cod.

When over, do a quick pressure release, and unlock the lid. Remove the quinoa and clean the inner pot with a paper towel. Press Sauté. Add the remaining butter and cod fillets and fry them for 2-3 minutes per side or until browned. Share the quinoa into four plates, and top with cod fillets.

Dill-Lemon Salmon with Caper Sauce

Total Time: 15 minutes | **Servings:** 4

Ingredients

4 salmon fillets	4 sprigs dill
Salt and black pepper to taste	1 lemon, sliced

Caper sauce

3 tbsp buttermilk	1 tbsp dill, chopped
3 tbsp mayo	2 tbsp capers, drained
1 lemon, juiced and zested	

Directions

To the pot, pour 1 cup of water and fit in a trivet. Season salmon with salt and pepper; lay on the trivet. Top with dill sprigs and lemon slices. Seal the lid, and set on Steam for 5 minutes. In a bowl, whisk all sauce ingredients. Do a quick release and remove the salmon; discard lemon and dill sprigs. Drizzle with caper sauce to serve.

Smoked Salmon Pilaf with Walnuts

Total Time: 20 minutes | **Servings:** 4

Ingredients

4 green onions, chopped (white part separated from green part)	
1 tbsp canola oil	Salt to taste
½ cup walnut pieces	1 smoked salmon fillet, flaked
1 cup basmati rice	2 tsp prepared horseradish
1 cup frozen corn, thawed	1 medium tomato, chopped

Directions

On Sauté, heat canola oil and sauté the white part of green onions for a minute, until starting to soften. Stir in the rice and corn, stirring occasionally for 2-3 minutes or until fragrant. Add in 2 cups water and salt. Seal the lid, select Pressure Cook on High, and set the time to 3 minutes.

After cooking, allow a natural release for 5 minutes. Fluff the rice gently with a fork. Stir in the flaked salmon, green parts of green onions, and horseradish. Add the tomato and let rest a few minutes to warm through. Top the pilaf with walnuts and serve. Enjoy!

Steamed Salmon with Sweet Chili Sauce

Total Time: 15 minutes | **Servings:** 2

Ingredients

Salmon

2 salmon fillets	Salt and black pepper to taste

Chili sauce

1 tbsp olive oil	1 tbsp honey
1 tbsp chili garlic sauce	1 tbsp hot water
½ lemon, juiced	1 tbsp chopped cilantro
2 cloves garlic, minced	½ tsp cumin

Directions

In a bowl, combine all sauce ingredients; set aside. Pour 1 cup water into the pot and fit in a trivet. Place salmon on the trivet and sprinkle with salt and pepper. Seal the lid, select Steam on High, and cook for 5 minutes. Do a quick pressure release. Transfer the salmon to a plate. Combine the sauce ingredients and pour over the salmon to serve.

Flavorful Vietnamese Salmon

Total Time: 15 minutes | **Servings:** 4

Ingredients

1 tbsp olive oil	1 cup vegetable broth
¼ cup brown sugar	Black pepper to taste
1 lime, zested and juiced	4 salmon fillets, cut into cubes
1 ½ tbsp soy sauce	2 scallions, sliced diagonally
3 tbsp fish sauce	2 tbsp chopped cilantro leaves
1 grated ginger	1 lime, cut into wedges

Directions

Set your Instant Pot to Sauté. Add in oil, sugar, lime zest, lime juice, soy sauce, fish sauce, ginger, broth, and pepper and let simmer for 3 minutes. Place in salmon, seal the lid, select Pressure Cook on High, and set the time to 5 minutes.

Do a quick pressure release. Carefully remove salmon onto serving plates and continue cooking until the sauce is reduced and syrupy on Sauté. Drizzle sauce over salmon, garnish with scallions, cilantro, and lime wedges and serve.

Effortless Seafood Jambalaya

Total Time: 25 minutes | **Servings:** 4

Ingredients

2 tbsp olive oil	1 cup white rice, long-grain
1 onion, chopped	½ lb shrimp, deveined
2 cups chicken broth	2 andouille sausages, sliced

Directions

Heat the olive oil in the Instant Pot on Sauté. Cook sausage and onion for 5 minutes. Pour in broth and rice and stir.

Seal the lid, select Pressure Cook, and set the time to 8 minutes. Once cooking is complete, perform a quick release. Press Sauté and stir in the shrimp. Cook for 3 minutes. Serve and enjoy!

Steamed Tilapia with Tomato-Olive Sauce

Total Time: 20 minutes | **Servings:** 2

Ingredients

2 tbsp butter
2 tilapia fillets
Salt and black pepper to taste
4 sprigs fresh rosemary
4 lemon slices
2 garlic cloves, thinly sliced
16 cherry tomatoes, halved
2 tsp green olives, sliced

Directions

Rub the fish with salt and pepper on both sides. Transfer to a foil-lined baking dish and top each fillet with 2 sprigs of rosemary and 2 slices of lemon. Set your Instant Pot to Sauté and melt butter. Cook the garlic for 30 seconds until slightly pale and fragrant. Stir in the tomatoes and olives and sauté for 3 minutes. Pour the tomato mix over the fish. Wipe clean. Pour in 1 cup of water and fit in a trivet. Place the baking dish on the trivet. Seal the lid, select Pressure Cook on High, and cook for 10 minutes. Do a quick release, unlock the lid and serve on a plate, topped with sauce.

Tomato Steamed Trout with Olives

Total Time: 25 minutes | **Servings:** 4

Ingredients

2 tbsp olive oil
1 small red onion, chopped
2 garlic cloves, minced
1 ½ cups chopped tomatoes
1 tsp tomato paste
1 cup fish broth
Salt and black pepper to taste
¼ tsp red chili flakes
¼ tsp dried dill
¼ tsp dried basil
4 trout fillets
¼ cup kalamata olives, pitted

Directions

Set your Instant Pot to Sauté, heat olive oil and sauté onion until softened, 3 minutes. Stir in garlic until fragrant, 30 seconds. Add tomatoes, tomato paste, fish broth, salt, pepper, dill, and basil. Allow boiling for 3 to 4 minutes.

Lay trout in tomato sauce and cover well with sauce. Seal the lid, select Pressure Cook on High, and set to 2 minutes. After cooking, perform a quick pressure release. Remove fish onto plates and stir Kalamata olives into sauce. Cook until sauce reduces, 4 minutes. Adjust the taste, spoon sauce over fish and serve warm. Garnish with chili flakes.

Penne Tuna Casserole with Cheese

Total Time: 20 minutes | **Servings:** 4

Ingredients

2 cups grated Monterey Jack cheese
2 tbsp olive oil
1 onion, chopped
1 large carrot, chopped
6 oz penne pasta
1 (12-oz) can full cream milk
1 cup vegetable broth
Salt to taste
2 tsp cornstarch
2 (5-oz) cans tuna, drained
1 cup chopped green beans

Directions

On Sauté, warm the oil and sauté onion and carrots for 3 minutes, until softened. Add in penne, three-fourths of cream milk, broth, and salt to the pot; stir to combine. Seal the lid, select Pressure Cook on High, and set to 5 minutes. After cooking, do a quick release and unlock the lid. Select Sauté and pour in the remaining cream milk.

In a bowl, mix cheese and cornstarch evenly and add the cheese mixture to the sauce while stirring, until the cheese melts and the sauce thickens. Add in tuna and green beans, and stir. Heat for 2 minutes. Serve right away.

Winter Succotash with Basil-Crusted Fish

Total Time: 25 minutes | **Servings:** 4

Ingredients

1 tbsp olive oil
½ small onion, chopped
1 garlic clove, minced
1 red chili, seeded and chopped
1 cup frozen corn
1 cup frozen mixed green beans
1 cup butternut squash, cubed
1 bay leaf
¼ tsp cayenne pepper
1 cup chicken stock
½ tsp Worcestershire sauce
Salt to taste
4 firm white fish fillets
¼ cup mayonnaise
1 tbsp Dijon mustard
1 ½ cups breadcrumbs
1 tomato, seeded and chopped
¼ cup chopped fresh basil

Directions

Season the fish fillets with salt. In a small bowl, mix the mayonnaise and mustard. Pour the breadcrumbs and basil into another bowl. Spread the mayonnaise mixture on all sides of the fish and dredge each piece in the basil breadcrumbs. Warm the olive oil in the pot and fry the fish for 6-7 minutes in total on Sauté mode. Set aside.

Add in onion, garlic, and chili to sauté for 4 minutes or until soft. Stir in corn, butternut squash, mixed beans, bay leaf, cayenne, stock, Worcestershire sauce, and salt. Seal the lid, select Pressure Cook on High, and set to 5 minutes. Once ready, do a quick release and unlock the lid. Stir in the tomato and remove bay leaf. Serve fillets with succotash.

White Wine Tilapia Foil Packs

Total Time: 15 minutes | **Servings:** 2

Ingredients

2 tbsp olive oil
2 tilapia fillets
2 garlic cloves, minced
2 tomatoes, chopped
1 tsp chopped rosemary
Salt and black pepper to taste
¼ cup white wine
1 cup water

Directions

Cut out 2 heavy-duty foil papers to contain each tilapia. Place each fish on each foil and arrange on top a drizzle of olive oil, garlic, tomatoes, rosemary, salt, pepper, and drizzle with wine. Wrap foil tightly to secure fish well.

Pour water into your Instant pot and fit in a trivet. Lay the fish packs on top. Seal the lid, select Pressure Cook on High, and set the time to 3 minutes. Do a quick release and remove fish packs. Place on serving plates and open. Serve.

Tuna Salad with Asparagus & Potatoes

Total Time: 15 minutes | **Servings:** 4

Ingredients

½ cup pimento-stuffed green olives
½ cup chopped roasted red peppers

4 tbsp olive oil	2 tbsp red wine vinegar
1 ½ lb potatoes, quartered	2 tbsp chopped fresh parsley
Salt and black pepper to taste	2 cans tuna, drained
8 oz asparagus, cut into three	

Directions

Pour 1 cup water into the inner pot and set a trivet. Place the potatoes on top. Seal the lid, select Pressure Cook on High, and set to 4 minutes. When ready, do a quick release; drain the potatoes. Wipe the pot dry and press Sauté.

Heat 2 tbsp olive oil and fry potatoes and asparagus for 5 minutes; season with salt. Pour asparagus and potatoes into a salad bowl. Sprinkle with 1 tbsp vinegar and mix to coat. In a bowl, pour 2 tbsp oil, vinegar, salt, and pepper; whisk to combine. To potatoes, add roasted red peppers, olives, parsley, and tuna; toss. Drizzle the dressing and serve.

Cheesy Tuna & Noodle One-Pot

Total Time: 25 minutes | **Servings:** 4

Ingredients

2 (3 oz) can tuna packed in oil, drained

3 tbsp unsalted butter	1 cup milk
16 oz egg noodles	5 oz frozen green peas
Salt and black pepper to taste	½ cup panko breadcrumbs
3 tbsp plain flour	½ cup grated Monterey Jack
1 ½ cups chicken broth	

Directions

Add the noodles and 6 cups of salted water in your Instant Pot. Seal the lid, select Pressure Cook on High, and set the cooking time to 3 minutes. After cooking, perform a quick pressure release. Drain the noodles and set them aside.

Clean the inner pot and press Sauté. Melt butter pot and stir in flour until lightly golden in color. Gradually stir in the broth until smooth liquid forms. Add milk and cook until thickened, 10 minutes. Season with salt and pepper.

Mix in tuna and green peas. Seal the lid, select Pressure Cook on High, and set to 1 minute. After cooking, do a quick release. Stir in breadcrumbs, cheese, and cook further on Sauté until cheese melts. Dish into plates and serve.

Tuna Fillets in Mango Sauce

Total Time: 20 minutes | **Servings:** 4

Ingredients

5 tbsp olive oil	1 tsp fresh ginger paste
4 tuna fillets	1 red onion, finely chopped
Salt and black pepper to taste	¼ tsp red chili flakes
1 cup chopped ripe mangoes	2 tsp chopped basil
1 cup fresh mango juice	2 tsp chopped parsley
1 tbsp apple cider vinegar	

Directions

Set your Instant Pot to Sauté, heat olive oil, season tuna with salt and pepper, and sear until golden on the outside and flaky within; set aside. To the pot, add ginger and red onion; cook for 5 minutes, stirring frequently. Pour in mango juice, mangoes, vinegar, chili flakes, and ½ cup of water. Seal the lid, select Pressure Cook on High, and set to 5 minutes. After cooking, do a quick pressure release. Stir in basil and parsley. Pour mango sauce over tuna and serve.

Dilled Tuna Cakes

Total Time: 30 minutes | **Servings:** 6

Ingredients

4 tbsp olive oil	4 tbsp plain flour
2 potatoes, peeled, chopped	1 egg, beaten
4 (7 oz) cans tuna in oil, drained	Salt and black pepper to taste
1 tsp cayenne pepper	¼ tsp dried dill
1 green onion, chopped	

Directions

Pour potatoes and 1 cup of water in your Instant Pot. Seal the lid, select Pressure Cook on High, and set the time to 6 minutes. When ready, do a quick release. Drain potatoes and transfer to a bowl. Mash with a grinder until thoroughly broken. Mix in tuna, cayenne, onion, flour, egg, salt, pepper, and dill until well combined. Form 6 patties out of the mixture. Wipe inner pot clean with paper towels, set the pot to Sauté, and heat olive oil. Fry the patties on both sides until golden on the outside, 6 to 8 minutes. Transfer to a wire rack to drain grease. Serve and enjoy!

Lemon Tuna Steaks with Capers

Total Time: 15 minutes | **Servings:** 2

Ingredients

4 tbsp olive oil	1 lemon, zested and juiced
2 tuna steaks	2 tbsp chopped thyme
Salt and black pepper to taste	3 tbsp drained capers

Directions

Pour 1 cup of water into your Instant Pot and fit in a trivet. Drizzle tuna with some olive oil and season with salt and pepper. Place it on the trivet. Seal the lid, select Pressure Cook, and set the time to 6 minutes. After cooking, do a quick release. Remove fish to a serving plate. Empty and clean inner pot. Set to Sauté and heat the remaining olive oil. Sauté lemon zest and juice, capers, and 2 tbsp of water for 3 minutes. Pour sauce over tuna and garnish with thyme.

Salmon Fillets with Parsley Pesto

Total Time: 15 minutes | **Servings:** 4

Ingredients

¼ cup olive oil	2 cups parsley leaves
4 salmon fillets	2 garlic cloves, minced
Salt and black pepper to taste	2 tbsp toasted pine nuts
1 lemon, juiced	3 tbsp grated Parmesan cheese
1 cup chicken broth	

Directions

Season salmon with salt and black pepper. In your Instant Pot, pour lemon juice and chicken broth. Fit in a trivet and place the salmon on top of the trivet. Seal the lid, select Steam mode, and set the cooking time to 5 minutes. After cooking, do a quick release and unlock the lid. In a food processor, add parsley, garlic, pine nuts, Parmesan, salt, and olive oil. Blend until smooth. Transfer the salmon to serving plates. Drizzle with the parsley pesto sauce and serve.

Crispy Snapper in Orange-Ginger Sauce

Total Time: 15 minutes | **Servings:** 4

Ingredients

½ red scotch bonnet pepper, minced
3 tbsp olive oil, divided
½ cup plain flour
4 red snapper fillets
Salt and black pepper to taste
2 green onions, chopped
3 sprigs thyme, leaves extracted
1 ½ tsp pureed ginger

1 garlic clove, minced
1 cup chicken broth
1 orange, zested and juiced
1 tbsp honey
4 orange slices to garnish
1 tbsp chopped parsley

Directions

Pour flour onto a flat plate. Season fish with salt, pepper, and dredge lightly in flour. Set your Instant Pot to Sauté, heat 2 tbsp of olive oil, and fry fish until golden, 1 minute. Transfer to a plate. Clean the inner pot. Heat remaining oil in the pot and sauté green onions, thyme, ginger, garlic, and scotch bonnet pepper for 1 minute. Mix in broth, orange zest, orange juice, and honey, allow heating for 1 minute, and lay fish in sauce. Seal the lid, select Pressure Cook, and cook for 1 minute. After cooking, do a quick release. Garnish with orange slices and parsley. Serve and enjoy!

Lime Halibut & Butternut Squash Soup

Total Time: 25 minutes | **Servings:** 4

Ingredients

3 tbsp butter
1 butternut squash, diced
1 Yukon gold potato, diced
1 yellow onion, chopped
2 garlic cloves, minced
1 tsp pureed ginger
2 tsp turmeric powder

1 tsp chili powder or to taste
4 cups chicken broth
Salt and black pepper to taste
4 halibut fillets, cubed
4 tbsp heavy cream
1 lime, juiced
2 tbsp chopped cilantro

Directions

Set your Instant Pot to Sauté and melt butter. Sauté squash, potato, and onion until sweaty, 5 minutes. Add garlic, ginger, turmeric, and chili powder. Stir-fry for 1 minute. Pour in chicken broth, salt, pepper, and fish.

Seal the lid, select Pressure Cook on High, and set to 12 minutes. After cooking, do a quick pressure release, and unlock the lid. Spoon out fish into a bowl and set aside. Using an immersion blender, pulse ingredients until smooth; stir in heavy cream and lime juice. Return fish to the soup, stir, and dish into bowls. Garnish with cilantro.

Cumin Salmon with Avocado Salsa

Total Time: 20 minutes | **Servings:** 4

Ingredients

2 tsp olive oil
1 tsp chili powder
1 tsp smoked paprika
½ tsp cumin powder
½ tsp garlic powder
Salt and black pepper to taste

4 salmon fillets
1 avocado, chopped
1 tomato, chopped
1 small red onion, chopped
½ lime, juiced
2 tbsp chopped cilantro

Directions

In a bowl, mix chili powder, paprika, cumin, garlic powder, salt, and pepper. Season salmon with spices. Set your Instant Pot to Sauté, heat olive oil, and fry salmon on both sides until brown and flaky within, 5 minutes per side. In another bowl, mix avocado, tomato, onion, lime juice, and cilantro. Plate salmon and top with avocado salsa.

Pinot Noir Poached Salmon

Total Time: 15 minutes | **Servings:** 4

Ingredients

1 cup Pinot Noir wine
2 tbsp red wine vinegar
5 thyme sprigs
2 celery stalks, chopped

1 tbsp sugar
Salt and black pepper to taste
4 salmon fillets
2 tbsp chopped parsley

Directions

In your Instant Pot, combine Pinot Noir wine, vinegar, 1 cup water, thyme sprigs, celery, sugar, salt, and black pepper and stir to combine. Place fish in the liquid. Seal the lid, select Steam on High, and the time to 5 minutes.

After cooking, perform a quick pressure release. Remove salmon to serving plates. Set the pot to Sauté, cook sauce further until reduced and syrupy, 3 to 4 minutes. Spoon sauce all over salmon, sprinkle with parsley, and serve.

Flounder Piccata

Total Time: 35 minutes | **Servings:** 4

Ingredients

3 tbsp butter, melted
3 slices prosciutto, chopped
½ small red onion, chopped
Salt and black pepper to taste

2 cups baby kale
½ cup whipping cream
4 flounder fillets
2 tbsp chopped fresh parsley

Directions

On Sauté, add half of butter and prosciutto, and cook until crispy, 3 minutes. Stir in red onion and cook for about 2 minutes. Fetch the kale into the pot and stir frequently, 4-5 minutes. Mix in whipping cream; transfer to a baking dish.

Lay the flounder fillets over the kale. Brush the fillets with the remaining butter and sprinkle with salt and pepper. Wipe the pot clean, and add 1 cup of water. Fit in a trivet and place baking dish on top. Seal the lid, select Pressure Cook on High, and set to 5 minutes. When done, allow a natural release for 10 minutes. Serve garnished with parsley.

Shrimp with Asparagus

Total Time: 20 minutes | **Servings:** 4

Ingredients

1 lb asparagus, trimmed, cut into 2-inch pieces
3 tbsp butter
4 garlic cloves, minced
¼ tsp dried dill
1 cup chicken broth
Salt and black pepper to taste
1 lb shrimp, deveined
¼ cup lemon juice
¼ tsp red chili flakes to garnish

Directions

Set your Instant Pot to Sauté, melt butter, and cook asparagus until softened, 5 minutes. Add garlic and dill and stir until fragrant, 30 seconds. Pour in broth, salt, pepper, and shrimp. Seal the lid, select Pressure Cook on High, and set to 3 minutes.

After cooking, perform a quick pressure release to let out steam, and unlock the lid. Stir in lemon juice, adjust taste with salt, black pepper, and spoon food into serving bowls. Garnish with chili flakes and serve.

Steamed Lemon Catfish

Total Time: 20 minutes | **Servings:** 4

Ingredients

5 lemongrass stalks, bottom half chopped
1 cup chicken stock
2 tbsp brown sugar
2 lemons, juiced
6 tbsp fish sauce
2 heads garlic, chopped
1 cup chopped cilantro
4 catfish fillets

Directions

Pour lemongrass, stock, sugar, lemon juice, fish sauce, garlic, and two-thirds of cilantro into the pot. On Sauté, let boil for 2 minutes. Place catfish in the pot and baste with sauce. Seal the lid, select Pressure Cook on High, and set the time to 2 minutes. After cooking, do a quick pressure release. Carefully place fish on a serving platter. Spoon sauce all over and garnish with remaining cilantro.

Garlic Lemon Shrimp

Total Time: 20 minutes | **Servings:** 6

Ingredients

1 lb jumbo shrimp, peeled and deveined
½ cup butter, divided
4 garlic cloves, minced
Salt and black pepper to taste
½ lemon, juiced
2 tbsp chopped parsley

Directions

Set your Instant Pot to Sauté, melt 2 tbsp of butter, and sauté garlic until fragrant, 30 seconds. Add shrimp, salt, and pepper, lemon juice, and 1 cup of water. Seal the lid, select Pressure Cook on High, and set the time to 2 minutes.

After cooking, do a quick pressure release to let out steam, and unlock the lid. Stir in remaining butter until melted. Spoon into serving plates and garnish with parsley.

Crabmeat & Broccoli Risotto

Total Time: 25 minutes | **Servings:** 4

Ingredients

¼ cup grated Pecorino Romano cheese
3 tbsp olive oil
1 lb broccoli, chopped
1 small onion, chopped
1 cup rice
¼ cup white wine
2 cups vegetable stock
8 oz lump crabmeat

Directions

Select Sauté on your Instant Pot, heat olive oil, and cook the onion for 3 minutes. Stir in rice and wine and cook for 3 minutes. Pour in vegetable stock and broccoli. Seal the lid, select Pressure Cook on High, and set the time to 8 minutes. After cooking, do a quick pressure release. Gently stir in crabmeat and cheese and let heat for 2 minutes. Serve.

Peppery Prawn & Potato Chowder

Total Time: 30 minutes | **Servings:** 4

Ingredients

2 tbsp olive oil
4 slices serrano ham, chopped
4 tbsp minced garlic
1 onion, chopped
2 Yukon Gold potatoes, chopped
16 oz frozen corn
2 cups vegetable broth
1 tsp dried rosemary
Salt and black pepper to taste
16 prawns, peeled and deveined
½ tsp red chili flakes
¾ cup heavy cream

Directions

In a bowl, toss prawns in garlic, salt, pepper, and flakes. Warm oil in your Instant Pot on Sauté and cook prawns for 5-6 minutes; set aside. Add in serrano ham and onion and cook for 3 minutes. Fetch out one-third of the ham into a bowl for garnish. Add potatoes, corn, broth, and rosemary to the pot. Seal the lid, select Pressure Cook on High, and set to 10 minutes. Do a quick pressure release. Stir in heavy cream. Top with prawns and reserved ham to serve.

Shrimp Paella with Andouille Sausages

Total Time: 30 minutes | **Servings:** 4

Ingredients

1 pound jumbo shrimp, peeled and deveined
1 tbsp melted butter
1 lb andouille sausages, sliced
1 white onion, chopped
4 garlic cloves, minced
½ cup dry white wine
1 cup Spanish rice
2 cups chicken stock
1 ½ tsp sweet paprika
1 tsp turmeric powder
Salt and black pepper to taste
1 lb baby squid, cut into rings
1 red bell pepper, chopped

Directions

Set your Instant Pot to Sauté and melt the butter. Brown the sausages for 3 minutes, stirring often. Remove to a plate and set aside. Sauté onion, garlic, and squid in the same fat for 5 minutes, until fragrant; pour in the wine. Use a wooden spoon to scrape off any browned bits from the bottom and cook until the wine reduces by half. Stir in rice and stock. Season with paprika, turmeric, pepper, and salt.

Seal the lid, select Pressure Cook on High, and set to 5 minutes. When done cooking, do a quick pressure release and unlock the lid. Select Sauté.

Add the shrimp to the pot and stir gently without mashing the rice. Cook for 6 minutes until pink and opaque. Return the sausage to the pot and mix in the bell pepper. Warm through for 2 minutes. Serve immediately.

Old Bay Crab Bisque

Total Time: 30 minutes | **Servings:** 4

Ingredients

1 tbsp butter	1 tsp dried dill
1 small red onion, chopped	1 tsp Old Bay seasoning
2 medium carrots, chopped	Salt and black pepper to taste
2 celery stalks, chopped	5 tsp paprika
2 garlic cloves, minced	2 cups chopped crab meat
½ cup diced tomatoes	1 cup heavy cream
3 cups chicken broth	1 tbsp chopped parsley

Directions

Set your Instant Pot to Sauté, melt butter, and sauté onion, carrots, and celery until softened, 5 minutes. Mix in garlic and cook until fragrant, 30 seconds. Add tomatoes, broth, dill, Old Bay seasoning, salt, pepper, paprika, and crab.

Seal the lid, select Pressure Cook on High, and set the time to 4 minutes. After cooking, allow a natural release for 10 minutes. Unlock the lid and fetch out crab meat onto a plate; set aside. Using an immersion blender, puree soup until smooth; stir in heavy cream. Spoon soup into bowls, top with crabmeat, and garnish with parsley to serve.

Paprika Shrimp Stew

Total Time: 20 minutes | **Servings:** 4

Ingredients

1 lb jumbo shrimp, peeled and deveined

2 tbsp smoked paprika	½ lemon, juiced
3 tbsp honey	Salt and black pepper to taste
1 tsp garlic powder	1 cup chicken broth
¼ tsp cayenne pepper	1 lemon, cut into wedges

Directions

In your Instant Pot, add shrimp, paprika, honey, garlic, cayenne powder, lemon juice, salt, black pepper, and chicken broth. Seal the lid, select Pressure Cook on High, and set the time to 4 minutes. After cooking, do a quick pressure release, and unlock the lid. Stir food and adjust the taste. Spoon into plates and serve with lemon wedges.

Calamari with Broad Beans & Kale

Total Time: 35 minutes | **Servings:** 4

Ingredients

2 tbsp olive oil	½ cup canned broad beans
4 green onions, chopped	Salt and black pepper to taste
2 garlic cloves, minced	½ cup chopped kale
1 lb prepared squid rings	2 tbsp chopped parsley
1 cup dry white wine	

Directions

Set the Instant Pot to Sauté and heat olive oil. Sauté onion and garlic for 3 minutes. Mix in squid, wine, beans, salt, and pepper. Cook until squid is opaque, 3 minutes. Pour in 1 cup water. Seal the lid, select Pressure Cook on High, and cook for 15 minutes. Do a quick pressure release. Add kale and cook for 2-3 minutes. Top with parsley to serve.

Thai Basil Scallops in Chili Sauce

Total Time: 20 minutes | **Servings:** 4

Ingredients

3 tbsp butter	½ cup coconut milk
4 garlic cloves, minced	1 lb scallops, tendons removed
¼ cup Thai basil, chopped	Salt and black pepper to taste
1 tsp red chili paste	1 lemon, cut into wedges

Directions

Set your Instant Pot to Sauté and melt butter. Sauté garlic, basil, and chili paste for 30 seconds. Add in scallops, coconut milk, and 1 cup water. Season to taste. Seal the lid, select Pressure Cook, and set the cooking time to 1 minute. Do a quick release. Serve with lemon wedges.

Cilantro Scallops in Mustard Sauce

Total Time: 20 minutes | **Servings:** 4

Ingredients

2 tbsp olive oil	1 lemon, zested and juiced
2 tbsp unsalted butter	3 tbsp heavy cream
1 lb scallops, tendons removed	1 tbsp Dijon mustard
Salt and black pepper to taste	3 tbsp chopped cilantro
4 garlic cloves, minced	

Directions

Set your Instant Pot to Sauté, melt butter, season scallops with salt and pepper, and sear until golden brown. Set aside. Add olive oil to the pot and sauté garlic for 30 seconds. Stir in lemon zest and juice, heavy cream, mustard, cilantro, and 1 cup water. Return the scallops. Seal the lid, select Pressure Cook, and cook for 2 minutes. Serve warm.

Rustic Seafood One-Pot

Total Time: 15 minutes | **Servings:** 4

Ingredients

2 tbsp olive oil	4 white fish fillets, cubed
1 lb clams, scrubbed	½ lb prepared squid rings
1 white onion, chopped	½ cup white wine
2 celery stalks, chopped	6 tomatoes, chopped
2 garlic cloves, minced	Salt and black pepper to taste

Directions

Discard any clams with broken or closed shells. Set your Instant Pot to Sauté, heat olive oil and sauté onion, garlic, and celery until softened, 3 minutes. Mix in fish, squid, white wine, 1 cup water, tomatoes, salt, pepper, and clams. Seal the lid, select Pressure Cook on High, and set to 2 minutes. When over, do a quick release. Serve.

Celery Mussels with Pancetta

Total Time: 25 minutes **Servings:** 4

Ingredients

18 oz canned chopped mussels, drained, liquid reserved
Salt to taste
2 thick pancetta slices, cubed
2 celery stalks, chopped
1 onion, chopped
1 tbsp flour
¼ cup white wine

1 parsnip, cut into chunks
1 tsp dried rosemary
1 bay leaf
1 ½ cups heavy cream
2 tbsp chopped fresh chervil

Directions

Set your Instant Pot to Sauté and cook pancetta for 5 minutes, until crispy. Remove to a paper towel-lined plate to drain fat; set aside. In the same fat, sauté celery and onion for 2 minutes. Stir in flour and pour in the wine. Cook for 1 minute or until reduced by about one-third.

Pour in 1 cup of water, mussel liquid, parsnip, salt, rosemary, and bay leaf. Seal the lid, select Pressure Cook, and set the time to 4 minutes. After cooking, perform a quick pressure release. Stir in mussels and heavy cream and cook for 2 minutes on Sauté. Remove the bay leaf. Scatter the pancetta over the top and garnish with the chervil to serve.

Best Crab Cake Ever

Total Time: 15 minutes | **Servings:** 4

Ingredients

1 tbsp olive oil
1 lb jumbo lump crabmeat
¼ cup mayonnaise
1 tsp hot sauce
1 green onion, chopped
2 tbsp Dijon mustard

2 tsp Worcestershire sauce
¾ cup panko breadcrumbs
1 egg, beaten
Salt and black pepper to taste
2 tbsp chopped dill

Directions

Pour 1 cup of water into your Instant Pot and fit in a trivet. Lightly grease a cake pan with olive oil and set aside. In a bowl, combine crabmeat, mayonnaise, hot sauce, green onion, mustard, Worcestershire sauce, panko breadcrumbs, egg, salt, black pepper, and dill. Pour the crabmeat mixture into the pan, cover with foil, and place on the trivet.

Seal the lid, select Pressure Cook, and set the time to 10 minutes. Do a quick pressure release. Remove the pan, take off the foil, and let cool firm up. Release the pan, slice the cake, and serve. Enjoy!

Wine-Steamed Mussels with Garlic

Total Time: 20 minutes | **Servings:** 4

Ingredients

1 ½ lb fresh mussels, debearded and washed
2 tbsp unsalted butter
3 shallots, chopped
4 garlic cloves, minced
2 Roma tomatoes, diced
1 lemon, zested

2 tbsp lemon juice
½ cup dry white wine
½ cup fish stock
2 tbsp chopped parsley
4 lemon wedges

Directions

Set your Instant Pot to Sauté, melt butter, and sauté shallots and garlic for 3 minutes. Stir in tomatoes, lemon zest, lemon juice, white wine, and fish stock. Cook for 2 minutes.

Mix in mussels. Seal the lid, select Pressure Cook, and set the time to 4 minutes. Do a quick release. Discard any closed mussel. Garnish with parsley and lemon wedges. Serve and enjoy!

Ginger Squid with Oyster Mushrooms

Total Time: 25 minutes | **Servings:** 4

Ingredients

1 cup chopped oyster mushrooms
3 tbsp olive oil
1 red bell pepper, sliced
2 garlic cloves, minced
1 lb squid rings
2 tsp ginger paste

1 cup chicken stock
1 tbsp soy sauce
1 tsp cornflour
2 tsp toasted sesame seeds
Salt and black pepper to taste

Directions

Set the pot to Sauté, heat oil, and sauté garlic, bell pepper, and mushrooms for 3 minutes. Mix in squid, ginger, stock, and soy sauce; season with salt and pepper.

Seal the lid, select Pressure Cook on High, and set the cooking time to 12 minutes. Do a quick pressure release, stir in the cornflour, and cook on Sauté until it is syrupy, about 1 minute. Top with sesame seeds and serve.

Chorizo Penne all' Arrabbiata & Seafood

Total Time: 25 minutes | **Servings:** 4

Ingredients

1 tbsp olive oil
1 onion, chopped
1 garlic, chopped
16 oz penne
1 (24-oz) jar Arrabbiata sauce
4 cups fish broth

1 chorizo, sliced
Salt and black pepper to taste
8 oz shrimp, peeled and deveined
8 oz scallops
12 clams, cleaned and debearded

Directions

On Sauté, warm the oil and add the chorizo, onion, and garlic; sauté for about 5 minutes. Stir in the penne, Arrabbiata sauce, and fish broth. Season with black pepper and salt and stir well.

Seal the lid, select Pressure Cook on High, and set the time to 2 minutes. When the time is over, do a quick pressure release and take out the lid. Select Sauté.

Stir in the shrimp, scallops, and clams. Cook for 5 minutes until the clams have opened and the shrimp and scallops are opaque. Discard any unopened clams. Spoon the seafood and chorizo pasta into bowls and serve. Enjoy!

SOUPS & STEWS

Lime & Cilantro Chicken Soup

Total Time: 25 minutes | **Servings:** 4

Ingredients

1 tbsp olive oil
1 cup green onions, chopped
2 green chilies, sliced
2 garlic cloves, minced
2 chicken breasts, cubed
4 cups chicken broth
2 tomatoes, chopped
Salt and black pepper to taste
¼ cup chopped cilantro
2 limes, juiced
2 avocados, pitted and sliced
1 cup sour cream for topping

Directions

Set your Instant Pot to Sauté. Heat olive oil and sauté green onions, chilies, and garlic until fragrant, 1 minute. Add chicken, broth, tomatoes, salt, and pepper. Seal the lid, select Pressure Cook on High, and set the time to 7 minutes. After cooking, allow a natural release for 10 minutes. Stir in cilantro and lime juice. Top with avocados and sour cream and serve.

Cumin Potato Soup with Peanuts

Total Time: 20 minutes | **Servings:** 4

Ingredients

2 tbsp olive oil
1 large brown onion, chopped
4 garlic cloves, minced
2 tbsp ginger puree
Salt and black pepper to taste
2 tsp cumin powder
¼ tsp cayenne powder
1 ½ lb russet potatoes, diced
1 cup crushed tomatoes
½ cup creamy peanut butter
4 cups chicken broth
2 tbsp chopped cilantro
3 tbsp toasted peanuts, chopped

Directions

Set your Instant Pot to Sauté, heat olive oil and sauté onion until softened, 3 minutes. Stir in garlic, ginger, salt, pepper, cumin powder, cayenne powder, and cook until fragrant, 1 minute. Pour in potatoes, tomatoes, peanut butter, and broth; mix well. Seal the lid, select Pressure Cook on High, and set the time to 8 minutes. After cooking, do a quick pressure release. Unlock the lid. Using an immersion blender, puree ingredients until smooth. Adjust taste with salt and pepper. Ladle the soup into individual bowls and top with cilantro and peanuts. Serve hot.

Italian Gremolata Prawn Soup

Total Time: 20 minutes | **Servings:** 4

Ingredients

1 small fennel bulb, chopped and fronds reserved
1 lb prawns, peeled and tails intact
1 tbsp olive oil
1 medium red onion, chopped
1 large carrot, chopped
1 celery stick, chopped
1 red chili, minced
6 garlic cloves, minced
¾ cup white wine
4 cups chicken stock
2 cups chopped tomatoes
½ cup canned pinto beans
Salt and black pepper to taste
1 lemon, zested and juiced
¼ cup chopped parsley
1 cup chopped spinach

Directions

Set your Instant Pot to Sauté, heat olive oil, and sauté fennel, onion, carrot, and celery until softened, 5 minutes. Stir in red chili and half of the garlic until fragrant, 30 seconds. Mix in wine, stock, tomatoes, prawns, and pinto beans.

Season with salt and black pepper. Seal the lid, select Soup on High, and set the time to 5 minutes. After cooking, do a quick release. Unlock the lid, stir in lemon juice, and adjust the taste with salt and pepper. In a bowl, mix the remaining garlic, lemon zest, parsley, and spinach to make gremolata. Ladle the soup into serving bowls and top with gremolata.

Chicken Soup with Tortilla Chips

Total Time: 30 minutes | **Servings:** 4

Ingredients

2 tbsp olive oil
4 cups water
3 oz tomato paste
2 tsp taco seasoning
1 tsp chili powder
½ tbsp ground cumin
Salt and black pepper to taste
1 garlic clove, minced
1 onion, chopped
2 celery stalks, chopped
1 chicken breast, cubed
2 tsp fresh lime juice
Broken tortilla chips for garnish
4 radishes, julienned
½ bunch cilantro, chopped

Directions

Set your Instant Pot to Sauté, heat the olive oil, and cook onion, garlic, chicken, celery, salt, and pepper for 5-6 minutes, until the chicken is no longer pink, stirring occasionally. Stir in taco seasoning, chili, ground cumin, tomato paste, then pour in the water.

Seal the lid, select Pressure Cook on High, and cook for 15 minutes. When done, perform a quick pressure release. Unlock the lid and stir in the lime juice. Top with radishes, cilantro, and tortilla chips to serve.

Hominy & Pork Soup

Total Time: 25 minutes | **Servings:** 4

Ingredients

2 tbsp olive oil
½ lb ground pork
Salt and black pepper to taste
½ tsp chili powder
1 tsp coriander powder
1 white onion, thinly sliced
½ bunch cilantro, chopped
4 cups chicken broth
1 cup chopped tomatoes
1 (28 oz) can hominy, rinsed
1 lemon, juiced
4 radishes, sliced for topping

Directions

Set your Instant Pot to Sauté, heat olive oil. Season the pork with salt, pepper, chili and coriander powders and brown it for 5 minutes in the pot. Add onion and cilantro and cook for 3 minutes. Pour broth, tomatoes, hominy, and stir.

Seal the lid, set on Pressure Cook on High, and set the time to 10 minutes. After cooking, do a quick pressure release. Stir in lemon juice; adjust the taste with salt and pepper. Dish food into serving bowls and top with radishes. Serve.

Jalapeño Corn Soup with Cheesy Topping

Total Time: 25 minutes | **Servings:** 4

Ingredients

2 tbsp olive oil
1 red onion, chopped
1 jalapeño pepper, chopped
½ cup cilantro stems, chopped
1 tsp paprika

1 lime, zested
2 cups corn kernels
4 cups chicken broth
½ cup celery stick, chopped

Topping

½ tbsp olive oil
1 cup corn kernels
1 lime, juiced

1 ½ tbsp cilantro, chopped
1 jalapeño, chopped
1 cup cotija cheese, crumbled

Directions

Set your Instant Pot to Sauté, heat the olive oil and red onion for 8 minutes. Mix in jalapeño, cilantro, celery, paprika, and lime zest. Pour in the corn kernels and chicken broth. Seal the lid, select Pressure Cook on High, and set the time to 5 minutes. When done, do a quick pressure release. Puree the soup using an immersion blender until smooth. In a bowl, toss to coat all topping ingredients, except for cotija cheese. Ladle the soup into bowls, spoon the topping over, and sprinkle with cotija cheese to serve.

Simmer Minestrone Soup

Total Time: 20 minutes | **Servings:** 4

Ingredients

1 tbsp olive oil
3 garlic cloves, minced
4 cups chicken stock
1 cup ditalini pasta
2 zucchinis, chopped
½ lb asparagus, sliced diagonally
1 leek, trimmed and sliced

¾ cup frozen peas
½ cup canned pinto beans
1 cup chopped kale
½ lemon, juiced
Salt and black pepper to taste
¼ cup chopped parsley
1 cup crumbled goat cheese

Directions

Set your Instant Pot to Sauté, heat oil, and sauté garlic until fragrant, 30 seconds. Pour in stock and pasta. Stir in zucchinis, asparagus, leek, peas, and pinto beans. Seal the lid, select Pressure Cook, and set the time to 5 minutes.

After cooking, do a quick pressure release. Unlock the lid, set to Sauté, and stir in kale and lemon juice; let wilt for 3 minutes. Adjust the taste. Mix in parsley and ladle soup into serving bowls. Top with goat cheese and serve.

Seafood Gumbo

Total Time: 35 minutes | **Servings:** 4

Ingredients

¼ cup + 2 tsp olive oil
1 lb jumbo shrimp
8 oz lump crabmeat
Salt to taste
¼ cup all-purpose flour
1 ½ tsp Cajun Seasoning
1 medium onion, chopped
1 red bell pepper, chopped

2 celery stalks, chopped
2 garlic cloves, minced
1 small banana pepper, minced
4 cups chicken broth
½ cup jasmine rice
2 green onions, finely sliced

Directions

Season the shrimp with salt and 2 tsp of olive oil; toss to coat. Add to the pot and cook for 5 minutes, until opaque and pink on Sauté; set aside. Heat the remaining ¼ cup of olive oil. Whisk in flour and cook until roux forms for 3-4 minutes, stirring constantly. Add in the Cajun seasoning, onion, bell pepper, celery, garlic, and banana pepper.

Cook for 5 minutes. Add the broth, rice, and crabmeat. Seal the lid, select Pressure Cook, and set the time to 8 minutes. Allow a quick release. Stir in the shrimp and cook for 3 minutes on Sauté. Garnish with green onions. Serve hot.

Cheddar Beer Soup

Total Time: 30 minutes | **Servings:** 4

Ingredients

4 tbsp butter
1 white onion, chopped
2 medium celery, chopped
2 medium carrots, chopped
2 garlic cloves, minced
Salt and black pepper to taste
¾ cup all-purpose flour

4 cups chicken broth
1 cup whole milk
12 oz wheat beer
2 ½ cups shredded cheddar
2 tbsp Dijon mustard
½ tsp Worcestershire sauce
½ cup crumbled bacon

Directions

Set your Instant Pot to Sauté, melt butter, and sauté onion, celery, and carrots until softened, 5 minutes. Stir in garlic until fragrant, 30 seconds. Season with salt and pepper.

Stir in flour until roux forms, and then mix in a few tbsp of broth until smooth. Pour in the remaining chicken broth and milk. Seal the lid, select Pressure Cook on High, and set the time to 1 minute. Allow a natural release for 10 minutes.

Puree ingredients until smooth using an immersion blender. Select Sauté and stir in beer, cheddar cheese, mustard, and Worcestershire sauce until cheese melts, 3 minutes. Spoon the soup into bowls and top with bacon and serve.

Vegan Mexican Sweetcorn Soup

Total Time: 30 minutes | **Servings:** 4

Ingredients

1 red bell pepper, deseeded and cut into chunks
3 tbsp olive oil
1 garlic clove, minced
2 cups sweet corn kernels
1 small potato, chopped
Salt and black pepper to taste

1 tsp Mexican spice mix
4 cups vegetable broth
¼ tsp dried thyme
1 cup heavy cream
2 tbsp chopped parsley

Directions

Set your Instant Pot to Sauté, heat olive oil, and sauté garlic for 30 seconds. Stir in corn, bell pepper, potato, salt, pepper, Mexican spice mix, broth, and thyme. Seal the lid, select Pressure Cook, and set the time to 10 minutes.

After cooking, do a natural pressure release for 10 minutes. Using an immersion blender, puree ingredients until smooth. Stir in heavy cream. Divide the soup between serving bowls, garnish with parsley and serve.

Miso & Sweet Potato Soup

Total Time: 35 minutes | **Servings:** 4

Ingredients

2 tsp olive oil
2 tbsp butter
1 white onion, chopped
3 garlic cloves, minced
4 cups chicken stock

2 tbsp white miso paste
2 large sweet potatoes, diced
Salt and black pepper to taste
4 chives, chopped

Directions

Set your Instant Pot to Sauté, heat olive oil and butter, and sauté onion and garlic until softened, 3 minutes. Add in ½ cup chicken stock, and when hot, stir in miso paste for 30 seconds. Pour in sweet potatoes and the remaining chicken stock. Seal the lid, select Pressure Cook on High, and set the cooking time to 15 minutes.

After cooking, allow a natural release for 10 minutes. Unlock the lid and, using an immersion blender, puree ingredients until smooth. Adjust taste with salt and black pepper. Mix in chives and spoon into bowls. Serve warm.

Traditional Florentine Soup

Total Time: 35 minutes | **Servings:** 4

Ingredients

1 pound Italian sausages, casings removed
1 tbsp olive oil
1 onion, chopped
2 garlic cloves, minced
1 zucchini, chopped
1 cup canned Cannellini beans
1 cup canned tomatoes, diced
½ tsp red chili pepper flakes

4 cups chicken broth
2 russet potatoes, sliced
2 cups kale, chopped
Salt and black pepper to taste
1 cup half and half
3 oz pancetta, cooked, chopped
Shredded Parmesan to serve

Directions

Set your Instant Pot to Sauté and heat olive oil. Cook pancetta for 5 minutes and set aside. Add in onion, garlic, and sausages, and sauté for 5 minutes. Stir in zucchini, beans, tomatoes, and red pepper flakes.

Pour in broth and stir. Add in potatoes and season with salt and pepper. Seal the lid, select Pressure Cook on High, and set to 15 minutes.

When ready, do a quick pressure release. Stir in the kale. Select Sauté and cook until wilted, about 3 minutes. Pour in the half and half and stir. Add in the pancetta and divide between bowls. Serve sprinkled with Parmesan cheese.

Red Lentil & Carrot Soup

Total Time: 15 minutes | **Servings:** 4

Ingredients

1 tbsp olive oil
1 small yellow onion, chopped
2 garlic cloves, minced
Salt and black pepper to taste
½ tsp curry powder
3 cups vegetable stock

3 carrots, cut into 1-inch slices
½ cup red lentils, rinsed
1 cup coconut milk
4 tbsp coconut cream
3 tbsp chopped parsley

Directions

Set your Instant Pot to Sauté, heat olive oil, and sauté onion until softened, 3 minutes. Stir in garlic, salt, pepper, curry powder, and allow releasing of fragrance for 1 minute. Stir in stock, carrots, red lentils, and coconut milk.

Seal the lid, select Pressure Cook mode on High, and set the time to 2 minutes. After cooking, do a quick pressure release. Unlock the lid. Using an immersion blender, puree ingredients until smooth. Adjust taste with salt and pepper. Ladle into individual soup bowls, top with coconut cream and parsley.

Mixed Mushroom Soup with Tofu

Total Time: 25 minutes | **Servings:** 4

Ingredients

1 tsp sesame oil
6 cups chicken stock
2 cups mixed mushrooms, sliced
¼ cup white wine vinegar
¼ cup soy sauce
2 tsp ginger paste

2 tsp garlic paste
1 tsp chili paste
¼ cup cornstarch
2 large eggs, beaten
8 oz firm tofu, cut into cubes
4 scallions, thinly sliced

Directions

In your Instant Pot, combine chicken stock (reserve ¼ cup), mushrooms, vinegar, soy sauce, ginger, garlic, and chili paste. Seal the lid, select Pressure Cook on High, and set to 2 minutes. After cooking, allow a natural release for 10 minutes. Unlock the lid and press Sauté.

In a bowl, combine the reserved chicken stock with cornstarch, and stir into the soup. Pour in eggs in a thin stream while mixing soup to form thin egg ribbons. Mix in tofu, half of the scallions, and sesame oil. Cook further for 2-3 minutes. Spoon the soup into bowls and garnish with remaining scallions.

Ground Beef Farfalle Soup

Total Time: 25 minutes | **Servings:** 6

Ingredients

2 tbsp olive oil
1 yellow onion, chopped
2 garlic cloves, minced
1 green bell pepper, chopped
½ lb ground beef
2 (14.5 oz) cans diced tomatoes
6 cups beef broth

½ tsp dried basil
¼ tsp dried oregano
½ tsp dried thyme
Salt and black pepper, to taste
8 oz farfalle pasta
1 cup ricotta cheese
1 cup shredded mozzarella

Directions

Set your Instant Pot to Sauté and warm the olive oil. Cook the onion, garlic, bell pepper, and ground beef for 5 minutes. Stir in tomatoes, broth, basil, oregano, thyme, salt, and black pepper. Put in the farfalle and stir.

Seal the lid, select Pressure Cook on High, and set the time to 4 minutes. When done, allow a natural release for 10 minutes. Unlock the lid and serve into bowls, topped with the ricotta and mozzarella cheese.

Split Pea Soup with Bacon & Ham

Total Time: 30 minutes | **Servings:** 4

Ingredients

8 bacon slices, chopped
16 oz dried split peas
1 onion, diced
1 celery stalk, chopped
2 carrots, diced
2 cups ham, diced
1 tsp dried rosemary
4 cups chicken stock
Salt and black pepper to taste
2 tbsp fresh parsley, chopped

Directions

Set your Instant Pot to Sauté and cook bacon until roasted and crisp, 5 minutes. Top with split peas, onion, celery, carrots, ham, rosemary, stock, salt, and pepper.

Seal the lid, select Pressure Cook on High, and set the time to 5 minutes. Once done, allow a natural release for 10 minutes. Whip soup continually until creamy. Spoon into bowls and serve warm topped with parsley.

Broccoli Soup with Ginger & Almonds

Total Time: 20 minutes | **Servings:** 4

Ingredients

1 avocado, halved, pitted, and peeled
1 tbsp butter
3 garlic cloves, minced
1 tbsp fresh ginger paste
1 tsp turmeric
1 tsp cumin powder
1 head broccoli, cut into florets
4 cups chicken broth
Salt and black pepper to taste
1 cup coconut milk
¼ cup sliced almonds

Directions

Set the pot to Sauté, melt butter, and sauté garlic, ginger, turmeric, and cumin until fragrant, 1 minute. Pour in broccoli and broth and season with salt and pepper. Seal the lid, select Pressure Cook, and set the time to 2 minutes.

After cooking, allow a natural release for 10 minutes. Unlock the lid, add avocado, and using an immersion blender, puree ingredients until smooth. Stir in coconut milk, adjust the taste and ladle into bowls. Top with almonds to serve.

Rosemary Pomodoro Soup

Total Time: 25 minutes | **Servings:** 4

Ingredients

¼ cup unsalted butter
1 medium onion, thinly sliced
2 garlic cloves, minced
2 cups canned whole tomatoes
4 cups chicken stock
10 sprigs rosemary, tied together
½ cup heavy cream
1 cup croutons for topping

Directions

Set your Instant Pot to Sauté, melt butter and sauté onion until softened, 3 minutes. Stir in garlic until fragrant, 30 seconds. Add tomatoes, stock, and rosemary. Seal the lid, select Pressure Cook on High, and set the time to 3 minutes.

After cooking, allow a natural release for 10 minutes. Unlock the lid. Discard the rosemary bundle. Using an immersion blender, puree until smooth. Mix in heavy cream, ladle the soup into four bowls, top with croutons, and serve.

Spiced Turnip Soup

Total Time: 40 minutes | **Servings:** 4

Ingredients

1 tbsp avocado oil
2 tbsp butter
1 large white onion, chopped
2 garlic cloves, minced
1 tbsp turmeric
1 tsp cumin powder
1 tsp coriander powder
3 large turnips, peeled, diced
3 cups vegetable stock
1 cup whole milk
2 tbsp toasted pine nuts
2 tsp chopped cilantro

Directions

Set your Instant Pot to Sauté, heat oil and butter, and sauté onion until softened, 3 minutes. Stir in garlic, turmeric, cumin, coriander, and cook for 1 minute. Add turnips and stock. Seal the lid, select Pressure Cook on High, and set to 15 minutes. After cooking, do a natural release.

Using an immersion blender, puree ingredients until smooth. Adjust the taste and mix in milk. Ladle into soup bowls and garnish with pine nuts and cilantro. Serve hot.

Provençal Tomato Soup

Total Time: 25 minutes | **Servings:** 5

Ingredients

2 tbsp olive oil
1 onion, chopped
2 garlic cloves, minced
2 (14-oz) cans pureed tomatoes
5 cups chicken broth
1 tsp herbs de Provence
1 tsp Worcestershire sauce
½ cup heavy cream

Directions

Set your Instant Pot to Sauté, heat the olive oil, and sauté the onion and garlic for 5 minutes, until browned and caramelized. Pour in tomatoes, broth, herbs de Provence, and Worcestershire sauce. Seal the lid, select Pressure Cook on High, and set to 6 minutes. When done, allow a natural release for 10 minutes. Pour in heavy cream and stir. Serve.

Caribbean Fish Soup

Total Time: 25 minutes | **Servings:** 4

Ingredients

4 tbsp butter
3 stalks celery, chopped
2 medium onions, chopped
Salt and black pepper to taste
4 cups chicken broth
4 Yukon gold potatoes, diced
4 bay leaves
1 Scotch bonnet pepper, minced
4 cod fillets, cubed
3 green onions, thinly sliced
1 tbsp chopped parsley

Directions

Set your Instant Pot to Sauté, melt butter and sauté celery and onions until softened, 5 minutes. Season with salt and black pepper. Pour in chicken broth. Stir in potatoes, bay leaves, Scotch bonnet pepper, and allow boiling.

Add fish, seal the lid, select Pressure Cook on High, and set the time to 10 minutes. After cooking, do a quick pressure. Carefully stir in the green onions to not break fish fillets and adjust the taste. Garnish with parsley and serve warm.

Spicy Red Pepper Soup

Total Time: 30 minutes | **Servings:** 4

Ingredients

2 tbsp butter
1 lb red bell peppers, diced
½ red onion, diced
5 garlic cloves
1 tsp dried basil
¼ tsp smoked paprika

4 cups chicken stock
2 tsp Sriracha sauce
Salt and black pepper to taste
¼ cup heavy cream
1 cup grated Parmesan cheese

Directions

Set your Instant Pot to Sauté, melt butter and sauté bell peppers and onion until softened, 5 minutes. Stir in garlic, basil, and paprika. Cook until fragrant, 30 seconds. Add chicken stock, Sriracha sauce, salt, and black pepper.

Seal the lid, select Pressure Cook on High, and set the time to 3 minutes. Allow a natural release for 10 minutes. Using an immersion blender, puree the soup until smooth. Stir in heavy cream. Serve warm topped with Parmesan cheese.

Chorizo Soup with Brown Rice

Total Time: 40 minutes | **Servings:** 4

Ingredients

2 tbsp olive oil
1 cup diced chorizo
1 medium onion, chopped
1 medium leek, chopped
1 red bell pepper, chopped

4 cups chicken stock
½ cup brown rice
Salt and black pepper to taste
1 tsp red chili flakes to garnish

Directions

Set your Instant Pot to Sauté, heat olive oil, add chorizo, and cook until brown, 5 minutes. Add and sauté onion, leek, and bell pepper, in the pot until softened, 5 minutes. Stir in stock and brown rice and season with salt and pepper.

Seal the lid, select Soup on High, and set the time to 10 minutes. After cooking, do a natural pressure release for 10 minutes. Garnish with red chili flakes and serve warm.

Button Mushroom & Brown Onion Soup

Total Time: 20 minutes | **Servings:** 4

Ingredients

3 tbsp butter
2 brown onions, chopped
2 cups sliced button mushrooms
2 tbsp all-purpose flour
4 cups chicken broth

¼ cup basmati rice, rinsed
1 bay leaf
Salt and black pepper to taste
2 tbsp chopped parsley

Directions

Set your Instant Pot to Sauté. Melt butter and sauté onions and mushrooms until softened, 5 minutes. Stir in flour until roux forms. Gradually mix in the broth a few tbsp at a time until smooth. Stir in rice, bay leaf, salt, and pepper. Seal the lid, select Soup and cook for 6 minutes on High. After cooking, allow a natural release. Adjust taste with salt and pepper. Spoon into bowls, garnish with parsley, and serve.

Squash Soup with Yogurt

Total Time: 25 minutes | **Servings:** 4

Ingredients

1 large butternut squash, deseeded and diced
1 tbsp olive oil
2 garlic cloves, minced
1 white onion, chopped
4 cups vegetable stock
2 cups Greek yogurt
1 avocado, pitted and peeled

1 lemon, juiced
¼ cup chopped dill
¼ cup chopped parsley
Salt and white pepper to taste
1 small red onion

Directions

Set your Instant Pot to Sauté, heat olive oil, and sauté the garlic and onion until softened, 5 minutes. Stir in squash and vegetable stock. Seal the lid, select Pressure Cook on High, and set the cooking time to 10 minutes. After cooking, do a quick release. Stir in Greek yogurt, avocado, lemon juice, dill, parsley, salt, and white pepper. Puree ingredients using an immersion blender until smooth. Spoon into serving bowls, garnish with parsley and red onion, and serve.

Coconut Chicken Soup

Total Time: 30 minutes | **Servings:** 4

Ingredients

2 cups coconut milk
3 cups chicken broth
2 tsp fresh ginger puree
1 stalk lemongrass, chopped
1 cup sliced cremini mushrooms
2 chicken breasts, cubed

1 lime, juiced
1 tsp coconut sugar
1 tsp Thai chili paste
1 tbsp fish sauce
¼ cup chopped cilantro
¼ cup fresh basil leaves

Directions

Set your Instant Pot to Sauté and mix in coconut milk, broth, ginger, and lemongrass; let boil, 5 minutes. Add mushrooms, chicken, lime juice, sugar, chili, and fish sauce. Seal the lid, select Pressure Cook on High, and set to 7 minutes. After cooking, perform a natural pressure release for 10 minutes, then a quick pressure release to let out the remaining steam. Unlock the lid and stir in cilantro and basil. Ladle the soup into individual bowls and serve warm.

Vietnamese Green Soup

Total Time: 15 minutes | **Servings:** 4

Ingredients

1 opo squash, halved, deseeded, and thinly julienned
1 tbsp coconut oil
1 onion, thinly sliced
1 tsp fish sauce

6 cups vegetable stock
Salt and white pepper to taste
½ cup frozen peas

Directions

Set your Instant Pot to Sauté, heat coconut oil, and sauté squash and onion until slightly softened, 3 minutes. Stir in stock, fish sauce, salt, white pepper, and frozen peas. Seal the lid, select Pressure Cook on High, and set the time to 1 minute. When cooking, do a quick pressure release. Ladle into soup bowls and serve.

Zucchini Leek Soup with Goat Cheese

Total Time: 25 minutes | **Servings:** 4

Ingredients

1 tbsp olive oil	½ tsp dried rosemary
1 white onion, chopped	1 tsp dried thyme
1 leek stalk, chopped	4 cups vegetable stock
3 large zucchinis, chopped	1 cup coconut cream
2 garlic cloves, minced	Salt and black pepper to taste
1 tsp dried basil	1 cup crumbled goat cheese

Directions

Set your Instant Pot to Sauté, heat olive oil, and sauté onion, leek, and zucchinis until softened, 5 minutes. Stir in garlic, basil, rosemary, and thyme. Cook until fragrant, 30 seconds. Add stock and coconut cream.

Seal the lid, select Pressure Cook on High, and set the time to 1 minute. After cooking, allow a natural release for 10 minutes. Unlock the lid and, using an immersion blender, puree ingredients until smooth. Season with salt and pepper. Spoon the soup into bowls and top with goat cheese.

Chili & Basil Tomato Soup

Total Time: 15 minutes | **Servings:** 4

Ingredients

3 lb tomatoes, peeled, chopped	Salt to taste
1 onion, chopped	1 cup milk
½ tsp chili flakes	½ cup crème fraîche
3 cups chicken broth	2 tbsp basil, chopped

Directions

To your Instant Pot, add tomatoes, broth, onion, and salt. Seal the lid, select Pressure Cook on High, and set the time to 5 minutes. Perform a quick pressure release. Add in milk and crème fraîche and stir. Transfer to a food processor and puree until smooth. Return to the pot, press Sauté and stir until heated through. Sprinkle with flakes and basil to serve.

Chicken Bean Soup

Total Time: 35 minutes | **Servings:** 4

Ingredients

15 oz canned black beans	1 jalapeño, seeded and diced
½ lb chicken breasts	1 (10-oz) can enchilada sauce
14 oz canned diced tomatoes	3 cups chicken broth
1 cup frozen corn kernels	1 cup milk
2 green onions chopped	1 cup mozzarella, shredded
1 green bell pepper, chopped	

Directions

In your Instant Pot, mix the chicken, beans, tomatoes, corn, green onions, bell pepper, jalapeño, enchilada sauce, and broth. Stir to combine. Seal the lid, select Pressure Cook on High, and set the time to 15 minutes. When done, allow a natural release for 10 minutes. Unlock the lid and remove the chicken to a cutting board. Using two forks, shred chicken into small strands and place back into the pot; stir in the milk. Serve topped with mozzarella.

Thai Shrimp Soup

Total Time: 20 minutes | **Servings:** 4

Ingredients

1 tbsp coconut oil	4 cups chicken broth
1 white onion, finely sliced	1 cup coconut milk
1 carrot, peeled and julienned	1 tbsp fish sauce
1 red bell pepper, sliced	1 lb shrimp, peeled and deveined
1 tsp grated ginger	3 green onions, diagonally sliced
2 garlic cloves, minced	2 tbsp chopped cilantro
1 long red chili, minced	2 limes, juiced
1 tbsp Thai green curry paste	

Directions

Set your Instant Pot to Sauté, heat coconut oil, and sauté onion, carrot, and bell pepper until softened, 5 minutes. Stir in ginger, garlic, red chili, and curry paste. Cook for 1 minute. Mix in broth, coconut milk, fish sauce, and shrimp.

Seal lid, select Pressure Cook on High, and set the time to 3 minutes. After cooking, perform a quick pressure release. Unlock the lid, stir in green onions and cilantro. Spoon the soup into serving bowls and drizzle lime juice on top.

Rich Bacon & Bean Soup

Total Time: 55 minutes | **Servings:** 4

Ingredients

3 tbsp butter	1 lb dried beans, soaked
1 onion, finely chopped	4 cups chicken broth
1 cup chopped fennel bulb	2 slices smoked bacon, chopped
2 carrots, finely chopped	2 tsp ground cumin
2 garlic cloves, minced	

Directions

Set your Instant Pot to Sauté, melt butter, and cook bacon for 5 minutes, until crispy; set aside. Add in onion, fennel, carrots, and garlic, and sauté for 5 minutes. Pour in broth, beans, and cumin. Stir to combine. Seal the lid, select Pressure Cook on High, and set to 25 minutes. Allow a natural release for 10 minutes. Top with bacon and serve.

Cheddar Asparagus Soup

Total Time: 30 minutes | **Servings:** 4

Ingredients

2 tbsp butter	1 ½ lb asparagus, chopped
1 onion, chopped	1 cup half-and-half
1 carrot, sliced	2 cups shredded cheddar
4 cups chicken broth	Salt and black pepper to taste
1 cup milk	

Directions

Set your Instant Pot to Sauté and melt butter. Cook onion, asparagus, and carrot for 3 minutes until tender. Pour in the broth. Seal the lid, select Pressure Cook mode on High, and set the time to 8 minutes. When done, allow a natural release for 10 minutes. Stir in milk, half-and-half, and cheddar until the cheese melts. Season to taste and serve.

Carrot & Lemongrass Soup

Total Time: 25 minutes | **Servings:** 4

Ingredients

2-inch long lemongrass, chopped
2 tbsp butter
1 red onion, diced
3 carrots, chopped
2 tsp ginger puree

4 cups chicken broth
1 cup coconut cream
Salt to taste
4 basil leaves, chopped

Directions

Set your Instant Pot to Sauté, melt butter, and sauté onion, carrots, and lemongrass until softened, 5 minutes. Stir in ginger until fragrant, 1 minute, and pour in the broth. Seal the lid, select Pressure Cook, and set the time to 1 minute. After cooking, allow a natural release for 10 minutes. Unlock the lid, add coconut cream, and using an immersion blender, puree ingredients until smooth; season with salt. Spoon the soup into serving bowls and garnish with basil.

German Soup with Bratwurst & Veggies

Total Time: 30 minutes | **Servings:** 6

Ingredients

4 tbsp butter
2 Yukon gold potatoes, cubed
4 shallots, chopped
1 celery stalk, chopped
2 carrots, chopped
¼ cup flour
6 cups chicken broth

1 tbsp Dijon mustard
½ head cabbage, shredded
1 lb cooked bratwurst, sliced
1 cup buttermilk
Black pepper to taste
3 cups shredded cheddar

Directions

Set your Instant Pot to Sauté and melt butter. Cook potatoes, shallots, celery, and carrots for 5 minutes, until tender. Stir in the flour and broth. Add in the mustard and stir until there are no lumps. Put the cabbage and bratwurst. Seal the lid, select Pressure Cook on High, and set the time to 5 minutes. When done, allow a natural release for 10 minutes. Unlock the lid and pour in the buttermilk and black pepper. Stir in the cheese until melted. Serve warm.

Rice & Chicken Soup

Total Time: 40 minutes | **Servings:** 4

Ingredients

2 tbsp olive oil
1 leek, chopped
2 chicken breasts, cubed
1 carrot, chopped
1 stalk celery, chopped

½ cup rice
5 cups chicken broth
1 cup frozen peas
Salt and black pepper to taste

Directions

Set the pot to Sauté and warm oil. Add in leek, carrot, and celery. Stir-fry for 5 minutes. Stir in chicken and brown for 6 minutes on all sides. Pour in broth, rice, salt, and pepper. Seal the lid, select Pressure Cook on High, and cook for 15 minutes. When ready, do a quick pressure release. Stir in peas for 3 minutes. Serve warm.

Tapioca Cold Fruit Soup

Total Time: 20 minutes + chilling time | **Servings:** 4

Ingredients

½ cup granulated sugar
4 tbsp tapioca
1 cup peach juice
2 apricots, cored and chopped

1 ½ cups raspberry juice
2 cups raspberries
1 cup strawberries, halved
1 cup blueberries

Directions

In your Instant Pot, combine sugar, 1 cup of water, tapioca, peach juice, and apricots. Seal the lid, select Pressure Cook on High, and set to 3 minutes.

Allow a natural release for 10 minutes. Stir in raspberry juice, raspberries, strawberries, and blueberries. Spoon soup into bowls; let cool. Then chill in the refrigerator for 45-60 minutes. Serve chilled.

Cream of Butternut Squash

Total Time: 25 minutes | **Servings:** 4

Ingredients

2 tbsp olive oil
2 lb butternut squash, cubed
2 sprigs parsley, chopped
1 onion, chopped
¼ tsp cumin

½-inch piece ginger, sliced
4 cups vegetable stock
½ cup sour cream
½ cup pumpkin seeds toasted

Directions

Set your Instant Pot to Sauté and warm olive oil. Add in onion and parsley and sauté until the onion is soft.

Place in squash and brown for 5 minutes, stirring often. Put in ginger, cumin, and stock, and stir. Seal the lid. Select Pressure Cook, cook for 10 minutes on High.

When done, do a quick pressure release. Pour mixture into a blender and puree until smooth. Stir in sour cream. Serve garnished with pumpkin seeds and a drizzle of olive oil.

Pumpkin-Ginger Soup

Total Time: 15 minutes | **Servings:** 4

Ingredients

2 tbsp chopped sage leaves
3 tbsp olive oil
1 medium pumpkin, chopped
1 red onion, finely chopped
1 tbsp ginger paste
3 cups vegetable stock

1 cup almond milk
½ tbsp chili powder
Salt and black pepper to taste
1 lime, juiced

Directions

Set your Instant Pot to Sauté, heat olive oil, and sauté pumpkin, onion, and ginger paste for 5 minutes. Mix in sage, stock, almond milk, chili powder, salt, and pepper.

Seal the lid, select Pressure Cook on High, and set the cooking time to 3 minutes. After cooking, do a quick pressure release. Stir in lime juice and ladle the soup into individual bowls. Serve and enjoy!

Everyday Scallion Lentil Soup

Total Time: 35 minutes | **Servings:** 4

Ingredients

2 tbsp olive oil
1 onion, chopped
1 cup dried lentils, rinsed
1 (28-oz) can diced tomatoes
2 cloves garlic, chopped

2 carrots, chopped
1 tbsp scallions, chopped
1 tsp paprika
Salt and black pepper to taste

Directions

Set your Instant Pot to Sauté and heat the olive oil. Cook the onion, garlic, and carrots for 5 minutes until tender. Stir in the paprika. Pour in 4 cups of water, lentils, tomatoes, salt, and pepper. Seal the lid, select Pressure Cook on High, and set to 10 minutes. When done, allow a natural release for 10 minutes. Stir in the scallions and serve.

Ginger Lamb Curry

Total Time: 1 hour 20 minutes | **Servings:** 4

Ingredients

¼ cup olive oil
2 lb lamb shoulder, cubed
4 green onions, sliced
2 tomatoes, peeled, chopped
2 tbsp garlic paste
1 tbsp ginger paste
1 ½ cups vegetable stock
1 potato, cubed
1 large carrot, sliced

2 tsp allspice
2 tsp ground coriander
1 tsp ground cumin
½ tsp curry powder
Salt to taste
½ tsp ground red chili pepper
2 bay leaves
2 tbsp mint leaves, chopped

Directions

Set your IP to Sauté and heat 2 tbsp of oil. Add in green onions and cook for 3 minutes until tender, stirring occasionally. Transfer to a food processor, place in tomatoes, garlic paste, and ginger paste, and blend until smooth.

Heat the remaining oil in the pot and add in the lamb. Cook for 6 minutes. Pour in the onion paste, vegetable stock, potato, carrot, allspice, coriander, cumin, curry powder, salt, red chili pepper, and bay leaves and stir. Seal the lid, select Pressure Cook on High, and set the time to 50 minutes. When done, allow a natural pressure release for 10 minutes. Unlock the lid and discard bay leaves. Garnish with mint leaves and serve right away.

Garlic Quinoa & Vegetable Stew

Total time: 25 minutes | **Servings:** 4

Ingredients

3 tbsp sesame oil
1 onion, chopped
2 cups vegetable broth
2 garlic cloves, minced

1 cup quinoa
¼ cup peanut butter
1 cup frozen vegetables, thawed
Salt and black pepper to taste

Directions

Set your Instant Pot to Sauté, warm sesame oil, and cook onion and garlic for 3 minutes, until tender. Stir in the broth, quinoa, salt, and pepper. Seal the lid.

Select Pressure Cook on High, and set the cooking time to 8 minutes. When ready, do a quick pressure and set the pot to Sauté. Put in peanut butter and vegetables and cook for 3 minutes. Serve and enjoy!

Swiss Cheese Stew with Pasta

Total Time: 30 minutes | **Servings:** 4

Ingredients

1 cup mushrooms, stems removed
2 tbsp olive oil
8 oz garganelli pasta
1 (12–oz) can evaporated milk
1 large egg

1 ½ tsp arrowroot starch
8 oz Swiss cheese, shredded
3 tbsp sour cream
3 tbsp grated cheddar cheese

Directions

Set your Instant Pot to Sauté, heat oil, and sauté mushrooms for 5 minutes; remove to a plate. Pour the pasta into the pot and add half of the evaporated milk and 3 cups of water.

Seal the lid, select Pressure Cook, and set the cooking time to 4 minutes. When ready, allow a natural pressure release for 10 minutes. Carefully unlock the lid.

In a bowl, whisk the remaining milk with egg. In another bowl, combine arrowroot with Swiss cheese. Pour the milk-egg and starch mixtures into the pot. Mix in mushrooms and sour cream. Sprinkle with cheddar cheese. Ladle the soup into individual bowls and serve.

Tunisian Lamb Stew

Total Time: 55 minutes | **Servings:** 4

Ingredients

2 russet potatoes, peeled and cut into wedges
2 tbsp olive oil
1 lb lamb shoulder, cubed
1 red onion, thinly sliced
8 cloves garlic, thickly sliced
2 tsp ras-el-hanout
1 tsp turmeric
1 tsp red chili flakes

1 tbsp rosemary leaves
¼ cup thyme leaves
¼ cup chopped parsley
2 tomatoes, roughly chopped
2 red bell peppers, cut into strips
2 cups vegetable stock
Salt to taste

Directions

Set your Instant Pot to Sauté, heat olive oil and brown lamb for 6-7 minutes. Add onion and garlic; cook until onion softens, 3 minutes. Stir in ras el hanout, turmeric, red chili flakes, rosemary, and thyme. Cook until fragrant, 3 minutes.

Mix in tomatoes, bell peppers, potatoes, stock, and salt. Seal the lid, select Pressure Cook on High, and set the time to 20 minutes. After cooking, allow a natural release for 10 minutes. Spoon into bowls, garnish with parsley, and serve.

Balsamic Fennel with White Beans

Total Time: 40 minutes | **Servings:** 4

Ingredients

2 tbsp olive oil
1 fennel bulb, thinly sliced
1 small red onion, chopped

1 cup dry white beans, soaked
3 cups vegetable broth
2 tbsp balsamic vinegar

Directions

Set your Instant Pot to Sauté, heat olive oil, and sauté onion and fennel until softened, 3 minutes. Add white beans, broth, and balsamic vinegar. Seal the lid, select Bean/Chili, and set the cooking time to 30 minutes. After cooking, do a quick pressure release to let out steam and unlock the lid. Stir food, dish into serving plates, and serve warm.

Pumpkin & Spinach Stew

Total Time: 25 minutes | **Servings:** 6

Ingredients

1 tbsp butter	2 (15-oz) cans chickpeas
1 white onion, chopped	1 ½ tsp cumin powder
4 garlic cloves, minced	½ tsp smoked paprika
2 lb pumpkin, cubed	1 tsp coriander powder
3 cups vegetable broth	Salt and black pepper to taste
1 (15-oz) can sundried tomatoes	4 cups baby spinach

Directions

Set your Instant Pot to Sauté. Combine butter, onion, and garlic in the pot, and cook for 5 minutes. Add in pumpkin, broth, tomatoes, chickpeas, cumin, paprika, coriander, salt, and pepper. Seal the lid, select Pressure Cook on High, and cook for 8 minutes. When done, perform a quick pressure release. Stir in spinach to wilt, 5 minutes on Sauté. Serve.

Harissa Beef Stew with Couscous

Total Time: 40 minutes | **Servings:** 4

Ingredients

1 lb beef stew meat, cubed	2 cups chicken broth
1 tbsp ras el hanout	2 tbsp tomato paste
Salt and black pepper to taste	1 cup couscous
3 carrots, peeled and julienned	2 tsp harissa paste
1 celery root, cut into chunks	¼ cup chopped cilantro
¾ cup pitted prunes, chopped	

Directions

Season beef with ras el hanout, salt, and pepper and add it to your Instant Pot. Pour in carrots, celery, prunes, broth, and tomato paste and stir. Seal the lid, select Pressure Cook on High, and set the time to 30 minutes.

Meanwhile, pour the couscous into a bowl, season with salt, and pour in 1 cup of boiling water. Cover the bowl with a napkin and allow water to absorb. Once Instant Pot beeps, perform a quick pressure release. Stir in the harissa paste and adjust the taste with salt and black pepper. Garnish with cilantro, and serve the beef stew with couscous.

Squid Potato Stew

Total Time: 20 minutes | **Servings:** 4

Ingredients

2 tbsp olive oil	1 ¼ cups squid rings, defrosted
1 white onion, chopped	1 cup chicken broth
4 potatoes, peeled and diced	Salt and black pepper to taste
2 garlic cloves, minced	¼ cup parsley leaves, chopped
¼ tsp curry powder	

Directions

Set your Instant Pot to Sauté and heat olive oil. Cook onion, garlic, curry powder, and potatoes for 3 minutes. Pour in squid rings, chicken broth, salt, and pepper.

Seal the lid, select Pressure Cook on High, and set the time to 10 minutes. After cooking, do a quick pressure release. Spoon stew into bowls and garnish with parsley. Serve.

Sausage & Red Kidney Stew

Total Time: 35 minutes | **Servings:** 4

Ingredients

6 bacon slices, chopped	3 cups chicken broth
½ lb kielbasa sausages, sliced	1 tsp honey
1 cup chopped tomatoes	1 cup ketchup
2 red bell peppers, diced	1 tbsp Worcestershire sauce
1 red onion, chopped	1 tsp mustard powder
1 cup red kidney beans, soaked	

Directions

Set your Instant Pot to Sauté and fry bacon until brown and crispy, 5 minutes; remove to a plate. Add sausages to inner pot and brown on both sides, 5 minutes. Set aside next to the bacon.

Wipe inner pot clean and combine bell peppers, onion, kidney beans, chicken broth, honey, ketchup, Worcestershire sauce, and mustard powder.

Seal the lid, select Pressure Cook on High, and set the time to 10 minutes. After cooking, do a quick pressure release. Stir in bacon and sausage, and simmer on Sauté mode for 5 minutes. Serve stew with bread or cooked white rice.

Beef Stew with Potatoes & Mushrooms

Total Time: 65 minutes | **Servings:** 4

Ingredients

2 tbsp olive oil	1 garlic clove, minced
1 lb beef stew meat, cubed	¼ cup red wine
1 tbsp flour	1 bay leaf
Salt and black pepper to taste	4 potatoes, cubed
½ tbsp paprika	1 cup canned tomatoes
1 onion, chopped	1 cup mushrooms, sliced
1 carrot, chopped	2 cups beef stock
1 celery stalk, chopped	

Directions

Set your Instant Pot to Sauté and heat olive oil. Toss the beef with flour, salt, and pepper until coated. Place into the pot and brown for 5-7 minutes until golden; set aside.

Add the onion, carrot, celery, garlic, mushrooms, salt, and pepper to the pot and cook for 5 minutes until tender. Pour in the remaining ingredients and stir to combine.

Seal the lid, select Meat/Stew, and set the cooking time to 35 minutes on High. When done, allow a natural release for 10 minutes. Unlock the lid and adjust the seasoning. Remove and discard bay leaf. Ladle the stew into individual bowls. Serve and enjoy!

Trout & Radish Stew

Total Time: 15 minutes | **Servings:** 4

Ingredients

4 tbsp olive oil, divided
1 red onion, thinly sliced
4 garlic cloves, minced
½ cup dry white wine
8 oz bottle clam juice
2 ½ cups chicken broth

½ lb radishes, diced
1 (15 oz) can diced tomatoes
Salt and black pepper to taste
¼ tsp red chili flakes
4 trout fillets, cut into cubes
1 lemon, juiced

Directions

Set your Instant Pot to Sauté. Heat olive oil and sauté the onion and garlic for 3 minutes until tender. Pour in the white wine and cook until reduced by one-third. Add the clam juice, chicken broth, radishes, tomatoes, salt, pepper, and red chili flakes. Stir well and add in the fish.

Seal the lid, select Pressure Cook on High, and set the time to 3 minutes. After cooking, do a quick pressure release, and unlock the lid. Stir and adjust the taste with salt and pepper. Mix in lemon juice. Serve warm and enjoy!

Spanish Chorizo Stew

Total Time: 20 minutes | **Servings:** 4

Ingredients

3 tbsp olive oil
1 onion, chopped
2 garlic cloves, minced
1 banana pepper, chopped
1 cup Spanish rice
¼ cup red salsa

1 cup canned tomatoes
2 cups vegetable stock
1 (16-oz) can pinto beans
Salt to taste
1 tbsp chopped fresh parsley
2 Spanish chorizo sausages, sliced

Directions

Heat the olive oil your Instant Pot on Sauté. Add chorizo, onion, garlic, and banana pepper and cook for 3 minutes, stirring occasionally. Mix in rice, salsa, tomatoes, vegetable stock, pinto beans, and salt. Seal the lid, select Pressure Cook, and set the cooking time to 8 minutes. When cooking is complete, do a quick release. Unlock the lid. Sprinkle with parsley. Serve and enjoy!

Mushroom Herb Stew

Total Time: 30 minutes | **Servings:** 4

Ingredients

2 tbsp sesame oil
1 ¼ lb mushrooms, chopped
2 yellow onions, chopped
4 garlic cloves, minced
2 cup chicken broth

1 tsp dried mixed herbs
¼ tsp red chili flakes
1 tsp dried thyme
Salt and black pepper to taste

Directions

Set your Instant Pot to Sauté, warm sesame oil, and cook the mushrooms, onions, garlic, mixed herbs, chili flakes, thyme, salt, and pepper. Pour in broth. Seal the lid, select Pressure Cook on High, and set to 10 minutes. After cooking, allow a natural release for 10 minutes. Unlock the lid. Serve.

Classic Beef Stew

Total Time: 50 minutes | **Servings:** 4

Ingredients

2 tbsp olive oil
1 lb beef stew meat, cubed
Salt and black pepper to taste
2 shallots, chopped
2 garlic cloves, minced
1 carrot, peeled and chopped

2 red bell peppers, chopped
2 tomatoes, chopped
2 bay leaves
1 tsp dried mixed herbs
1 ½ cups beef broth
1 tsp cornstarch

Directions

Heat olive oil in your Instant Pot on Sauté. Season beef with salt and pepper and brown on all sides, 5 minutes; set aside. Add shallots, garlic, carrot, bell peppers to the pot and cook for 5 minutes. Stir in tomatoes, herbs, bay leaves, and broth and return the beef. Seal the lid, select Pressure Cook on High, and set the time to 20 minutes. Allow a natural release for 10 minutes. Remove and discard the bay leaves. Stir in cornstarch and press Sauté. Cook for 1 to 2 minutes until the sauce thickens. Adjust the taste and serve.

Beef Stew with Red Wine

Total Time: 50 minutes | **Servings:** 4

Ingredients

2 lb stewing beef, fat trimmed, cubed
1 lb red potatoes, cut into pieces
3 tbsp olive oil
½ cup white flour
Salt and pepper to taste
2 bay leaves
2 garlic cloves, minced
1 tbsp tomato paste

3 carrots, peeled and chopped
½ cup red wine
½ fennel bulb, sliced
1 onion, chopped
2 ½ cups beef stock
¼ cup chopped parsley

Directions

Season the beef with salt and pepper, then roll in the flour. Set your Instant Pot to Sauté, heat olive oil, and cook beef for 8 minutes in total; transfer to a bowl. Stir in wine and cook until reduced by half, scraping off bits at the bottom.

Return meat and add onion, garlic, bay leaves, carrots, fennel, potatoes, tomato paste, and stock. Seal the lid, select Pressure Cook, and cook for 20 minutes. When done, allow a natural release for 10 minutes. Stir in parsley. Serve.

Zucchini Stew with Gruyère Cheese

Total Time: 15 minutes | **Servings:** 4

Ingredients

3 tbsp melted butter
4 zucchinis, sliced
Salt to taste

½ cup grated Gruyere cheese
2 cups tomato sauce
1 cup shredded mozzarella

Directions

Put the zucchini, tomato sauce, and 1 cup of water in your Instant Pot. Sprinkle with mozzarella cheese. Seal the lid, select Pressure Cook for 5 minutes. Perform a quick pressure release. Top with Gruyere cheese and butter.

PASTA & SIDE DISHES

Pappardelle with Tomatoes & Mozzarella

Total Time: 20 minutes | **Servings**: 4

Ingredients

2 tbsp olive oil
2 cups dried pappardelle
Salt and black pepper to taste
2 garlic cloves, minced
1 cup cherry tomatoes, halved
A handful of baby arugula
1 cup grated mozzarella cheese
¼ cup grated Parmesan cheese

Directions

Add pappardelle, 6 cups of water, and salt to your Instant Pot. Seal the lid, select Pressure Cook on High, and set to 3 minutes. After cooking, do a quick pressure release. Drain pasta through a colander; set aside. Wipe the pot clean with a napkin and set your Instant Pot to Sauté.

Heat olive oil and stir-fry garlic until fragrant, 30 seconds. Add tomatoes and cook until softened, 2-3 minutes. Stir in pasta, arugula, and mozzarella cheese. Season with salt and pepper. Allow arugula to wilt for 1 to 2 minutes. Garnish with Parmesan cheese and serve.

Hazelnut Pesto Tagliatelle

Total Time: 15 minutes | **Servings**: 4

Ingredients

4 tsp olive oil
1 ½ cups tagliatelle
Salt and black pepper to taste
1 cup spinach
3 tbsp hazelnuts
1 garlic clove, minced
¼ cup grated Parmesan cheese
2 tbsp basil, chopped

Directions

Place the pasta in your Instant Pot and cover it with salted water. Seal the lid, select Pressure Cook, and set the time to 4 minutes. After cooking, do a quick pressure release. Drain pasta through a colander and pour it into a bowl.

Meanwhile, in a food processor, combine spinach, hazelnuts, garlic, olive oil, basil, salt, and black pepper. Blend until smooth. Pour pesto over pasta and toss until well mixed. Divide between plates and garnish with Parmesan cheese.

Ground Beef Bucatini in Pepper Sauce

Total Time: 35 minutes | **Servings**: 4

Ingredients

4 tbsp olive oil
2 cups bucatini
1 lb ground beef
Salt and black pepper to taste
1 garlic clove, minced
1 bay leaf
¼ cup dry white wine
2 yellow bell peppers, chopped
4 tomatoes, chopped

Directions

Add bucatini, 6 cups of water, and salt to your Instant Pot. Seal the lid, select Pressure Cook on High, and set the time to 3 minutes. After cooking, do a quick pressure release, and unlock the lid. Drain pasta through a colander; set aside.

Wipe inner pot clean with paper towels and set to Sauté. Heat olive oil and brown the ground beef for 5 minutes. Season to taste. Add garlic and bay leaf, cook further for 3 minutes. Pour in wine and half cup of water; cook further for 3 minutes.

Top with bell peppers and tomatoes. Seal the lid, select a Pressure Cook on High, and set the time to 2 minutes. After cooking, perform a natural pressure release for 10 minutes, and then a quick pressure release to let out the remaining steam. Unlock the lid and stir the sauce and adjust the taste. Plate bucatini and top with beef sauce. Serve warm.

Watercress Rigatoni with Smoked Salmon

Total Time: 15 minutes | **Servings**: 4

Ingredients

1 tbsp olive oil
1 ½ cups rigatoni
2 garlic cloves, minced
2 oz smoked salmon, flaked
1 cup watercress leaves
Salt and black pepper to taste

Directions

Add pasta, 5 cups of water, and salt to your Instant Pot. Seal the lid, select Pressure Cook on High, and set to 3 minutes. Do a quick pressure release. Drain rigatoni through a colander; set aside. Wipe inner pot clean and set to Sauté. Heat olive oil in the inner pot and stir-fry garlic until fragrant, 30 seconds. Stir in salmon and watercress; cook for 2 minutes. Toss in rigatoni, season with salt and pepper, and plate. Serve warm.

Bacon & Mushroom Cavatelli

Total Time: 35 minutes | **Servings**: 4

Ingredients

2 tbsp olive oil
2 cups dried cavatelli
4 bacon slices, chopped
1 white onion, finely chopped
½ cup button mushrooms, sliced
2 garlic cloves, minced
2 cups chopped tomatoes
2 tsp tomato paste
6 ½ cups water
Salt and black pepper to taste
2 tbsp chopped parsley
2 tbsp sour cream

Directions

Add cavatelli, 6 cups of water, and salt to your Instant Pot. Seal the lid, select Pressure Cook on High, and set the time to 3 minutes. After cooking, do a quick release, and unlock the lid. Drain pasta through a colander and set aside. Wipe inner pot clean and set to Sauté. Heat 1 tbsp of olive oil and cook bacon until crispy and brown, 5 minutes. Transfer to a paper towel-lined plate and set aside. Add remaining olive oil to the inner pot.

Sauté the onion and mushrooms until softened, 5 minutes. Stir in garlic for 30 seconds. Add tomatoes, tomato paste, ½ cup of water, salt, and pepper. Seal the lid, select a Pressure Cook on High, and set the time to 2 minutes. After cooking, allow a natural release for 10 minutes. Unlock the lid and stir in parsley, bacon, and sour cream until well mixed. Adjust taste with salt and black pepper. Mix in pasta until well coated in sauce, then plate and serve.

Buttered Pea Spaghetti

Total Time: 15 minutes | **Servings:** 4

Ingredients

2 tbsp butter
16 oz green spaghetti
1 cup frozen green peas
1 cup cooking cream

A pinch of nutmeg powder
Salt and black pepper to taste
¼ cup shaved Parmesan cheese
2 tbsp mint, chopped

Directions

Add green spaghetti, 6 cups of water, and salt to your Instant Pot. Seal the lid, select Pressure Cook on High, and set the cooking time to 3 minutes. After cooking, do a quick pressure release, and unlock the lid. Drain pasta through a colander and pour in a large bowl. Wipe inner pot clean with a paper towel and set the pot to Sauté.

Melt the butter in the inner pot and sauté frozen peas until softened and warmed through. Mix in cooking cream, nutmeg, salt, and pepper. Cook for 1 minute and toss pasta in the sauce. Top with Parmesan cheese and mint and serve.

Saffron Tagliatelle with Creamy Sauce

Total Time: 15 minutes | **Servings:** 4

Ingredients

1 tbsp olive oil
2 tbsp butter
16 oz tagliatelle
1 brown onion, chopped
2 garlic cloves, minced
2 tsp cornflour

2 cups heavy cream
½ tsp saffron powder
1 egg yolk
½ lemon, juiced
Salt and black pepper to taste

Directions

Add the tagliatelle, 6 cups of water, and salt to your Instant Pot. Seal the lid, select Pressure Cook on High, and set the time to 3 minutes. After cooking, do a quick pressure release. Drain pasta through a colander. Set aside.

Wipe inner pot clean and set to Sauté. Heat olive oil and butter in the inner pot and sauté onion until softened, 3 minutes. Stir in garlic until fragrant, 30 seconds, whisk in the cornflour, and cook for 1 minute. Gradually stir in heavy cream until smoothly combined and whisk in saffron and egg yolk. Make sure to mix fast to prevent the egg from cooking. Stir in lemon juice, salt, pepper, and then pasta until well combined. Serve warm.

Red Wine Spaghetti with Tomatoes

Total Time: 40 minutes | **Servings:** 4

Ingredients

1 tbsp olive oil
16 oz spaghetti
1 medium onion, chopped
2 garlic cloves, minced
1 lb ground pork
1 tbsp tomato puree
1 tsp granulated sugar
1 tbsp dried oregano

1 tsp red chili flakes
1 red bell pepper
2 red chilies, chopped
½ cup red wine
½ cup chicken broth
1 (28 oz) can diced tomatoes
Salt and black pepper to taste

Directions

In your Instant Pot, add spaghetti, 5 cups of water, and salt. Seal the lid, select Pressure Cook on High, and set to 3 minutes. After cooking, perform a quick pressure release; drain pasta and set aside. Clean the pot and press Sauté.

Heat olive oil and sauté onion until softened, 3 minutes. Mix in garlic and cook until fragrant, 30 seconds. Add pork, and brown, 5 minutes. Stir in tomato puree, sugar, oregano, flakes, bell pepper, and chilies. Cook for 3 minutes. Stir in wine, broth, tomatoes, and season with salt and pepper. Seal the lid, select Pressure Cook on High, and set to 10 minutes. Allow a natural release for 10 minutes. Divide pasta into plates and top with pork sauce. Serve.

Egg Noodles with Sausage & Pancetta

Total Time: 20 minutes | **Servings:** 4

Ingredients

1 tbsp olive oil
3 oz pancetta, chopped
1 onion, sliced
¼ cup dry white wine
1 cup chicken stock

Salt and black pepper to taste
5 oz wide egg noodles
4 cups shredded green cabbage
1 ½ lb smoked sausage, sliced

Directions

Set to Sauté your Instant Pot and heat the olive oil. Cook the pancetta for 6 minutes. With a slotted spoon, transfer to a paper towel-lined plate to drain. Sauté onion for 2 minutes, until softened. Pour in the wine and simmer until the wine reduces while scraping the bottom of the pot with a wooden spoon. Pour in stock, salt, pepper, and noodles.

Top with cabbage and sausages. Seal the lid, select Pressure Cook on High, and set the time to 3 minutes. When the cooking time is over, do a quick pressure release and unlock the lid. Serve topped with pancetta.

Italian Tri-Color Rotini with Spinach & Nuts

Total Time: 20 minutes | **Servings:** 4

Ingredients

2 tbsp olive oil
1 lb tri-color rotini pasta
1 onion, chopped
3 cloves garlic, minced
12 white mushrooms, sliced
1 zucchini, sliced
1 tsp dried oregano
1 tsp dried basil

Salt and black pepper to taste
Freshly grated Parmesan cheese
¼ cup pine nuts
6 cups baby spinach
1 cup vegetable stock
½ cup tomato paste
3 tbsp light soy sauce

Directions

Set your Instant Pot to Sauté and heat olive oil. Stir-fry onion and garlic until fragrant, 3 minutes, stirring occasionally. Season with salt and pepper. Put in the mushrooms, zucchini, oregano, and basil and cook for 3 minutes, until tender. Pour in stock, rotini, spinach, tomato paste, 3 cups water, and soy. Seal the lid, select Pressure Cook on High, and cook for 4 minutes. When done, do a quick pressure release. Top with Parmesan cheese and pine nuts and serve.

Gemelli with Asparagus & Snap Peas

Total Time: 15 minutes | **Servings:** 4

Ingredients

3 tbsp butter
16 oz gemelli pasta
1 head broccoli, cut into florets
¼ lb asparagus, spears only
2 zucchinis, chopped
¼ cup snap peas

3 tbsp vegetable stock
¼ cup heavy cream
2 tbsp chopped parsley
A pinch of nutmeg powder
Salt and black pepper to taste
2 tbsp shaved Parmesan cheese

Directions

Add gemelli pasta, 6 cups of water, and salt to your Instant Pot. Fit a steamer basket over pasta and add broccoli, asparagus, zucchinis, and peas. Seal the lid, select Steam on High, and set the time to 3 minutes. After cooking, do a quick pressure release. Remove steamer basket with vegetables. Drain pasta through a colander. Set aside.

Wipe inner pot clean and set to Sauté. Melt butter and sauté steamed vegetables for 2 minutes. Add stock and mix in heavy cream until heated. Mix in parsley, nutmeg, salt, and pepper. Allow flavors to incorporate for 1 minute. Add in the pasta and toss to coat well. Top with Parmesan cheese and serve.

Rich Shrimp Fra Diavolo

Total Time: 15 minutes | **Servings:** 4

Ingredients

2 tbsp olive oil
2 tbsp unsalted butter
3 garlic cloves, minced
2 green onions, chopped
½ tsp red pepper flakes
Salt and black pepper to taste

16 oz linguine
1 lb shrimp, peeled and deveined
1 bunch asparagus, chopped
1 lemon, zested and juiced
¼ cup parsley leaves

Directions

Set your Instant Pot to Sauté, heat olive oil, and sauté garlic and green onions until fragrant and softened, 1 minute. Season with red flakes, salt, pepper, and cook further for 1 minute. Pour in 5 cups water, linguine, and butter, and stir.

Seal the lid, select Pressure Cook on High, and set the time to 4 minutes. After cooking, do a quick pressure release. Arrange shrimp and asparagus on top. Seal the lid, select Pressure Cook on High, and set to 2 minutes. Do a quick pressure release, and unlock the lid. Add lemon zest, and juice, parsley, and stir food. Adjust the taste and serve.

Seafood Spaghetti

Total Time: 15 minutes | **Servings:** 4

Ingredients

1 tbsp butter
1 white onion, chopped
4 garlic cloves, minced
½ tsp red chili flakes
2 cups crushed tomatoes
4 cups chicken broth

Salt and black pepper to taste
½ cup red wine
16 oz dried penne pasta
20 frozen jumbo shrimp
½ cup heavy cream
1 cup grated Parmesan cheese

Directions

Set your Instant Pot to Sauté, melt butter and stir-fry onion and garlic for 3 minutes. Add flakes, tomatoes, broth, salt, pepper, and wine. Pour in penne and shrimp. Seal the lid, select Pressure Cook on High, and set the time to 4 minutes. Do a quick pressure release and press Sauté. Stir in heavy cream. Garnish with Parmesan cheese and serve.

Mustard Short Ribs with Egg Noodles

Total Time: 60 minutes | **Servings:** 4

Ingredients

3 tbsp melted butter
4 lb beef bone-in short ribs
1 cup beef broth
6 oz egg noodles
2 tbsp prepared horseradish

6 tbsp Dijon mustard
1 garlic clove, minced
Salt and black pepper to taste
1 ½ cups breadcrumbs

Directions

Season the short ribs on all sides with salt. Pour 1 cup of broth into your Instant Pot. Put in a trivet and place the short ribs on top. Seal the lid, choose Pressure Cook on High for 25 minutes. After cooking, allow a natural release for 10 minutes, and unlock the lid. Remove the trivet and short ribs. Add the egg noodles and 2 cups of water.

Seal the lid, select Pressure Cook on High, and set the time to 4 minutes. Do a quick pressure release. In a bowl, mix horseradish, mustard, garlic, and pepper. Brush the sauce on all sides of the short ribs and reserve any extra sauce.

Preheat oven to 420°F. In another bowl, mix butter and breadcrumbs. Coat the ribs with crumbs. Place the ribs in a foil-lined roasting pan. Bake for 15 minutes, turning once. Serve the beef and noodles, along with the extra sauce.

Sicilian-Style Cavatappi Pasta

Total Time: 30 minutes | **Servings:** 4

Ingredients

½ cup shaved Parmigiano Reggiano
1 tbsp olive oil
4 shallots, chopped
2 cloves minced garlic
3 cups mushrooms, sliced
½ tsp dried parsley
½ tsp dried basil
¼ tsp dried oregano

¼ tsp red pepper flakes
2 cups milk
¼ cup flour
16 oz cavatappi pasta
2 cups frozen peas, thawed
1 cup canned pinto beans

Directions

Set your Instant Pot to Sauté and warm olive oil. Place in the mushrooms, garlic, parsley, basil, oregano, red flakes, and shallots; cook until tender, 5 minutes. Stir in 3 cups water, milk, and flour. Place in the remaining ingredients, except for Parmigiano shavings and pinto beans.

Seal the lid, select Pressure Cook on High, and set to 8 minutes. When done, allow a natural release for 10 minutes. Stir in pinto beans and cook until everything is heated on Sauté. Scatter with Parmigiano shavings and serve.

Spaghetti Carbonara with Broccoli

Total Time: 25 minutes | **Servings**: 4

Ingredients

1 tbsp butter
1 lb spaghetti
1 head broccoli, cut into florets
1 garlic clove, crushed
Salt and black pepper to taste
4 eggs
8 oz bacon
1 cup Pecorino cheese, grated

Directions

Place spaghetti, 4 cups of water, and salt into your Instant Pot. Seal the lid, select Pressure Cook, and set the time to 5 minutes. When done, do a quick pressure release. Remove pasta with a perforated spoon to a bowl. Place a steamer basket inside and add in broccoli. Seal the lid and cook for 4 minutes on High. When ready, do a quick pressure release.

In a bowl, whisk eggs with cheese and pepper. Wipe the pot clean. Set to Sauté and add in bacon and garlic. Cook for 5 minutes, until crispy; discard garlic and set aside. Add in butter, return pasta to pot and reheat for 30 seconds.

Add in the egg mixture and stir until the eggs thicken into a sauce. Top with broccoli and serve.

Butternut Squash Pasta with Pancetta

Total Time: 15 minutes | **Servings**: 4

Ingredients

4 oz pancetta, cooked and crumbled
2 tbsp olive oil
1 (4-lb) butternut squash
2 tbsp fresh sage, chopped
5 cloves garlic sliced
Salt to taste
¼ tsp nutmeg
1 cup Gruyere cheese, grated

Directions

Set your Instant Pot to Sauté and heat oil. Place in the sage and garlic and cook until the sage is crispy, 2 minutes; set aside. Cut the butternut squash in half, lengthwise, and deseed. Wipe inner pot clean. Pour in 1 cup water and fit in a trivet. Put the butternut squash on the trivet. Seal the lid, select Pressure Cook on High, and set the time to 3 minutes.

When ready, do a quick pressure release. Unlock the lid and remove the squash. Take a fork and make spaghetti by scraping the butternut squash lengthwise; season with salt.

Pour the sage mixture over and sprinkle with nutmeg. Top with Gruyere cheese and pancetta to serve.

Scallion Smoked Sausage Farfalle

Total Time: 20 minutes | **Servings**: 4

Ingredients

1 lb smoked Italian sausages, sliced
1 tbsp olive oil
1 medium onion, chopped
3 garlic cloves, minced
5 cups chicken broth
1 (10 oz) can diced tomatoes
½ cup heavy cream
16 oz farfalle
Salt and black pepper to taste
1 ¼ cups grated pepper jack
4 scallions, chopped to garnish

Directions

Set your Instant Pot to Sauté, heat oil and cook sausages, and onion until lightly brown, 4 minutes. Add garlic and cook until fragrant, 30 seconds. Pour in broth, tomatoes, heavy cream, farfalle, salt, and pepper. Seal the lid, select Pressure Cook on High, and set the time to 4 minutes. After cooking, do a quick pressure release. Set the pot to Sauté and adjust the taste with salt and pepper. Add cheese to pasta and mix until melted. Garnish with scallions to serve.

Cheesy Pizza-Pasta Salad

Total Time: 15 minutes | **Servings**: 4

Ingredients

¼ cup olive oil
8 oz bow tie pasta
6 sprigs oregano
¼ cup chopped basil
3 garlic cloves, minced
1 cup cubed mozzarella cheese
1 ½ cups Parmesan, shaved
1 cup black olives, sliced
7 oz pepperoni, thinly sliced
¼ cup red wine vinegar
Salt and black pepper to taste

Directions

In your Instant Pot, add pasta, 5 cups of water, and salt. Seal the lid, select Pressure Cook on High, and set to 3 minutes. After cooking, do a quick pressure release. Drain pasta and pour it into a salad bowl. Add oregano, basil, garlic, mozzarella, Parmesan, olives, pepperoni, olive oil, vinegar, salt, and pepper. Toss until well mixed. Serve.

Pumpkin Noodles with Walnuts

Total Time: 15 minutes | **Servings**: 4

Ingredients

2 tbsp butter
16 oz pasta noodles
1 medium yellow onion, diced
2 garlic cloves, minced
2 cups pumpkin puree
4 cups vegetable broth
Salt and black pepper to taste
4 oz cream cheese, softened
¼ cup walnuts, chopped
¼ tsp red chili flakes
½ tsp nutmeg powder
3 tbsp chopped parsley

Directions

In your Instant Pot, add noodles, onion, garlic, pumpkin puree, broth, salt, and pepper. Seal the lid, select Pressure Cook on High, and set the time to 5 minutes. After cooking, do a quick pressure release, and unlock the lid. Set the pot to Sauté and stir in butter, cream cheese, and half of the walnuts. Cook until cream cheese melts. Adjust taste with salt, black pepper, red chili flakes, and nutmeg powder. Dish food and garnish with parsley. Serve.

Spicy Linguine with Bacon & Tomatoes

Total Time: 25 minutes | **Servings**: 4

Ingredients

2 tbsp olive oil
16 oz linguine
4 bacon slices, chopped
1 white onion, chopped
Salt and black pepper to taste
A pinch of red chili flakes
1 (14-oz) can tomato sauce
½ cup chicken broth
½ cup grated Parmesan cheese

Directions

To your Instant Pot, add pasta, 6 cups of water, and salt. Seal the lid, set on Pressure Cook on High, and set the time to 3 minutes. After cooking, do a quick pressure release, and unlock the lid. Drain pasta through a colander; set aside.

Clean the inner pot and select Sauté. Add bacon and fry until brown and crispy, 5 minutes. Transfer to a paper towel-lined plate to drain grease and set aside. Heat olive oil in the inner pot with bacon fat and sauté onion until softened, 3 minutes. Season with salt, pepper, and flakes. Stir in tomato sauce and chicken broth. Seal the lid, set on Pressure Cook on High, and cook for 3 minutes. After cooking, perform a quick pressure release, and unlock the lid. Adjust taste with salt, black pepper, and stir in pasta until well coated in sauce. Dish food, sprinkle Parmesan cheese on top, and serve warm.

Parmesan Spaghetti with Herbs

Total Time: 15 minutes | **Servings**: 4

Ingredients

4 tbsp olive oil	2 tbsp chopped oregano
16 oz spaghetti	2 tbsp chopped parsley
3 garlic cloves, minced	Salt and black pepper to taste
3 tbsp chopped basil	½ cup grated Parmesan cheese

Directions

Add spaghetti, 6 cups of water, and salt to your Instant Pot. Seal the lid, select Pressure Cook on High, and set the time to 2 minutes. After cooking, do a quick pressure release, and unlock the lid. Drain pasta through a colander. Set aside.

Wipe the pot clean and set the pot to Sauté. Heat 2 tbsp olive oil and stir-fry garlic, basil, oregano, and parsley. Cook for 1 minute and toss spaghetti in sauce. Season with salt and pepper, drizzle with olive oil and serve with Parmesan.

Feta & Arugula Rigatoni

Total Time: 15 minutes | **Servings**: 4

Ingredients

3 tbsp olive oil, divided	Salt and black pepper to taste
1 lemon, zested and juiced	16 oz whole-wheat rigatoni
½ tsp red pepper flakes	2 cups baby arugula
½ cup crumbled feta cheese	2 tbsp chopped chives
½ cup Greek yogurt	

Directions

In a bowl, mix lemon zest and juice, flakes, and 1 tbsp of olive oil. Add feta and combine; set aside to marinate for 5 minutes. In a bowl, combine Greek yogurt, salt, pepper, and remaining olive oil until well mixed; set aside. To your Instant Pot, add rigatoni and 6 cups of salted water. Seal the lid, select Pressure Cook, and cook for 4 minutes.

After cooking, do a quick pressure release. Drain pasta pour into yogurt mixture. Toss with two spoons until well coated in the sauce. Top with marinated feta, arugula, and mix again. Garnish with chives and serve.

Pasta Salad with Roasted Peppers

Total Time: 15 minutes | **Servings**: 4

Ingredients

2 roasted red bell peppers, chopped

5 tbsp olive oil	2 tbsp basil pesto
8 oz conchiglie	Salt and black pepper to taste
2 garlic cloves, minced	3 tbsp chopped basil
2 tbsp lemon juice	

Directions

Add conchiglie, 5 cups of water, and salt to your Instant Pot. Seal the lid, select Pressure Cook, and set the cooking time to 3 minutes. After cooking, do a quick pressure release, and unlock the lid. Drain pasta through a colander.

In a large bowl, whisk the olive oil with garlic, bell peppers, lemon juice, pesto, salt, and black pepper. Toss pasta in dressing and mix in fresh basil. Adjust taste with salt and black pepper, and serve.

Macaroni with Hummus & Olives

Total Time: 10 minutes | **Servings**: 4

Ingredients

8 oz cups macaroni	¼ cup chopped basil
¾ cup hummus	Salt and black pepper to taste
1 tsp garlic paste	¼ cup black olives, pitted
½ cup cherry tomatoes, halved	½ tsp oregano

Directions

Cover macaroni with salted water in your Instant Pot. Seal the lid, select Pressure Cook, and set to 4 minutes. After cooking, do a quick pressure release, and unlock the lid. Drain pasta through a colander and transfer to a bowl.

In a bowl, add hummus, garlic, tomatoes, oregano, basil, salt, pepper, and olives. Stir well, and top the pasta to serve.

Mediterranean Fettuccine

Total Time: 15 minutes | **Servings**: 4

Ingredients

2 tbsp olive oil	¼ tsp mustard powder
1 cup heavy cream	Salt and black pepper to taste
16 oz dried fettuccine	2 tbsp capers, drained
1 ¼ cups grated Parmesan	1 tbsp dried oregano

Directions

Add fettuccine, 6 cups of water, and salt to your Instant Pot. Seal the lid, select Pressure Cook on High, and set the time to 4 minutes. After cooking, do a quick pressure release and Unlock the lid. Drain pasta through a colander. Set aside.

Set the pot to Sauté. Heat olive oil and mix in heavy cream, oregano, mustard powder, and 1 cup of Parmesan until the cheese melts, 2 minutes. Season with salt and pepper. Toss fettuccine in the sauce until well coated. Transfer to serving plates. Garnish with remaining Parmesan cheese and capers.

Sriracha Mac n' Cheese

Total Time: 15 minutes | **Servings**: 4

Ingredients

1 ½ cups Gruyere cheese, grated
6 cups water
A pinch of salt
1 lb elbow macaroni

2 large eggs
1 tsp ground mustard
1 tsp sriracha sauce
1 ½ cups half and half

Directions

Place the macaroni, water, and salt into your Instant Pot. Seal the lid, select Pressure Cook on High, and set the time to 4 minutes. In a bowl, whisk the eggs with ground mustard, sriracha sauce, and half and half; set aside. Do a quick release and unlock the lid. Set to Sauté. Toss in the egg mixture, stir in Gruyere cheese until melted, and serve.

Basil Spaghetti with Chicken Tomatoes

Total Time: 15 minutes | **Servings**: 4

Ingredients

2 tbsp olive oil
2 chicken breasts, cubed
Salt and black pepper to taste
16 oz spaghetti
1 cup dry white wine

2 cups cherry tomatoes, halved
¼ cup heavy cream
1 lemon, zested and juiced
2 tbsp basil, chopped

Directions

Warm oil in your Instant Pot on Sauté. Season chicken with salt and pepper and cook until golden brown. Pour in the wine, 4 cups of water, and spaghetti. Seal the lid, hit Pressure Cook, and cook for 4 minutes. Do a quick pressure release. Press Sauté and stir in tomatoes, heavy cream, lemon zest and juice. Cook for 2 minutes. Top with basil.

Swedish Steamed Cabbage

Total Time: 15 minutes | **Servings**: 4

Ingredients

3 tbsp olive oil
1 roasted bell peppers, chopped
1 large cabbage, shredded
Salt and black pepper to taste

1 tsp white vinegar
1 tsp poppy seeds

Directions

Pour 1 cup of water into your Instant Pot, fit in a steamer basket, and add in the cabbage. Seal the lid, select Pressure Cook on High, and set the time to 1 minute. After cooking, do a quick pressure release, and unlock the lid. Transfer cabbage to a bowl and add olive oil, salt, black pepper, bell pepper, vinegar, and poppy seeds; toss well. Serve.

Cardamom Polenta with Mozzarella

Total Time: 25 minutes | **Servings**: 4

Ingredients

4 tsp butter
1 cup polenta
4 cups chicken broth

1 tsp cardamom powder
½ cup shredded cheddar
¼ cup half and half

Directions

Set your Instant Pot to Sauté. Combine polenta and chicken broth in the inner pot until boiling. Seal the lid. Select Pressure Cook on High, and set the time to 7 minutes. After cooking, allow a natural release for 10 minutes. Unlock the lid and whisk in cardamom, butter, cheddar cheese, and half and half. Spoon into serving bowls and serve.

Simple Basil Spaghetti

Total Time: 15 minutes | **Servings**: 4

Ingredients

¼ cup olive oil
1 ½ cups water
3 cups dry red wine
16 oz spaghetti

Salt to taste
8 garlic cloves, minced
½ cup grated Parmesan cheese
4 basil leaves, cut into strips

Directions

In your Instant Pot, add water, red wine, spaghetti, and salt. Seal the lid, select Pressure Cook on High, and set to 3 minutes. After cooking, perform a quick pressure release. Drain pasta and set aside. Clean inner pot and press Sauté. Heat olive oil and sauté garlic until fragrant, 30 seconds. Return pasta to the inner pot and stir to coat thoroughly. Top with Parmesan cheese and mix until cheese melts. Spoon pasta into serving plates and garnish with basil.

Scallop & Arugula Spaghetti

Total Time: 20 minutes | **Servings**: 4

Ingredients

1 tbsp butter
1 ¼ lb scallops, peeled, deveined
¼ cup white wine
8 oz spaghetti
½ cup tomato puree

½ tsp red chili flakes
1 tsp grated lemon zest
1 tbsp lemon juice
6 cups arugula

Directions

Melt butter in your Instant Pot on Sauté and add scallops. Cook for 6 minutes. Pour in the wine and simmer for 2 minutes. Add spaghetti, 6 cups water, tomato puree, and chili flakes; stir. Seal the lid, select Pressure Cook, and cook for 5 minutes. Do a quick pressure release. Stir in the lemon zest, juice, and arugula until wilted and soft. Serve.

Roasted Peppers & Potatoes with Feta

Total Time: 15 minutes | **Servings**: 4

Ingredients

½ cup roasted red bell peppers, diced
2 tbsp olive oil
1 cup vegetable broth
1 lb russet potatoes, cubed

Salt and black pepper to taste
4 oz crumbled feta cheese
½ jar hot sauce

Directions

Set your Instant Pot to Sauté, heat olive oil, pour potatoes, and season with salt and pepper. Stir-fry until the potatoes begin to crisp. Pour in vegetable broth, seal the lid, select Pressure Cook mode on High, and set the time to 6 minutes.

After cooking, do a quick pressure release to let out steam, and unlock the lid. Drain potatoes through a colander and transfer to a large bowl. Add bell peppers, feta cheese, and hot sauce; mix well. Dish and serve warm.

Red Chili Couscous with Broccoli

Total Time: 15 minutes | **Servings**: 4

Ingredients

2 tbsp olive oil
½ cup couscous
1 head broccoli, cut into florets

2 garlic cloves, minced
1 red chili, seeded and chopped
Salt and black pepper to taste

Directions

Pour 1 cup of water into your Instant Pot and fit in a trivet. Place the broccoli on the trivet. Seal the lid, select Steam, and set the time to 1 minute. Do a quick pressure release. Remove broccoli to a bowl. Take out water and the trivet.

In another bowl, cover the couscous with boiled water. Let sit for 2-3 minutes until all the water is absorbed. Fluff up with a fork and set aside. Press Sauté and warm the olive oil. Add in garlic, red chili, salt, and pepper and cook for 1 minute. Stir in broccoli for 30 more seconds. Serve the couscous topped with broccoli mixture.

Oregano Quinoa with Almonds

Total Time: 15 minutes | **Servings**: 4

Ingredients

2 tbsp olive oil
1 cup quinoa
1 cup almond milk

½ tsp dried oregano
3 tbsp toasted flaked almonds

Directions

Combine quinoa, oregano, almond milk, olive oil, and 1 cup of water in your Instant Pot. Seal the lid, select Pressure Cook, and set the time to 8 minutes. Perform a quick pressure release. Fluff the quinoa with a fork. Top with flaked almonds. Serve and enjoy!

Avocado & Tomato Pearl Barley Salad

Total Time: 60 minutes | **Servings**: 4

Ingredients

4 tbsp olive oil
1 cup pearled barley, rinsed
1 garlic clove, minced

½ cup cherry tomatoes, halved
1 avocado, sliced

Dressing

2 tbsp extra-virgin olive oil
1 lime, juiced
1 spring onion, sliced

2 tbsp parsley, finely chopped
Salt and black pepper, to taste

Directions

Place the barley, 4 cups water, 4 tbsp of olive oil, salt, and garlic into your Instant Pot. Seal the lid, select Pressure Cook, and set to 30 minutes. Allow a natural release for 10 minutes. Drain the barley; let cool for 10 minutes. In a bowl, combine all dressing ingredients, add in barley and toss to combine. Top with cherry tomatoes and avocado.

Prosciutto & Sweet Potato Gratin

Total Time: 15 minutes | **Servings**: 4

Ingredients

1 ½ lb sweet potatoes, quartered
Salt and black pepper to taste
½ cup heavy cream
1 cup shredded Provolone

10 oz prosciutto, chopped
¾ cup frozen peas, thawed
½ cup grated Pecorino Romano
3 tbsp chopped fresh chives

Directions

Pour 1 cup of water into your Instant Pot and put in a trivet. Arrange sweet potatoes on top. Seal the lid, select Pressure Cook, and set to 4 minutes. After cooking, do a quick pressure release. Use a large fork to break the potatoes into pieces. Empty the water of the pot. Put the potatoes back in the pot and season with salt and pepper.

Mix in the heavy cream, Provolone cheese, and prosciutto. Gently stir in the peas. Select Sauté and cook for 3-4 minutes. Sprinkle with Pecorino cheese and chives to serve.

Creamy Custards with Ham & Emmental

Total Time: 15 minutes | **Servings**: 4

Ingredients

2 Serrano ham slices, halved widthwise
1 tbsp olive oil
4 large eggs
1 oz cottage cheese

¼ cup half and half
¼ cup grated Emmental cheese
¼ cup caramelized onions

Directions

Set your Instant Pot to Sauté, heat the olive oil and cook the ham for 2 minutes, turning occasionally; remove to a plate. Rush the inside of four ramekins with the ham fat. Set aside. Beat eggs with cottage cheese, and half and half.

Stir in Emmental cheese. Lay a piece of ham on the bottom of each custard cup. Share the onions among the cups as well as the egg mixture. Pour 1 cup of water into the inner pot and fit in a trivet. Arrange the ramekins on top. Seal the lid, select Pressure Cook on High, and set to 7 minutes. Perform a quick pressure release. Let chill before serving.

Broccoli & Cauliflower Gruyere Side

Total Time: 20 minutes | **Servings**: 4

Ingredients

1 cauliflower, cut into florets
1 broccoli, cut into florets
½ tsp garlic powder
½ tsp onion powder
1 cup chicken broth

Salt and black pepper to taste
1 cup evaporated milk
¼ cup grated Gruyere cheese
1 cup grated cheddar cheese

Directions

In your Instant Pot, add cauliflower, broccoli, garlic, onion, broth, salt, and pepper. Seal the lid, select Pressure Cook on High, and set the time to 3 minutes. After cooking, allow a natural release for 10 minutes, and unlock the lid. Set the pot to Sauté. Add evaporated milk, cheeses and stir until they melt. Spoon into bowls and serve.

Rice & Beans with Avocado

Total Time: 15 minutes | **Servings:** 6

Ingredients

1 ½ cups brown rice
1 cup canned red kidney beans
1 cup salsa
½ bunch parsley, chopped
3 cups vegetable broth

2 cups water
Salt and black pepper to taste
1 avocado, pitted and sliced
1 large lime, cut into wedges

Directions

In your Instant Pot, add brown rice, kidney beans, salsa, broth, and water. Season with salt and pepper. Seal the lid, select Pressure Cook on High, and time to 8 minutes. After cooking, allow a quick release. Unlock the lid, fluff rice and beans, and spoon into bowls. Garnish with parsley and top with avocado and lime wedges to serve.

Honey-Glazed Carrots

Total Time: 15 minutes | **Servings:** 4

Ingredients

¼ cup butter, melted
3 large carrots, cut into chunks
1 cup vegetable stock

2 tbsp honey
1 tbsp chopped parsley
Salt and black pepper to taste

Directions

Add carrots, vegetable stock, salt, and pepper to your Instant Pot. Seal the lid, select Pressure Cook on High, and set the time to 2 minutes. After cooking, do a quick pressure release. Using a slotted spoon, fetch out carrots into a baking sheet. Brush with butter and honey and cook under the broiler for 4 minutes. Top with parsley and serve.

Brussel Sprout Rice with Spring Onions

Total Time: 35 minutes | **Servings:** 4

Ingredients

2 tbsp sesame oil
1 lb Brussels sprouts, sliced
1 cup jasmine rice
4 spring onions, sliced

1 tbsp light soy sauce
1 garlic clove, minced
Salt and black pepper to taste

Directions

Set your Instant Pot to Sauté and warm sesame oil. Add in spring onions, garlic, Brussels sprouts, salt, and pepper and cook for 5 minutes until tender. Mix in rice and 2 cups of water. Seal the lid, and cook on Pressure Cook for 10 minutes. When done, allow a natural release for 10 minutes. Fluff the rice with a fork, stir in soy sauce and serve.

Buttery Celeriac & Potato Mash

Total Time: 30 minutes | **Servings:** 4

Ingredients

3 tbsp butter, softened
Salt and black pepper to taste
1 lb potatoes, chopped
½ lb celeriac, chopped

½ cup milk
1 garlic clove, minced
2 tbsp chives, chopped

Directions

Place celeriac and potatoes into your Instant Pot and cover with salted water. Seal the lid, select Steam, and set the time to 10 minutes. When done, allow a natural release for 10 minutes. Unlock the lid and drain the celeriac and potatoes.

Use a potato masher to mash the potatoes and slowly pour in the milk until uniform and smooth. Add in butter, black pepper, and garlic; whisk until smooth. Taste and adjust the seasoning. Serve scattered with chives.

Chili Snap Peas with Bacon

Total Time: 15 minutes | **Servings:** 4

Ingredients

3 bacon slices, chopped
2 garlic cloves, minced
1 ½ cups snap peas

1 cup vegetable broth
¼ tsp red chili flakes
2 tsp lemon juice

Directions

Set your Instant Pot to Sauté and brown bacon until crispy, 5 minutes. Transfer to a paper towel-lined plate to drain grease. Sauté garlic until fragrant, 30 seconds, and top with snap peas, vegetable broth, and red chili flakes.

Seal the lid, select Pressure Cook on High, and set the time to 1 minute. After cooking, do a quick pressure release to let out steam, and unlock the lid. Stir in bacon and lemon juice. Spoon into serving plates and serve.

Scallion Corn with Cream Cheese

Total Time: 15 minutes | **Servings:** 4

Ingredients

3 tbsp butter
2 cups canned sweet corn kernels
½ cup whole milk
8 oz cream cheese
½ cup heavy cream

1 tsp cayenne pepper
1 tsp sugar
Salt and black pepper to taste
2 tbsp scallions, chopped

Directions

In your Instant Pot, add sweet corn, milk, cream cheese, butter, heavy cream, cayenne pepper, sugar, salt, and pepper. Seal the lid, select Pressure Cook, and set the time to 5 minutes. After cooking, perform a quick pressure release to let out steam, and unlock the lid. Stir food vigorously until creamy. Ladle into bowls, garnish with scallions, and serve.

Power Green Rice

Total Time: 30 minutes | **Servings:** 4

Ingredients

2 tbsp olive oil
1 onion, chopped
1 cup frozen green peas
1 cup rice, rinsed

1 garlic clove, minced
Salt and black pepper to taste
3 tbsp cilantro, chopped
½ lime, juiced

Directions

Set your Instant Pot to Sauté and heat the oil. Cook in onion and garlic for 5 minutes. Mix in rice and 2 cups of water.

Season with pepper and salt and stir to combine. Seal the lid, select Pressure Cook, and set to 7 minutes.

When done, allow a natural release for 10 minutes. Unlock the lid and stir in the peas and lime juice until heated through. Sprinkle with cilantro to serve.

Quick & Easy Steamed Potatoes

Total Time: 15 minutes | **Servings:** 4

Ingredients

2 tbsp butter, melted	Salt and black pepper to taste
4 large potatoes	2 tbsp chopped parsley

Directions

Pierce holes all around potatoes using a fork. Pour 1 cup of water into your Instant Pot, fit in a trivet, and put potatoes on the trivet. Seal the lid, select Pressure Cook, and set the time to 6 minutes. After cooking, perform a quick release. Remove potatoes, break the top parts opened, and season with salt and pepper. Top with butter and parsley. Serve.

Delicious Steamed Veggies

Total Time: 15 minutes | **Servings:** 4

Ingredients

2 tbsp olive oil	1 lb asparagus, cut into thirds
1 cup vegetable broth	1 ½ lb russet potatoes, halved
½ lb carrots, cut into chunks	1 lemon, juiced
1 lb green beans, trimmed	1 tsp oregano

Directions

Pour vegetable broth in your Instant Pot, fit in a trivet, and pour carrots, green beans, asparagus, oregano, and potatoes on top. Seal the lid, select Pressure Cook, and set the time to 2 minutes. After cooking, do a quick pressure release, and unlock the lid. Using tongs, remove vegetables to a bowl and drizzle with lemon juice and olive oil. Serve.

Bacon & Bell Pepper Wild Rice Pilaf

Total Time: 35 minutes | **Servings:** 4

Ingredients

1 tbsp olive oil	2 cups chicken broth
2 bacon slices, chopped	4 garlic cloves, minced
1 onion, chopped	½ tsp dried thyme
1 celery stalk, finely chopped	½ tsp ground nutmeg
1 cup wild rice	2 tbsp parsley, chopped
4 roasted bell pepper strips	Salt and black pepper to taste

Directions

Set your Instant Pot to Sauté and heat the olive oil. Add in the onion, garlic, bacon, and celery and sauté for 5 minutes. Stir in the wild rice, thyme, nutmeg, salt, and pepper for 1 minute. Pour in the chicken broth and stir.

Seal the lid, select Pressure Cook, and set to 10 minutes. When done, allow a natural release for 10 minutes. Fluff the rice with a fork. Transfer to a plate and arrange the red pepper strips on top. Sprinkle with parsley and serve.

Mushroom & Spinach Risotto

Total time: 25 minutes | **Servings:** 4

Ingredients

4 tbsp butter	¼ tsp dried thyme
1 red onion, chopped	1 cup Carnaroli rice
3 garlic cloves, minced	2 cups vegetable broth
2 celery sticks, chopped	2 cups baby spinach
8 oz button mushrooms, sliced	¼ cup grated Parmesan cheese
Salt and black pepper to taste	

Directions

Set your Instant Pot to Sauté and melt 2 tbsp of butter. Cook onion, garlic, celery, and mushrooms for 5 minutes. Stir in salt, pepper, thyme, rice, and broth. Seal the lid, select Pressure Cook on High, and set the time to 8 minutes. When done, perform a quick pressure release. Unlock the lid and set to Sauté. Add in the remaining butter and spinach and cook for 2 minutes until the spinach wilts. Top with Parmesan cheese and stir. Serve immediately.

Mixed Quinoa & Rice with Mushrooms

Total Time: 35 minutes | **Servings:** 4

Ingredients

1 cup mixed quinoa and brown rice

2 tbsp olive oil	½ fennel bulb, chopped
1 tbsp butter	1 cup button mushrooms, sliced
1 onion, chopped	2 cups vegetable stock
2 garlic cloves, minced	½ cup Parmesan shavings
2 baby carrots, chopped	Salt and black pepper to taste

Directions

Set your Instant Pot to Sauté and heat the oil. Place in the onion, garlic, carrots, fennel, and mushrooms and sauté for 5 minutes until tender. Stir in quinoa, brown, and rice for 1 minute. Pour in the stock and stir to deglaze the bottom of the pot. Adjust the seasoning with salt and pepper. Seal the lid and select Pressure Cook. Set the cooking time to 12 minutes on High. When done, allow a natural release for 10 minutes. Carefully unlock the lid and stir in the butter to melt. Scatter over the Parmesan shavings and serve warm with pork chops. Enjoy!

Cremini Mushrooms in BBQ Sauce

Total Time: 15 minutes | **Servings:** 4

Ingredients

1 ½ cups cremini mushrooms, chopped

1 tbsp olive oil	2 garlic cloves, crushed
2 tbsp barbecue sauce	1 tbsp chopped parsley

Directions

Combine mushrooms, 1 cup of water, barbecue sauce, and garlic in your Instant Pot. Seal the lid, select Pressure Cook on High, and set the time to 1 minute. After cooking, do a quick pressure release, and unlock the lid. Using a slotted spoon, fetch out mushrooms into a bowl; discard garlic. Drizzle with olive oil and toss well. Garnish with parsley.

Potato & Kale Gratin

Total Time: 25 minutes | **Servings:** 4

Ingredients

2 lb potatoes, thinly sliced
1 cup kale, steamed
1 tbsp dill, chopped

1 cup crème fraîche
3 oz of cheddar cheese
Salt to taste

Directions

Put half of the potatoes in a greased baking dish and season with salt. Spread kale over potatoes, sprinkle with half of the cheese, then top with the remaining potatoes. Pour over crème fraîche and finish with the remaining cheese. Add 1 cup of water to your Instant Pot and fit in a trivet. Place the baking dish on the trivet. Seal the lid, select Pressure Cook, and cook for 15 minutes on High. When done, perform a quick pressure release. Serve garnished with dill.

Double-Cheese Macaroni

Total Time: 15 minutes | **Servings:** 2

Ingredients

1 tbsp butter
8 oz elbow macaroni
½ tsp mustard powder
A pinch of cayenne pepper

1 cup milk
¼ cup Greek yogurt
1 ½ cups cheddar cheese
¼ cup Parmesan cheese, grated

Directions

Place the macaroni and 4 cups of salted water into your Instant Pot. Seal the lid, select Pressure Cook, and set to 4 minutes on High. When ready, do a quick pressure release. Drain pasta and return to the pot. Mix in the milk, mustard, butter, cayenne, Greek yogurt, and cheeses. Stir for 1 minute until the cheeses melt. Adjust the seasoning and serve.

Rice Pilaf with Turmeric & Cilantro

Total Time: 20 minutes | **Servings:** 4

Ingredients

1 tbsp olive oil
1 onion, thinly sliced
1 tsp turmeric
1 cup rice, rinsed

½ tsp lemon zest
1 lemon, juiced
2 cups vegetable stock
2 tbsp chopped cilantro

Directions

Set your Instant Pot to Sauté and heat olive oil. Place in onion and cook for 3 minutes, stirring occasionally. Stir in rice to coat. Add in lemon zest and juice, turmeric, and stock; mix. Seal the lid, select Pressure Cook, and set to 8 minutes on High. Do a quick pressure release and fluff the rice with a fork. Stir through the cilantro and serve.

Scallion & Cauliflower Rice

Total Time: 20 minutes | **Servings:** 2

Ingredients

2 tbsp oil
2 scallions, sliced
1 garlic clove, minced

2 cups cauliflower rice
Salt and black pepper to taste
¼ tsp hot sauce

Directions

Set your Instant Pot to Sauté and heat the oil. Place in the scallions and garlic and cook for 2-3 minutes, stirring often. Stir in cauli rice. Cook for 7-8 minutes. Add in the hot sauce and mix well. Season with salt and pepper and serve hot.

The Original Lebanese Hummus

Total Time: 60 minutes | **Servings:** 4

Ingredients

¼ cup olive oil
1 lb dried chickpeas, soaked
¼ cup tahini
2 medium cloves garlic

Juice from 1 lemon
½ tsp ground cumin
¼ tsp sumac
2 tbsp parsley, chopped

Directions

Cover chickpeas with water in your Instant Pot. Seal the lid, select Pressure Cook, and set the time to 35 minutes. When done, allow a natural release for 15 minutes. Drain the chickpeas and reserve the liquid. Place the chickpeas in a food processor, add 1 cup of the reserved liquid, and the remaining ingredients. Blend until smooth and creamy.

Greek-Style Potato Salad

Total Time: 30 minutes | **Servings:** 2

Ingredients

3 small potatoes, peeled
3 cups water
2 tbsp Greek yogurt
2 tbsp light mayonnaise
1 garlic clove, minced

1 tsp lemon zest
1 tbsp dill, chopped
½ small red onion, sliced
Salt and black pepper to taste

Directions

Place the potatoes, salt, and water into your Instant Pot. Seal the lid, select Steam, and set the time to 10 minutes on High. When done, allow a natural release for 10 minutes. Drain the potatoes and set aside to cool before slicing them. Mix together the remaining ingredients, except for dill. Add to the potatoes; toss to coat. Serve sprinkled with dill.

Chive & Herb Potatoes

Total Time: 20 minutes | **Servings:** 4

Ingredients

3 tbsp butter
2 lb baby potatoes, washed
½ tsp dried rosemary
½ tsp dried thyme
½ tsp dried tarragon

½ tsp garlic powder
Salt and black pepper to taste
2 cups vegetable stock
Chopped chives for garnish

Directions

In a bowl, mix rosemary, thyme, tarragon, garlic powder, salt, and pepper. Set your Instant Pot to Sauté and melt butter. Place in potatoes and cook for 5-6 minutes, stirring frequently. Pour in herb mixture and stock. Seal the lid, select Pressure Cook, and set to 7 minutes. Perform a quick pressure release. Serve topped with chives.

Cheddar-Parmesan Vegetable Rice

Total Time: 25 minutes | **Servings**: 4

Ingredients

1 cup jasmine rice, rinsed
¼ cup frozen mixed vegetables
½ tsp garlic powder
½ tsp onion powder
2 cups chicken broth
Salt and black pepper to taste
¼ cup grated Parmesan cheese
1 cup grated cheddar cheese

Directions

In your Instant Pot, add jasmine rice, mixed vegetables, garlic, onion, chicken broth, salt, and pepper. Seal the lid, select Pressure Cook on High, and set the time to 6 minutes.

After cooking, allow a natural release for 10 minutes. Set the pot to Sauté. Add cheeses and stir until melted. Spoon food into bowls and serve warm.

Homemade Baba Ganoush with Nachos

Total Time: 15 minutes | **Servings**: 2

Ingredients

¼ cup olive oil
1 lb eggplants, sliced
2 tbsp tahini
1 garlic clove
1 ¼ tbsp lemon juice
1 tsp parsley. chopped
Salt and black pepper to taste
Nacho tortilla chips

Directions

Pour 1 cup of water into your Instant Pot and fit in a trivet. Place the eggplants on the trivet. Seal the lid, select Steam on High, and cook for 6 minutes. Do a quick pressure release. In a food processor, blend eggplants and the remaining ingredients, except for parsley, until smooth. Season to taste and sprinkle with parsley. Serve with tortilla chips.

Parmesan Asparagus

Total Time: 15 minutes | **Servings**: 4

Ingredients

2 tbsp butter, softened
1 lb asparagus, chopped
2 garlic cloves, minced
Salt and black pepper to taste
2 tbsp grated Parmesan cheese

Directions

In your Instant Pot, place 1 cup of water and a trivet. Cut out a foil sheet, place asparagus on top as well as garlic and butter. Season with salt and pepper. Wrap foil and place asparagus packet on the trivet. Seal the lid, select Pressure Cook on High, and set the time to 8 minutes. When ready, do a quick pressure release. Remove foil pack, put asparagus onto a platter, and top with Parmesan cheese to serve.

Buttered Baby Carrots

Total Time: 15 minutes | **Servings**: 4

Ingredients

2 tbsp butter
1 lb baby carrots, peeled
¼ tsp salt
2 tbsp honey
1 orange, juiced and zested
A pinch of cinnamon
2 tbsp sesame seeds
1 cup water

Directions

Pour water in your Instant Pot and fit in a trivet. Place carrots on the trivet. Seal the lid, select Steam. Cook for 2 minutes. Do a quick release. Remove carrots. Press Sauté and melt butter. Add in salt, honey, orange juice, zest, and cinnamon; cook for 5 minutes. Add the mixture to the carrots and toss to coat. Scatter sesame seeds over. Serve.

Blue Cheese Polenta

Total Time: 20 minutes | **Servings**: 4

Ingredients

2 tbsp unsalted butter
½ cup polenta
2 cups chicken stock
¼ cup heavy cream
½ cup blue cheese, crumbled
Salt and black pepper, to taste

Directions

Place the polenta and chicken stock into the inner pot. Seal the lid, select Pressure Cook, and set the time to 7 minutes on High. When done, perform a quick pressure release. Stir in butter, heavy cream, and blue cheese until smooth and the cheese fully melted. Adjust the seasoning. Serve.

Pecan & Cherry Stuffed Pumpkin

Total time: 25 minutes | **Servings**: 4

Ingredients

1 (2-pound) pumpkin, halved lengthwise, stems trimmed
2 tbsp olive oil
5 toasted bread slices, cubed
1 ½ cups vegetable broth
1 tsp dried parsley
1 tsp onion powder
Salt and black pepper to taste
½ cup dried cherries
½ cup chopped pecans

Directions

Brush the pumpkin with some oil. Pour 1 cup of water into your Instant Pot and fit in a trivet. Place the pumpkin, skin-side down, on the trivet. Seal the lid, select Pressure Cook, and set the cooking time to 15 minutes on High. When ready, do a quick pressure release. Remove the pumpkin and water. Press Sauté, pour in the remaining ingredients, and cook until the liquid is reduced by half. Divide the filling between pumpkin halves and top with pecans. Serve.

Pecorino Mac & Cheese

Total time: 15 minutes | **Servings**: 6

Ingredients

3 tbsp butter
1 lb elbow macaroni
1 cup heavy cream
½ cup whole milk
2 ½ cups mozzarella, grated
½ cup Pecorino Romano, grated

Directions

In your Instant Pot, mix 6 cups of salted water and macaroni. Seal the lid, select Pressure Cook on High, and set the cooking time to 4 minutes. When ready, do a quick pressure release. Stir in the heavy cream, milk, and butter. Gradually add mozzarella cheese, stirring often, until melted. Serve sprinkled with Pecorino Romano cheese.

STOCKS & SAUCES

Chicken Bone Stock

Total Time: 50 minutes | **Servings**: 6

Ingredients

2 lb roasted chicken carcasses
1 large yellow onion, chopped
6 celery stalks, chopped
4 large carrots, chopped
4 cloves garlic, smashed
6 sprigs thyme
6 sprigs rosemary
1 tbsp whole black peppercorns
2 tbsp white vinegar

Directions

In your Instant Pot, add chicken carcasses, onion, celery, carrots, garlic, thyme, rosemary, peppercorns, vinegar, and 8 cups of water. Seal the lid, select Soup/Broth on High, and set to 30 minutes. Allow a natural release for 10 minutes. Strain stock through a fine mesh into a clean bowl. Discard solids and pour the liquid into jars. Cover and allow cooling. Refrigerate and use for up to 3 months.

Beef Bone Stock

Total Time: 100 minutes | **Servings**: 6

Ingredients

2 lb beef bones
1 large yellow onion, chopped
2 celery stalks, chopped
2 large carrots, chopped
4 cloves garlic, smashed
6 sprigs thyme
6 sprigs rosemary
1 tbsp black peppercorns
2 tbsp white vinegar

Directions

Preheat oven to 380 F. In a baking sheet, spread beef bones, onion, celery, carrots, garlic, and spray with cooking spray. Roast in the oven until browned, 45 minutes. Transfer beef mixture to your Instant Pot and top with thyme, rosemary, peppercorns, vinegar, and 8 cups of water. Seal the lid, select Soup/Broth on High, and set the time to 40 minutes.

Allow a natural release for 10 minutes. Unlock the lid and strain stock through a fine mesh into a clean bowl. Discard solids and pour the liquid into jars. Cover, let cool, and discard the fat layer. Refrigerate and use for up to 3 months.

Pork Stock

Total Time: 60 minutes | **Servings**: 6

Ingredients

2 lb pork leg bones, rinsed well
1 finger ginger, sliced
½ cup white wine

Directions

To the inner pot, add pork leg bones, ginger, white wine, and 8 cups of water. Seal the lid, select Soup/Broth on High and set to 40 minutes. After cooking, do a natural release for 10 minutes. Strain stock through a fine mesh into a clean bowl. Discard solids and pour the liquid into jars; cover and let cool. Refrigerate and use for up to 2 weeks.

Carrot-Coconut Stock

Total Time: 50 minutes | **Servings**: 6

Ingredients

1 large yellow onion, chopped
8 large carrots, chopped
4 cloves garlic, smashed
1 lemongrass stalk, chopped
8 cilantro sprigs
1 tbsp black peppercorns
2 tbsp white wine vinegar
6 cups coconut water

Directions

To the inner pot, add onion, carrots, garlic, lemongrass, cilantro, peppercorns, vinegar, coconut water, and 2 cups of water. Seal the lid, select Soup/Broth on Low and set the time to 30 minutes. After cooking, allow a natural release.

Unlock the lid. Strain stock through a fine mesh into a clean bowl. Discard solids and pour the liquid into jars. Cover and allow cooling. Refrigerate and use for up to 1 month.

Seafood & Mushroom Stock

Total Time: 50 minutes | **Servings**: 4

Ingredients

2 tbsp olive oil
1 lb shrimp shells and heads
2 large yellow onions, chopped
6 celery stalks, chopped
2 cups sliced mixed mushrooms
4 large carrots, chopped
4 cloves garlic, smashed
1 tbsp black peppercorns
½ cup white wine

Directions

On Sauté, heat olive oil and brown shrimp shells and heads, onions, garlic, celery, mushrooms, and carrots, for 5 minutes. Top with peppercorns, white wine, and 8 cups of water. Seal the lid, select Soup/Broth on High for 30 minutes. After cooking, allow a natural release for 10 minutes. Strain stock through a fine mesh into a clean bowl. Discard solids and pour the liquid into jars. Cover and allow cooling. Refrigerate and use for up to 3 months.

Green Veggie Stock

Total Time: 30 minutes | **Servings**: 6

Ingredients

1 large yellow onion, chopped
6 celery stalks, chopped
1 leek stalk, roughly chopped
1 cup spinach
4 large carrots, chopped
4 cloves garlic, smashed
1 bay leaf
6 sprigs thyme
1 tbsp parsley, chopped
1 tbsp tarragon, chopped
1 tbsp black peppercorns
2 tbsp white wine vinegar
4 cups coconut water
6 cups water

Directions

Add onion, celery, leek, spinach, carrots, garlic, bay leaf, thyme, parsley, tarragon, peppercorns, white wine vinegar, coconut water, and water to your Instant Pot. Seal the lid, select Soup/Broth on High, and set the time to 10 minutes. After cooking, allow a natural release for 10 minutes. Unlock the lid. Strain stock through a fine mesh into a clean bowl. Discard solids and pour the liquid into jars. Cover and allow cooling. Refrigerate and use for up to 1 month.

Asian-Style Vegetable Stock

Total Time: 40 minutes | **Servings:** 6

Ingredients

1 tbsp olive oil
1 white onion, diced
1 knob ginger, washed and sliced
10 garlic cloves, crushed
5 celery stalks, chopped
3 carrots, peeled and sliced
10 scallions, cut into thirds
1 tbsp salt
1 bunch of cilantro, chopped

Directions

Set your Instant Pot to Sauté and heat olive oil. Brown onion, ginger, garlic, celery, and carrots, 10 minutes. Add scallions, salt, cilantro, and 8 cups of water. Seal the lid, select Soup/Broth on High for 10 minutes.

When ready, allow a natural release for 10 minutes. Strain stock through a fine mesh into a clean bowl. Discard solids, pour the liquid into jars, cover, and let cool. Refrigerate and use for up to 3 months.

Basil Vegetable Stock

Total Time: 30 minutes | **Servings:** 4

Ingredients

1 large yellow onion, chopped
6 celery stalks, chopped
4 large tomatoes
4 large carrots, chopped
4 cloves garlic, smashed
1 bay leaf
6 sprigs fresh oregano
1 small bunch basil leaves
1 tbsp black peppercorns
2 tbsp apple cider vinegar
6 cups chicken broth
2 cups water

Directions

In your Instant Pot, add onion, celery, tomatoes, carrots, garlic, bay leaf, oregano, basil, peppercorns, apple cider vinegar, chicken broth, and water. Seal the lid, select Soup/Broth on High and set the time to 10 minutes. After cooking, allow a natural release for 10 minutes. Unlock the lid. Strain stock through a fine mesh into a clean bowl. Discard solids and pour the liquid into jars. Cover and allow cooling. Refrigerate and use for up to 2 months.

Curried Ginger Broth

Total Time: 50 minutes | **Servings:** 4

Ingredients

2 tbsp black peppercorns
1 tbsp cumin seeds
2 tbsp coriander seeds
1 tbsp turmeric
15 curry leaves, torn
1-inch finger ginger, sliced
2 green chilies, chopped
2 yellow onions, chopped
6 garlic cloves, minced
¼ cup white vinegar
6 cups chicken broth

Directions

Set your Instant Pot to Sauté and add peppercorns, cumin seeds, coriander seeds, turmeric, and curry leaves. Toast for 2 minutes or until fragrant. Stir in ginger, green chilies, onions, garlic, white vinegar, broth, and 2 cups of water. Seal the lid, select Soup/Broth on High, and set to 30 minutes. After cooking, allow a natural release for 10 minutes.

Unlock the lid and strain stock through a fine mesh into a clean bowl. Discard solids. Pour the liquid into jars. Refrigerate and use for up to 3 months.

Chili Marinara Sauce

Total Time: 35 minutes | **Servings:** 6

Ingredients

4 tbsp olive oil
1 small white onion, chopped
5 garlic cloves, minced
8 cups tomatoes, crushed
4 tbsp tomato paste
½ cup red wine
½ cup water
Salt and black pepper to taste
2 tsp dried basil
2 tsp dried oregano
2 tbsp dried parsley
2 tbsp Italian seasoning
1 tsp granulated sugar
1 tsp red chili powder

Directions

Set your Instant Pot to Sauté, heat olive oil, and sauté onion and garlic until softened, 3 minutes. Add in tomatoes, tomato paste, red wine, water, salt, pepper, basil, oregano, parsley, Italian seasoning, sugar, and chili. Seal the lid, select Pressure Cook on High, and set the time to 25 minutes. After cooking, allow a natural release. Let cool. Spoon into jars, cover, and refrigerate. Use for up to 5 days.

Caribbean Hot Sauce

Total Time: 20 minutes | **Servings:** 4

Ingredients

8 cups habanero peppers, heads removed
3 tbsp salt
1 ¼ cups water
6 garlic cloves, crushed
¼ cup tequila
¼ cup agave nectar
¼ cup apple cider vinegar

Directions

Add habanero peppers, salt, water, and garlic to the inner pot. Seal the lid, select Pressure Cook on High, and set to 2 minutes. After cooking, allow a natural release for 10 minutes. Stir in tequila, agave nectar, and vinegar. Using an immersion blender, process ingredients until smooth. Spoon into jars and refrigerate. Use for up to 2 months.

Alfredo Sauce

Total Time: 15 minutes | **Servings:** 4

Ingredients

4 tbsp butter
1 cup chicken broth
4 garlic cloves, minced
4 leaves basil, chopped
¼ cup chopped parsley
2 cups heavy cream
8 oz cream cheese, softened
1 cup grated Parmesan cheese

Directions

To the inner pot, add chicken broth, garlic, basil, and parsley. Seal the lid, select Pressure Cook on High, and set the cooking time to 1 minute. After cooking, perform a quick pressure release. Unlock the lid and press Sauté. Vigorously whisk in butter, heavy cream, and cream cheese until melted and well-combined, 3 minutes. Mix in Parmesan cheese to melt and turn Instant Pot off. Spoon into bowls and serve.

Tomato Pizza Sauce

Total Time: 25 minutes | **Servings:** 8

Ingredients

2 lb tomatoes crushed with juice
4 tbsp tomato paste
1 cup chicken broth
3 tsp dried oregano
Salt and black pepper to taste

Directions

Add tomatoes, tomato paste, chicken broth, oregano, salt, and black pepper to the inner pot. Seal the lid, select Pressure Cook on High, and set the time to 5 minutes. After cooking, allow a natural release for 10 minutes. Unlock the lid, stir sauce, turn Instant Pot off and let cool. Spoon into jars, cover, and refrigerate. Use for up to 5 days.

Simple Buffalo Sauce

Total Time: 15 minutes | **Servings:** 4

Ingredients

½ cup unsalted butter
1 cup hot sauce
¼ tsp Worcestershire sauce
1 ½ tbsp white vinegar

Directions

Set your Instant Pot to Sauté mode and adjust to medium heat. In your Instant Pot, combine hot sauce, butter, Worcestershire sauce, and white vinegar. Allow cooking until bubbling, 7 to 10 minutes. Spoon into jars or serve.

Green Pea-Lime Butter Sauce

Total Time: 20 minutes | **Servings:** 4

Ingredients

2 tbsp unsalted butter
1 garlic clove, minced
¼ cup chopped cilantro
1 cup green peas
1 cup chicken broth
¼ cup squeezed lime juice

Directions

Set your Instant Pot to Sauté and melt butter. Sauté garlic and cilantro until fragrant, 1 minute. Add in peas and broth. Seal the lid, select Pressure Cook on High, and set the time to 3 minutes. After cooking, allow a natural release for 10 minutes. Spoon mixture into a blender and add lime juice; process until smooth. Pour into a bowl to serve.

Basil-Mascarpone & Blue Cheese Sauce

Total Time: 15 minutes | **Servings:** 4

Ingredients

2 tbsp butter
1 cup heavy cream
1 ½ cups mascarpone cheese
1 cup crumbled blue cheese
1 tsp dried basil
Salt and black pepper to taste

Directions

Select Sauté and boil heavy cream until thickened, while occasionally stirring. Whisk in mascarpone cheese, blue cheese, and butter to melt for 2 minutes. Stir in basil, salt, and pepper. Press Cancel. Spoon sauce into serving cups.

Walnut Butterscotch Sauce

Total Time: 15 minutes | **Servings:** 4

Ingredients

3 tbsp unsalted butter
¼ cup brown sugar
3 tbsp water
1 tbsp rum
1 ½ cups heavy cream
2 tbsp chopped walnuts

Directions

Set your Instant Pot to Sauté, mix brown sugar and water in your Instant Pot, and cook until dissolved, continuously stirring, 3 minutes. Allow bubbling for 3 to 4 more minutes. Stir in rum and cook further for 1 minute. Turn Instant Pot off. Whisk in butter and heavy cream. Fold in walnuts and spoon sauce into serving bowls to cool before serving.

Italian Pasta Sauce

Total Time: 45 minutes | **Servings:** 6

Ingredients

2 tbsp olive oil
2 tbsp butter
1 lb ground beef
1 small white onion, chopped
5 garlic cloves, minced
6 cups chopped tomatoes
4 tbsp tomato paste
2 cups tomato ketchup
½ cup red wine
2 tsp dried oregano
2 tbsp dried parsley
2 tbsp Italian seasoning
Salt and black pepper to taste
2 tbsp maple syrup

Directions

Set your Instant Pot to Sauté, heat olive oil and butter, and cook beef until brown, 5 minutes. Add and sauté onion until softened, 3 minutes. Stir in garlic and cook until fragrant, 30 seconds. Add tomatoes, tomato paste and ketchup, wine, ½ cup of water, oregano, parsley, Italian seasoning, salt, pepper, and maple syrup. Seal the lid. Select Pressure Cook and set the time to 25 minutes. After cooking, allow a natural release for 10 minutes; unlock the lid. Stir sauce, turn Instant Pot off, and let cool. Spoon into jars, cover, and refrigerate. Use for up to 5 days.

Red Wine Onion Gravy

Total Time: 25 minutes | **Servings:** 4

Ingredients

2 tbsp butter
1 shallot, finely chopped
1 tsp plain flour
1 tbsp red wine vinegar
2 cups red wine
1 cup thinly sliced red onion
1 cup chicken stock
1 tsp dried oregano
1 tbsp Dijon mustard

Directions

Set your Instant Pot to Sauté, melt half of the butter, and sauté shallots until softened, 2 minutes. Stir in flour until a sand-like consistency form. Mix in vinegar until thick paste forms and stir in the red wine while scraping the stuck bits at the bottom. Stir in onion, stock, oregano, and mustard. Seal the lid, select Pressure Cook on High, and set to 2 minutes. After cooking, allow a natural release for 10 minutes. Press Sauté. Mix in remaining butter and serve.

Pineapple Sauce

Total Time: 25 minutes | **Servings:** 4

Ingredients

3 tbsp cornflour mixed with ¼ cup water
2 cups chopped pineapples
3 garlic cloves, minced
½ cup pineapple juice
½ lemon, zested and juiced

¼ cup white vinegar
1 cup maple syrup
2 tsp red chili flakes
1 tsp salt

Directions

Add pineapples and garlic to a blender and process until coarsely mixed. Pour into the inner pot and top with pineapple juice, lemon zest, lemon juice, white vinegar, maple syrup, chili flakes, salt, and 1 cup of water.

Seal the lid, select Pressure Cook on High, and set the time to 1 minute. After cooking, allow a natural release for 10 minutes. Unlock the lid and select Sauté mode, and stir in cornflour mixture. Cook until sauce thickens, 2 to 3 minutes. Turn Instant Pot off and spoon sauce into a glass jar. Cover and refrigerate. Use for up to a week.

Pop's BBQ Sauce

Total Time: 25 minutes | **Servings:** 4

Ingredients

3 tbsp olive oil
1 brown onion, chopped
6 garlic cloves, minced
2 cups ketchup
½ cup brown sugar

2 tbsp chili powder
½ cup apple cider vinegar
4 tbsp Worcestershire sauce
Salt and black pepper to taste

Directions

Set your Instant Pot to Sauté, heat oil, and sauté onion until softened, 3 minutes. Stir in garlic and cook until fragrant, 30 seconds. Add in ketchup, brown sugar, chili powder, vinegar, Worcestershire sauce, salt, and pepper and cook for 15 minutes until sticky, stirring occasionally; let cool. Spoon into jars, cover, and refrigerate for up to 5 days.

Speedy White Sauce with Yogurt

Total Time: 15 minutes | **Servings:** 4

Ingredients

1 tbsp olive oil
2 tbsp butter
2 tbsp flour
1 egg yolk
½ cup chicken broth

Salt and black pepper to taste
1 ½ cups yogurt
2 tbsp lemon juice
2 tbsp dill, chopped

Directions

In a bowl, combine yogurt and egg yolk until well mixed; set aside. Set your Instant Pot to Sauté and heat olive oil and butter. Add flour and stir constantly until well combined, 1 minute. Pour in chicken broth and continue stirring until uniform. Season with salt and pepper. Transfer to a bowl and slowly mix in yogurt mixture. Return to the pot and stir until just heated. Spoon into a bowl, drizzle with lemon juice and sprinkle with dill to serve.

Creamy Zucchini Sauce

Total Time: 15 minutes | **Servings:** 4

Ingredients

6 tbsp olive oil
2 zucchinis, sliced into ribbons
3 garlic cloves, minced
2 red chilies, minced
3 tbsp chopped basil

1 cup chicken broth
1 lemon, juiced
½ cup heavy cream
4 tbsp grated Parmesan cheese

Directions

Set your Instant Pot to Sauté, heat olive oil and sauté zucchinis until softened, 3 minutes. Stir in garlic and cook until fragrant, 30 seconds. Mix in chilies, basil, chicken broth, and lemon juice. Seal the lid, select Pressure Cook on High, and set the time to 5 minutes. After cooking, do a quick pressure release and unlock the lid. Using an immersion blender, puree ingredients until smooth. Select Sauté mode and stir in heavy cream and Parmesan cheese until the cheese melts. Spoon sauce into bowls to serve.

Dijon Peppercorn Sauce

Total Time: 15 minutes | **Servings:** 4

Ingredients

3 tbsp black peppercorns, crushed
3 tbsp butter
2 tsp smoked paprika
1 tsp Dijon mustard
1 shallot, minced

½ cup brandy
1 cup beef stock
¼ cup heavy cream
Salt to taste

Directions

Set your Instant Pot to Sauté and toast peppercorns until fragrant, 1 minute. Add butter to melt. Stir in paprika and shallot, and cook for 2-3 minutes. Pour in brandy and beef stock. Seal the lid, and select Pressure Cook on High. Set the cooking time to 5 minutes. After cooking, do a quick release and unlock the lid. Whisk in heavy cream and mustard until well combined and heated through. Adjust taste with salt and spoon into sauce cups.

Sweet & Sour Sauce

Total Time: 15 minutes | **Servings:** 4

Ingredients

1 ½ tbsp olive oil
3 tbsp rice vinegar
1 tbsp light soy sauce
2 tbsp granulated sugar
1 tbsp ketchup
1 small white onion, quartered

1 small carrot, chopped
1 green bell pepper, chopped
1 garlic clove, minced
1 tsp ginger paste
1 cup pineapple chunks
1 cup vegetable broth

Directions

In a bowl, combine rice vinegar, soy sauce, sugar, and ketchup. Set your Instant Pot to Sauté, heat oil and sauté onion, carrot, and bell pepper until softened, 5 minutes. Stir in garlic and ginger for 1 minute. Stir in the vinegar mixture, pineapples, and broth. Seal the lid, select Pressure Cook, and set to 2 minutes. Do a quick pressure release. Serve.

Arrabbiata Sauce

Total Time: 20 minutes | **Servings:** 4

Ingredients

1 red serrano chili pepper, minced
2 tbsp olive oil
2 garlic cloves, minced
1 lb tomatoes, peeled, chopped
1 tbsp tomato paste

1 tbsp zested lemon
A pinch of granulated sugar
1 tbsp balsamic vinegar
1 tsp dried marjoram

Directions

Set your Instant Pot to Sauté, heat oil, and sauté serrano chili and garlic until fragrant, 1 minute. Stir in tomatoes, tomato paste, lemon zest, 1 cup of water, and sugar. Seal the lid, select Pressure Cook on High, and set the time to 3 minutes. After cooking, allow a natural release for 10 minutes. Using an immersion blender, puree ingredients until almost smooth. Stir in balsamic vinegar and marjoram. Spoon sauce into glass jars and keep in the refrigerator for up to 1 week.

Enchilada Sauce

Total Time: 15 minutes | **Servings:** 4

Ingredients

3 tbsp olive oil
3 tbsp all-purpose flour
½ tsp garlic powder
2 tsp chili powder
1 tsp cumin powder

Salt and black pepper to taste
2 tbsp tomato paste
2 cups vegetable broth
1 tsp white vinegar

Directions

Set your Instant Pot to Sauté mode and adjust to medium heat. Heat olive oil in your Instant Pot and mix in all-purpose flour; cook until golden, 1 minute. Add garlic powder, chili powder, cumin powder, salt, and black pepper. Stir and cook until fragrances release, 1 minute. Mix in tomato paste and vegetable broth. Seal the lid, select Pressure Cook on High, and set the time to 1 minute. After cooking, do a quick pressure release and unlock the lid. Stir in white vinegar and turn Instant Pot off. Pour into jars, cover, and cool.

Favorite Black Bean Sauce

Total Time: 45 minutes | **Servings:** 4

Ingredients

1 tsp cornstarch, mixed in 3 tbsp water
2 tbsp coconut oil
4 garlic cloves, minced
2 tbsp ginger paste
2 scallions, chopped
1 ½ cups chicken broth

1 cup black beans, soaked
2 tbsp rice wine
1 tbsp tamarind sauce
1 tsp brown sugar
½ tsp rice vinegar

Directions

Set the pot to Sauté, heat coconut oil, and sauté garlic, scallions, and ginger until fragrant, 2 minutes. Stir in broth, beans, rice wine, tamarind sauce, sugar, and vinegar. Seal the lid, select Pressure Cook on High, and set to 25 minutes.

After cooking, perform natural pressure release for 10 minutes. Unlock the lid, and using an immersion blender, puree until smooth. Press Sauté and stir in the slurry until thickened, 2 minutes. Spoon sauce into a bowl to serve.

Velouté Sauce

Total Time: 15 minutes | **Servings:** 4

Ingredients

2 tbsp unsalted butter
2 tbsp all-purpose flour
1 cup chicken broth, warmed

3 tbsp heavy cream
2 tbsp squeezed lemon juice
Salt and black pepper to taste

Directions

Set your Instant Pot to Sauté, melt butter and whisk in flour. Cook until golden, 1 minute. Stir in chicken stock until smooth; cook further for 2 to 3 minutes. Turn Instant Pot off. Whisk in heavy cream, lemon juice, salt, and pepper.

Basic White Sauce

Total Time: 15 minutes | **Servings:** 6

Ingredients

2 tbsp butter
1 medium onion, chopped
12 garlic cloves, minced
1 bay leaf
1 cup chicken broth
6 black peppercorns

1 cup whole milk
¼ cup white breadcrumbs
2 tbsp heavy cream
A pinch of nutmeg powder
Salt and black pepper to taste

Directions

Combine onion, garlic, bay leaf, chicken broth, and peppercorns in your Instant Pot. Seal the lid, select Pressure Cook on High, and set the time to 3 minutes. After cooking, do a quick pressure release. Unlock the lid and set to Sauté.

Strain mixture through a colander and return warm liquid to the inner pot. Stir in milk and breadcrumbs and continue cooking for 4 to 5 minutes. Whisk in butter, heavy cream, nutmeg, salt, and pepper. Spoon into sauce cups and serve.

Custard Sauce

Total Time: 15 minutes | **Servings:** 4

Ingredients

1 tbsp cornflour
1 cup whole milk
1 egg, cracked into a bowl

2 tbsp granulated sugar
½ tsp vanilla extract

Directions

In a bowl, mix cornflour with 3 tablespoons of milk until smooth. Pour the remaining milk into your Instant Pot. Seal the lid, select Pressure Cook, and set the time to 1 minute. Do a quick pressure release. Blend egg, sugar, and vanilla in a food processor.

Whisk hot milk into cornflour mixture until smoothly combined and pour back into the pot. Cook on Sauté, continuous stirring for 2 minutes. Pour milk mixture into a food processor and blend until mixed. Serve chilled.

Almond Satay Sauce

Total Time: 15 minutes | **Servings**: 4

Ingredients

4 scallions, roughly chopped
2 garlic cloves, minced
2 tsp ginger paste
2 tsp brown sugar
½ cup almond butter
1 tsp fish sauce

2 tbsp soy sauce
1 tsp squeezed lemon juice
1 tbsp Sriracha sauce
Salt to taste
2 tbsp chopped almonds

Directions

In a blender, add scallions, garlic, ginger, brown sugar, almond butter, fish sauce, soy sauce, lemon juice, and Sriracha. Process until smooth. Pour blended ingredients into the inner pot.

Select Sauté, and cook the sauce until thickened, 3-5 minutes. Stir and adjust the taste with salt. Spoon sauce into bowls, garnish with almonds, and serve.

Gorgonzola Sauce

Total Time: 15 minutes | **Servings**: 6

Ingredients

2 cups crumbled Gorgonzola cheese
2 tbsp butter
1 cup heavy cream
2 tbsp dry white wine

2 tsp chopped sage
Salt and white pepper to taste

Directions

Set your Instant Pot to Sauté, melt butter and stir in heavy cream and white wine. Seal the lid, select Pressure Cook on High, and set the cooking time to 1 minute. After cooking, do a quick pressure release.

Select Sauté and keep boiling heavy cream until thickened like a white sauce; occasionally stir. Whisk in Gorgonzola cheese until melted. Stir in sage, salt, and white pepper. Cook further for 1 minute. Spoon into cups to serve.

Teriyaki Sauce

Total Time: 15 minutes | **Servings**: 4

Ingredients

1 cup soy sauce
1 cup pineapple juice
2 tbsp mirin
3 tbsp brown sugar

1 clove garlic, minced
1 tsp ginger paste
Black pepper to taste
2 tsp cornstarch

Directions

In your Instant Pot, mix soy sauce, pineapple juice, mirin, ½ cup of water, brown sugar, garlic, ginger, and black pepper, until well combined. Seal the lid, select Pressure Cook on High, and set the cooking time to 1 minute.

After cooking, perform a quick pressure release to let out steam. Unlock the lid and press Sauté. Stir in cornstarch until dissolved. Cook sauce until thickened, 1 minute. Spoon into jars, cover, and allow cooling.

White Chocolate Fudge Sauce

Total Time: 15 minutes | **Servings**: 4

Ingredients

¼ cup white chocolate, chopped
4 tbsp unsalted butter
2 cups heavy cream

3 tbsp granulated sugar
2 tbsp brandy

Directions

In your Instant Pot, add heavy cream, sugar, butter, and white chocolate. Select Sauté and cook for 4 minutes.

After cooking, do a quick release, and unlock the lid. Whisk brandy into the mixture and pour into a serving jar. Serve.

Citrus-Apple Sauce

Total Time: 10 minutes | **Servings**: 4

Ingredients

1 large orange, zested
1 cup squeezed orange juice
1 cup apple juice

2 cinnamon sticks
2 tbsp honey
½ lemon, juiced

Directions

Place orange zest and juice, apple juice, and cinnamon in your Instant Pot. Seal the lid, select Pressure Cook. Set the time to 4 minutes on High. Do a quick release. Remove and discard cinnamon sticks. Mix in honey and add lemon juice.

French Chocolate Sauce

Total Time: 15 minutes | **Servings**: 4

Ingredients

2 cups heavy cream
¼ cup plain chocolate,

chopped
2 tbsp brandy

Directions

Add heavy cream to your Instant Pot. Select Sauté mode and cook heavy cream until thickened while occasionally stirring, 3-4 minutes. Whisk in chocolate and brandy until chocolate melts. Press Cancel and spoon sauce into cups.

Orange-Cranberry Sauce

Total Time: 25 minutes | **Servings**: 6

Ingredients

2 cups fresh cranberries
1 orange, juiced and zested

½ cup agave syrup

Directions

To your Instant Pot, add all ingredients and 1 cup of water. Seal the lid, select Pressure Cook, and set to 5 minutes.

When ready, do a quick release. Carefully unlock the lid. Transfer the contents to a bowl. Mash the cranberries to make a smoother sauce. Spoon into jars, close, and let cool completely. Store in the refrigerator.

SWEETS & DESSERTS

Holiday White Chocolate Oreo Cake

Total Time: 60 minutes + cooling time | **Servings:** 6

Ingredients

12 Oreo cookies, smoothly crushed
2 tbsp salted butter, melted
16 oz cream cheese, softened
½ cup granulated sugar
2 large eggs, room temperature
1 tbsp plain flour
¼ cup heavy cream
2 tsp vanilla extract
16 whole Oreo cookies, crushed
1 cup whipped cream
2 tbsp chocolate sauce

Directions

Line the bottom of a 7-inch springform pan with foil, grease lightly with cooking spray, and set aside.

In a bowl, combine smoothly crushed Oreo cookies with butter and press into the bottom of the pan. Freeze for 15 minutes. In another bowl, add cream cheese, and beat using a mixer until smooth. Add sugar to whisk further until homogeneous. Beat eggs one by one until mixed. Whisk in flour, heavy cream, and vanilla until well combined.

Fold in 8 coarsely crushed cookies and pour mixture onto crust in the springform pan. Cover pan tightly with foil. Pour 1 ½ cups of water into the inner pot and set to a trivet with slings. Place the pan on the trivet.

Seal the lid, set to Manual/Pressure Cook on High, and set time to 35 minutes. After cooking, allow a natural pressure release for 10 minutes.

Holding slings, remove trivet with cake pan onto a flat surface. Remove foil and transfer to a cooling rack to chill. Refrigerate for 8 hours. Top with whipped cream, remaining cookies, and swirl with chocolate sauce. Slice and serve.

New York-Style Cheesecake

Total Time: 65 minutes + cooling time | **Servings:** 4

Ingredients

2 tbsp melted salted butter
12 graham crackers
1 ½ tbsp brown sugar
16 oz cream cheese, softened
1 cup granulated sugar
1 tsp vanilla extract
2 eggs
½ cup sour cream
2 tbsp cornstarch
2 pinches salt

Directions

Pour graham crackers into a plastic bag and gently break into crumbs by pounding a rolling pin on top. Transfer to a bowl and mix in butter and brown sugar. Pour mixture into a 7-inch springform and use a spoon to press to fit.

Set aside in the refrigerator to harden. In a bowl, using an electric hand mixer, whisk cream cheese and sugar until smooth. Add vanilla, eggs, sour cream, cornstarch, and salt. Remove the cake pan from the refrigerator and pour cream cheese mixture on top. Spread evenly using a spatula and cover the pan with foil.

Pour 1 cup of water into your Instant Pot, fit in a trivet, and place the cake pan on top. Seal the lid, select Manual/Pressure Cook on High, and set time to 40 minutes.

After cooking, allow a natural release for 10 minutes. Unlock the lid and carefully remove the cake pan. Allow cooling for 10 minutes and chill in the refrigerator for 3 hours. Remove from refrigerator; slice and serve.

Chocolate Crème de Pot

Total Time: 30 minutes + chilling time | **Servings:** 6

Ingredients

¼ cup bittersweet chocolate, melted
½ cup whole milk
1 ½ cups heavy cream
5 large egg yolks
¼ cup caster sugar
A pinch of salt
Whipped cream for topping
1 tbsp chocolate sprinkles

Directions

Set your Instant Pot to Sauté, mix in the milk and heavy cream, and let boil. In a bowl, beat egg yolks, sugar, and salt until well combined. Gradually, whisk the egg mixture into the cream until well mixed. Also, mix in melted chocolate; cook until thickened, 2 to 3 minutes. Spoon mixture into 6 custard cups and clean inner pot.

Pour 1 cup of water into your Instant Pot, fit in a trivet with slings, and arrange 3 cups on top. Stand the other cups on the touching rims of the other cups. Seal the lid, set to Pressure Cook on High, and set to 6 minutes.

When done, allow a natural release for 10 minutes. Remove cups onto a flat surface to cool. Chill further in the refrigerator for 6 hours. When ready to serve, remove from the fridge, swirl the top with whipping cream, and decorate with chocolate sprinkles.

French Apricot Cobbler

Total Time: 50 minutes | **Servings:** 4

Ingredients

3 tbsp butter, melted
4 cups sliced apricots
½ cup + ¼ cup brown sugar
2 tbsp + ¾ cup plain flour
½ tsp cinnamon powder
¼ tsp nutmeg powder
1 ½ tsp salt, divided
1 tsp vanilla extract
½ tsp baking powder
½ tsp baking soda

Directions

In a 7-inch heatproof bowl, mix apricots, ½ cup of brown sugar, 2 tbsp of flour, cinnamon, nutmeg, ½ tsp of salt, vanilla, and ¼ cup of water; set aside. In another bowl, mix the remaining flour, salt and brown sugar, baking powder and soda, and butter. Spoon mixture over apricot mixture and spread to cover.

Pour 1 cup of water into your Instant Pot, fit in a trivet, and place heatproof bowl on top. Seal the lid, select Pressure Cook on High, and set to 25 minutes. After cooking, allow a natural release for 10 minutes. Remove bowl and serve.

Holiday Molten Brownie Pudding

Total Time: 45 minutes | **Servings**: 6

Ingredients

7 tbsp butter, melted
1 cup caster sugar
2 eggs, cracked into a bowl
¼ cup plain flour
¼ cup cocoa powder

1 tsp vanilla extract
¼ cup chocolate chips
¼ cup milk chocolate chip
Vanilla ice cream for serving

Directions

Pour 1 cup of water and fit in a trivet with slings. Grease the inner parts of a 7-inch baking dish with 1 tbsp of butter; set aside. In a bowl, using an electric hand mixer, whisk sugar and eggs. In another bowl, combine flour and cocoa powder. Pour into wet ingredients and mix until well combined. Add the remaining butter and vanilla; mix.

Pour mixture into a baking dish and sprinkle the top with the two types of chocolate chips. Place on the trivet. Seal the lid, set to Pressure Cook on High, and set to 30 minutes. After cooking, do a quick pressure release t, and unlock the lid. Carefully take out the baking dish and scoop fudge into dessert cups. Top with vanilla ice cream and serve.

Cointreau Pudding Cake with Dates

Total Time: 50 minutes | **Servings**: 4

Ingredients

3 tbsp unsalted butter, melted
½ tsp baking soda
½ tsp cinnamon powder
¼ tsp cloves powder
¼ tsp allspice
¼ tsp salt
¾ cup plain flour

1 tsp baking powder
6 tbsp hot water
2 tbsp Cointreau orange liqueur
2 tbsp whole milk
1 egg, lightly beaten
½ cup chopped dates
½ cup salted caramel sauce

Directions

In a bowl, combine baking soda, cinnamon, cloves, allspice, salt, flour, and baking powder. In another bowl, mix hot water, Cointreau, butter, and milk. Pour into dry ingredients and mix until well mixed. Whisk in egg and fold in dates.

Lightly grease 4 medium ramekins with cooking spray, divide mixture among them, and cover with foil. Pour 1 cup of water into your Instant Pot, fit in a trivet with slings, and place ramekins on top. Seal the lid, select Pressure Cook on High, and set the time to 25 minutes. After cooking, perform a natural pressure release for 10 minutes. Unlock the lid and carefully remove ramekins, invert onto dessert plates, and drizzle caramel sauce on top.

Chocolate Pudding in a Jar

Total Time: 30 minutes + chilling time | **Servings**: 4

Ingredients

1 tbsp coconut oil
3 ¼ cups whole milk
¼ cup maple syrup
1 ½ tbsp vanilla extract

3 medium eggs, cracked
4 tbsp cocoa powder
1 ¼ tsp gelatin
¼ cup collagen

Directions

In a blender, add milk, maple syrup, vanilla, coconut oil, eggs, and cocoa powder. Process until smoothly combined. Add gelatin and collagen; blend again until smooth. Pour mixture into 4 large mason jars and cover. Pour 1 cup of water into your Instant Pot, fit in a trivet, and stand mason jars on top.

Seal the lid, select Manual/Pressure Cook on High, and set the time to 5 minutes. After cooking, allow a natural release for 10 minutes, and unlock the lid. Carefully remove jars and allow cooling. Refrigerate overnight and serve.

Sunday Raspberry Cheesecake

Total Time: 70 minutes + cooling time | **Servings**: 4

Ingredients

12 large raspberries + more for garnishing
2 tbsp melted butter
12 graham crackers
16 oz cream cheese, softened
1 cup granulated sugar
1 tsp vanilla extract

3 tbsp maple syrup
2 eggs
2 tsp cinnamon powder
½ cup heavy cream

Directions

Pour graham crackers into a plastic bag and gently break into crumbs by pounding with a rolling pin. Transfer biscuit to a bowl and mix in butter. Pour mixture into a 7-inch springform pan and press to fit with a spoon. Refrigerate.

In a bowl, whisk cream cheese and sugar until smooth. Add vanilla, raspberries, maple syrup, eggs, cinnamon, and heavy cream and mix until well combined. Remove the cake pan from the refrigerator and pour cream cheese mixture on top. Spread and cover the pan with foil. Pour 1 cup of water into the pot, fit in a trivet, and place cake pan on top.

Seal the lid, select Manual/Pressure Cook on High, and set to 40 minutes. After cooking, allow a natural pressure release for 10 minutes, and then a quick pressure release. Unlock the lid and carefully remove the pan. Allow cooling for 10 minutes and chill in the fridge for 3 hours. Release cake pan, garnish with 3 to 4 raspberries, slice, and serve.

Almond Sugar Cookie Fudge

Total Time: 15 minutes + chilling time | **Servings**: 6

Ingredients

2 tbsp butter
1 ½ cups white chocolate chips
2 cups condensed milk

1 ¼ cups sugar cookie mix
1 tsp almond extract

Directions

Set Instant Pot to Sauté mode. Put in white chocolate chips, condensed milk, almond extract, sugar cookie mix, and butter. Melt chocolate fully while continuously stirring, 10 minutes. Pour mixture into the cake pan and refrigerate for 2 hours. Remove and release pan after. Slice fudge into squares and serve.

Cinnamon Apple Crisps

Total Time: 25 minutes | **Servings:** 4

Ingredients

4 tbsp unsalted butter, melted
5 Granny Smith apples, chopped
½ tsp nutmeg powder — ¼ cup plain flour
2 tsp cinnamon powder — ½ tsp salt
1 tbsp honey — ¼ cup brown sugar
1 cup water — 1 cup vanilla ice cream
¾ cup old fashioned rolled oats

Directions

In your Instant Pot, mix apples, nutmeg, cinnamon, honey, and water. In a medium bowl, combine butter, rolled oats, flour, salt, and brown sugar. Drop tablespoons of the mixture all over the apples. Seal the lid, set to Manual/Pressure Cook on High, and cook for 5 minutes. After cooking, allow a natural pressure release for 10 minutes. Spoon dessert into serving bowls, top with vanilla ice cream, and serve immediately.

Caramel Corns

Total Time: 15 minutes | **Servings:** 4

Ingredients

4 tbsp butter — 3 tbsp brown sugar
1 cup sweet corn kernels — ¼ cup whole milk

Directions

Set your Instant Pot to Sauté, melt butter, and mix in corn kernels. Once heated and popping, cover the top with a clear instant pot safe lid, and continue cooking until corn stops popping for 3 minutes.

Open the lid and transfer popcorns to a bowl. Press Cancel and wipe the inner pot clean. Select Sauté. Combine in brown sugar and milk and cook with frequent stirring until sugar dissolves and sauce coats the back of the spoon, 3-4 minutes. Turn Instant Pot off. Drizzle caramel sauce all over corns and toss to coat thoroughly. Cool and serve.

Monkey Bread with Pecans

Total Time: 50 minutes + overnight rising | **Servings:** 6

Ingredients

½ cup butter, melted
16 frozen unbaked dinner rolls, thawed
¼ cup light brown sugar — ½ cup powdered sugar
1 ½ cinnamon powder — 2 tsp whole milk
¼ cup toasted pecans, chopped

Directions

Grease a bundt pan with cooking spray and set aside. Divide each dinner roll into half. Set aside. In a shallow bowl, mix sugar, cinnamon, and pecans. Coat bread rolls in sugar mixture, in butter, and then place in the bundt pan, making sure to build layers. Cover the pan with foil and allow rising overnight on the counter.

The next morning, pour 1 cup of water into your Instant Pot, fit in a trivet, and place bundt pan on top. Seal the lid, select Pressure Cook on High, and set time to 25 minutes. After cooking, allow a natural release for 10 minutes.

Unlock the lid, remove the pan, take off the foil, and allow complete cooling. In a bowl, whisk sugar with milk until smooth. Invert bread onto a serving platter and drizzle with the sugar glaze. Slice and serve.

Effortless Soda Cake

Total Time: 40 minutes + cooling time | **Servings:** 6

Ingredients

1 ½ cups orange soda — 1 tbsp caster sugar for decorating
1 (15.25 oz) box orange cake mix

Directions

Lightly grease a bundt pan with cooking spray and set aside. In a bowl, mix orange soda and orange cake mix until well combined. Pour into the bundt pan, cover with a paper towel, and then with a foil.

Pour 1 cup of water into your Instant Pot, fit in a trivet, and place the pan on top. Seal the lid, select Manual/Pressure Cook on High, and set time to 30 minutes. After cooking, do a quick pressure release. Remove pan, take off the foil and paper towel, and allow cooling. Turn over onto a platter, decorate with caster sugar, slice, and serve.

Nutty Yogurt Pudding

Total Time: 40 minutes | **Servings:** 4

Ingredients

2 cups condensed milk — 1 tsp cardamom powder
1 ½ cups Greek yogurt — ¼ cup mixed nuts, chopped
1 tsp cocoa powder

Directions

Lightly grease 4 medium ramekins with cooking spray. Set aside. In a bowl, combine condensed milk, Greek yogurt, cocoa powder, and cardamom powder. Pour mixture into ramekins and cover with foil.

Pour 1 cup of water into the pot, fit in a trivet, and place ramekins on top. Seal the lid, select Manual/Pressure Cook on High, and set time to 15 minutes. After cooking, perform a natural pressure release for 15 minutes. Unlock the lid, remove ramekins, take off the foil, and cool slightly. Top with nuts and serve immediately.

Country Berry Pudding

Total Time: 35 minutes + chilling time | **Servings:** 4

Ingredients

1 ½ cups strawberries and raspberries, mashed
1 tsp melted butter — A pinch of salt
3 tbsp butter, softened — 1 cup milk
½ cup caster sugar — 1 lemon, zested and juiced
½ cup plain flour — 2 eggs, beaten

Directions

Grease 4 medium ramekins with melted butter and set aside. Put softened butter in a medium bowl and whisk with an electric hand mixer until creamy. Add sugar, flour, salt, and continue whisking until smooth. Beat in milk, lemon zest, and lemon juice until well-combined. While still whisking, add eggs gradually until smoothly mixed.

Fold in berries, divide the mixture into ramekins, and cover with foil. Pour 1 cup of water into your Instant Pot, fit in a trivet, and place ramekins on top.

Seal the lid, select Pressure Cook on High and set to 20 minutes. After cooking, do a quick pressure release, and unlock the lid. Carefully remove ramekins, let cool, and refrigerate for 4 hours. Serve.

Pineapple Upside Down Yellow Cake

Total Time: 50 minutes | **Servings:** 4

Ingredients

2 tbsp butter, melted
1 (18.5-oz) box yellow cake mix

¼ cup brown sugar
1 cup pineapple slices

Directions

In a medium bowl, prepare cake mix according to instruction on the box. Set aside. Grease a 7-inch springform pan with butter, sprinkle brown sugar at the bottom of the pan and arrange pineapple slices on top.

Pour cake batter all over and cover the pan with foil. Pour 1 cup of water into your Instant Pot, fit in a trivet, and place cake pan on top. Seal the lid, select Pressure Cook on High, and set to 18 minutes. After cooking, allow a natural release for 10 minutes. Carefully remove the cake pan, take off the foil and let cool for 10 minutes. Turn the cake over onto a plate, slice, and serve.

Jamaican Coconut Pudding

Total Time: 20 minutes + cooling time | **Servings:** 4

Ingredients

¼ cup granulated sugar
2 egg yolks
2 cups coconut milk
2 tbsp coconut cream
2 tbsp flour

1 tbsp cornstarch
Pinch of salt
1 tsp vanilla extract
½ cup coconut flakes, toasted

Directions

Set your Instant Pot to Sauté and warm coconut milk and coconut cream for 2 minutes; set aside. In a bowl, beat egg yolks with sugar and add flour, cornstarch, and salt and whisk until smooth. Put 1 tbsp of the coconut milk mixture into the egg mixture and whisk again. Pour mixture into the pot. Mix in vanilla extract.

Seal the lid, select Pressure Cook on High, and set the time to 2 minutes. After cooking, do a quick pressure release and unlock the lid. Stir and spoon pudding into dessert bowls. Allow complete cooling and chill in the refrigerator for at least 1 hour. To serve, top pudding with coconut flakes.

Mom's Lemon Pudding

Total Time: 15 minutes + chilling time | **Servings:** 4

Ingredients

1 tbsp butter, melted
2 lemons, zested
¼ cup lemon juice
2 ½ cups whole milk
¼ cup cornstarch

¼ tsp salt
1 cup granulated sugar
2 eggs
2 egg yolks

Directions

In a pot, combine milk, lemon zest, cornstarch, salt, and sugar. Place over medium heat on a stovetop until boiling, 2 minutes. Turn off the heat.

In a medium bowl, beat eggs and egg yolks. Slowly whisk in milk mixture until well combined. Mix in butter and then lemon juice. Pour mixture into 4 medium ramekins and cover with foil.

Pour 1 cup of water into your Instant Pot, fit in a trivet, and place ramekins on top. Seal the lid, select Pressure Cook on High, and set the cooking time to 5 minutes.

After cooking, perform a quick pressure release. Unlock the lid, remove ramekin onto a flat surface, take off the foil, and allow complete cooling. Chill in the refrigerator before serving.

Yummy Caramel Cheesecake

Total Time: 70 minutes + cooling time | **Servings:** 4

Ingredients

¼ cup butter, melted
2 cups graham crackers
3 tbsp brown sugar
2 (8 oz) cream cheese, softened
½ cup granulated sugar

2 tbsp plain flour
1 tsp vanilla extract
3 eggs
1 cup caramel sauce

Directions

Pour graham crackers into a plastic bag and crush biscuits with a rolling pin. Pour into a bowl and mix in brown sugar and butter. Spread mixture at the bottom of a 7-inch springform pan and use a spoon to press to fit. Freeze in the refrigerator for 10 minutes.

In a bowl, using an electric hand mixer, whisk cream cheese and sugar until smooth. While mixing, add flour gradually and vanilla until well combined. Beat in eggs on low speed until blended. Remove pan from oven and pour mixture over crust; cover the pan with foil.

Pour 1 cup of water into your Instant Pot, fit in a trivet, and place the cake pan on top. Seal the lid, select Manual/Pressure Cook on High, and set to 40 minutes.

After cooking, allow a natural release for 10 minutes. Carefully remove the pan, and take off the foil. Let cool for 10 minutes, pour caramel sauce all over the cake, and refrigerate for 3 hours. Remove and release cake pan. Slice the cheesecake and serve.

Blackberry Yogurt Jars

Total Time: 8 hrs 20 min + cooling time | **Servings:** 4

Ingredients

8 cups whole milk

½ cup plain yogurt

2 tbsp vanilla bean paste

1 cup blackberries

Directions

Pour milk into your Instant Pot. Seal the lid, select Yogurt, and press Adjust until the display shows "Boil." When done, press Cancel and unlock the lid. Stir the milk, remove the pot, and allow cooling up to 100°F. Check the temperature with a food thermometer.

Whisk in yogurt and vanilla bean paste. Return the inner pot to Instant Pot. Seal the lid, select Yogurt mode, and set the cooking time to 8 hours. After cooking, the display will show "Yogt." Refrigerate the yogurt for a few hours.

Mash the blackberries in a bowl using a fork. Divide them between mason jars and top with yogurt. Serve.

Homemade Apricot Yogurt

Total Time: 8 hours 20 minutes + cooling time | **Servings:** 4

Ingredients

4 cups whole milk

2 packets yogurt starter

4 tsp apricot spread

Directions

Set your Instant Pot to Sauté, pour in the milk, and bring to a boil. Remove to a heat-proof bowl and cool until a thermometer has reached a temperature of 110°F. Clean the inner pot.

In a bowl, pour 1 cup of cooled milk and mix in yogurt starter. Return to the pot and add in the remaining cooled milk; stir to combine. Seal the lid, select Yogurt, and cook for 8 hours. When done, do a quick pressure release. Unlock the lid and gently stir the yogurt. Divide the apricot spread between jars, top with yogurt, and let sit for 6 hours to thicken. Chill in the fridge and serve.

Key Lime Pie

Total Time: 75 minutes + cooling time | **Servings:** 4

Ingredients

4 tbsp unsalted butter, melted

1 cup graham crackers

3 large egg yolks

2 tbsp granulated sugar

9 key limes, juiced

1 tbsp zested key lime

1 (14 oz) can condensed milk

Topping

½ cup heavy cream

¼ cup granulated sugar

1 tsp zested key lime

Directions

Pour graham crackers into a plastic bag and gently crush using a rolling pin. Pour the biscuit into a bowl and mix in butter. Pour mixture into a greased springform and use a spoon to press to fit. Freeze in the refrigerator to compact.

Using an electric hand mixer, whisk egg yolks and sugar in a large bowl until the yolk is pale yellow and thickened. While mixing, add lime juice, lime zest, and condensed milk.

Remove the cake pan from the refrigerator and pour in the lime juice mixture. Cover with foil. Pour 1 cup of water into your Instant Pot, fit in a trivet, and place pan on top.

Seal the lid, select Manual/Pressure Cook on High, and set time to 40 minutes. After cooking, allow a natural release for 10 minutes. Unlock the lid and carefully remove the cake pan. Allow cooling for 10 minutes.

Whisk heavy cream in a bowl while slowly adding sugar until stiff. Spoon mixture into a piping bag and press decorative mounds on the cake. Sprinkle with lime zest and chill cake in the refrigerator for 3 hours. Slice and serve.

Coconut Rice Dessert Cups

Total Time: 35 minutes | **Servings:** 6

Ingredients

1 cup rice

2 cups milk

1 cup water

1 tsp vanilla extract

¼ tsp ground cinnamon

A pinch of salt

¼ cup sugar

1 cup coconut flakes

Directions

Place the rice, milk, water, sugar, and salt into your Instant Pot and stir to combine. Seal the lid, select Pressure Cook, and set time to 12 minutes on High.

When done, perform a natural pressure release for 10 minutes; remove the lid. Stir in the vanilla extract and cinnamon to blend. Spoon the dessert into cups and top with the coconut flakes. Serve chilled.

Easy Toffee Dessert

Total Time: 45 minutes | **Servings:** 4

Ingredients

¼ cup butter

¼ cup granulated sugar

1 tbsp cocoa powder

½ tsp ginger powder

2 medium eggs

1 cup self-rising flour

2 tbsp whole milk

½ cup caramel sauce

Directions

In a medium bowl, cream butter and sugar until light and fluffy. Mix in cocoa powder and ginger powder until well combined. Beat in eggs, while adding flour a little at a time, until properly mixed and then whisk in milk.

Pour half of the mixture into a large ramekin bowl, top with caramel sauce, and cover with remaining batter. Cover bowl with foil. Pour 1 cup of water into your Instant Pot, fit in a trivet, and place the bowl on top.

Seal the lid, select Pressure Cook on High, and set to 15 minutes. After cooking, allow a natural release for 10 minutes. Unlock the lid, carefully remove the bowl, and take off the foil. Allow to sit for 5 minutes before serving.

Strawberry Pancake Bites

Total Time: 30 minutes | **Servings:** 4

Ingredients

¼ cup olive oil
1 cup pancake mix
¾ cup water
2 large eggs
½ cup strawberries, chopped

Directions

In a medium bowl, combine pancake mix, water, eggs, strawberries, and olive oil. Spoon mixture into 4 large silicone muffin cups and cover with foil.

Pour 1 cup of water into your Instant Pot, fit in a trivet, and place muffin cups on top. Seal the lid, select Pressure Cook, and set to 10 minutes on High. After cooking, allow a natural release for 10 minutes. Unlock the lid, carefully remove cups, and take off the foil. Empty pancake bites onto plates and serve.

White Chocolate Blueberry Minis

Total Time: 60 minutes + cooling time | **Servings:** 4

Ingredients

4 tbsp butter, melted
2 cups graham crackers
2 (8 oz) cream cheese, softened
½ cup caster sugar
½ tsp vanilla extract
1 tbsp honey
1 egg
¼ cup grated white chocolate
½ cup blueberries, mashed
10 blueberries for garnish
2 tbsp heavy cream

Directions

Crush graham crackers in a plastic bag using a rolling pin and transfer to a bowl. Mix in butter and pour the mixture into 4 greased ramekins. Press with a spoon fit and freeze crust in the refrigerator.

Meanwhile, in a bowl, whisk cream cheese and sugar until smooth. While mixing, add vanilla, honey, and egg until well blended. Mix in chocolate, blueberries, and heavy cream.

Remove ramekins from the fridge and pour in filling; cover ramekins with foil. Pour 1 cup of water into your Instant Pot, fit in a trivet, and place the cake pan on top.

Seal the lid, select Manual/Pressure Cook on High, and set the time to 25 minutes. After cooking, perform a natural pressure release for 10 minutes. Unlock the lid, carefully remove ramekins, and take off the foil. Allow cooling for 10 minutes, and then chill the cake in the refrigerator for 2 hours. When ready to serve, garnish with blueberries.

Original Crema Catalana

Total Time: 40 minutes + chilling time | **Servings:** 2

Ingredients

2 egg yolks, room temperature
3 tsp sugar
1 cup milk
1 cinnamon stick
1 strip lemon peel
½ tbsp cornstarch
1 tbsp superfine sugar for topping
1 cup water

Directions

Warm the milk, cinnamon, and lemon peel in your Instant Pot on Sauté. When everything is heated, remove to a bowl and allow to infuse, about 30 minutes. Then, remove the cinnamon and lemon peel.

In a bowl, beat the eggs with the sugar and cornstarch until the sugar dissolves. Slowly add the egg mixture into the milk and gently stir until everything is well mixed. Divide the mixture between ramekins and cover with foil.

Pour water into your Instant Pot and fit in a trivet. Place the ramekins on the trivet. Seal the lid, select Steam, and set the cooking time to 20 minutes.

When done, do a natural release for 10 minutes. Remove the foil. Let cool for 30 minutes, then refrigerate for 30 minutes. Sprinkle sugar on top of the ramekins and place under the broiler until sugar is caramelized. Serve.

Awesome Nutella Cakes

Total Time: 35 minutes | **Servings:** 6

Ingredients

1 cup Nutella
2 large eggs
¼ cup plain flour
14 blueberries + for serving

Directions

In a medium bowl, whisk Nutella and eggs until smoothly combined. Add flour and mix well. Grease 6 holes of a silicone egg bite tray with cooking spray and fill halfway with Nutella mixture. Drop two blueberries into each hole and cover with the remaining Nutella mixture.

Wrap muffin tray with foil. Pour 1 cup of water into your Instant Pot, fit in a trivet, and place egg bite tray on top. Seal the lid, select Manual/Pressure Cook on High, and set to 18 minutes. After cooking, do a quick pressure release, and unlock the lid. Carefully remove the tray, take off the foil, allow cooling for 10 minutes, and pop out dessert bites. Serve immediately or chill for later use.

Vanilla Tapioca Pudding

Total Time: 55 minutes + chilling time | **Servings:** 4

Ingredients

1 cup tapioca pearls
3 cups whole milk
¼ tsp salt
2 eggs
½ cup granulated sugar
1 tsp vanilla extract

Directions

In your Instant Pot, add tapioca, milk, and salt. Seal the lid, select Pressure Cook on High, and set the cooking time to 15 minutes. After cooking, perform a natural pressure release for 20 minutes. Unlock the lid and select Sauté.

Beat eggs in a bowl and mix in 2 tbsp of tapioca liquid until well combined. Pour mixture into tapioca along with sugar and vanilla. Mix until adequately combined. Cook in the pot for 10 minutes. Dish tapioca into dessert bowls, leave it cool, and chill for 1 hour. Serve after.

Morning Banana Pudding

Total Time: 20 minutes + chilling time | **Servings:** 4

Ingredients

2 tbsp cold butter, cut into 4 pieces
1 cup whole milk
2 cups half-and-half
¾ cup + 1 tbsp sugar
4 egg yolks
3 tbsp cornstarch
1 tsp vanilla extract
2 medium banana, sliced
1 cup heavy cream

Directions

Set your Instant Pot to Sauté. Mix in milk, half-and-half, and ½ cup of sugar. Heat while occasionally stirring until sugar dissolves, 3 minutes.

Beat egg yolks in a bowl and add ¼ cup of sugar. Whisk until combined. Add cornstarch and mix well. Scoop ½ cup of the milk mixture into the egg mix and whisk again until smooth. Pour mixture into the inner pot. Seal the lid, select Pressure Cook on High, and cook for 2 minutes.

After cooking, do a quick release and unlock the lid. Press Cancel and stir in butter and vanilla until butter melts. Lay banana pieces into 4 dessert cups and top with pudding.

In a bowl, whisk heavy cream with remaining sugar; spoon mixture on top of the pudding. Refrigerate for 1 hour.

Old-Fashioned Chocolate Fudge

Total Time: 50 minutes + cooling time | **Servings:** 4

Ingredients

¼ cup olive oil
1 (16 oz) box brownie mix
2 eggs
1 ½ cups chocolate chips
¼ cup chocolate syrup
3 tbsp whole milk
5 tbsp heavy cream
4 tbsp sprinkles

Directions

In a bowl, combine brownie mix, olive oil, eggs, ½ cup of chocolate chips, syrup, and milk.

Lightly grease a silicone egg bite tray with cooking spray and fill with chocolate mixture 2/3 way up. Cover muffin tray loosely with foil.

Pour 1 cup of water into your Instant Pot, fit in a trivet, and place egg bite tray on top. Seal the lid, select Pressure Cook on High, and set the time to 20 minutes.

After cooking, allow a natural release for 10 minutes; unlock the lid. Remove the tray, take off the foil, allow cooling for 5 minutes, and pop out dessert bites.

While dessert cools, empty and clean the pot, and select Sauté. Add remaining chocolate chips and heavy cream to inner pot and cook with continuous stirring until chocolate chips melt and well mixed with heavy cream, 5 minutes.

Pour mixture into a bowl and roll in dessert bites until well coated. Drizzle sprinkles on top and cool in the refrigerator for 20 to 30 minutes.

Serve and enjoy!

White Chocolate-Milk Faux Muffins

Total Time: 15 minutes | **Servings:** 4

Ingredients

1 (36 oz) white chocolate chip, melted
½ cup whole milk

Directions

In a medium bowl, mix white chocolate with milk until well combined. Lightly grease a silicone egg bite tray with cooking spray and fill with chocolate mixture two-thirds way up. Cover egg tray loosely with foil.

Pour 1 cup of water into your Instant Pot, fit in a trivet, and place egg bite tray on top. Seal the lid, select Manual/Pressure Cook on High, and set time to 12 minutes. After cooking, perform a quick pressure release to let out steam, and unlock the lid. Carefully remove the tray, take off the foil, allow cooling for 5 minutes, and pop out dessert bites.

Maple-Orange French Toast

Total time: 40 minutes | **Servings:** 4

Ingredients

6 bread slices, cubed
2 large eggs
1 cup milk
2 tsp vanilla extract
1 tsp ground cinnamon
Zest from 1 orange
1 cup water
Maple syrup for topping

Directions

Beat the eggs with the milk, vanilla extract, cinnamon, and orange zest in a mixing bowl. Add in the bread cubes and mix to coat. Pour this mixture into a previously greased pan and cover with aluminium foil. Pour the water into your Instant Pot and fit in a trivet. Place the covered pan on top.

Seal the lid, select Pressure Cook on High, and set to 15 minutes. After cooking, allow a natural release for 5 minutes. Unlock the lid, remove the pan, and take off the foil; let cool for 5 minutes. Drizzle with maple syrup to serve.

Spanish Churro Bites

Total Time: 30 minutes | **Servings:** 4

Ingredients

1 (21 oz) box cinnamon swirl crumb cake & muffin mix
1 brown sugar packet (included in cake mix box)
1 tsp cinnamon powder
2 eggs
1 cup heavy cream
4 tbsp brown sugar
1 tbsp granulated sugar

Directions

In a medium bowl, whisk muffin mix, brown sugar mix, ½ teaspoon of cinnamon powder, eggs, and heavy cream until smoothly combined. Lightly grease a silicone egg bite tray with cooking spray and fill with cinnamon mixture two-thirds way up. Cover muffin tray with foil.

Pour 1 cup of water into your Instant Pot, fit in a trivet, and place egg bite tray on top. Seal the lid, select Pressure Cook on High, and set the cooking time to 12 minutes.

After cooking, perform a quick pressure release to let out steam, and unlock the lid. Carefully remove the tray, take off the foil, allow cooling for 5 minutes, and pop out dessert bites.

Pour brown sugar onto a plate and lightly roll in warm churro bites. On another plate, mix the remaining cinnamon powder with granulated sugar and roll in churro bites a second time. Serve.

Mini Biscuit Cheesecakes

Total Time: 50 minutes | **Servings:** 12

Ingredients

8 oz cream cheese, softened
¼ cup granulated sugar
2 tbsp sour cream
¼ tsp vanilla extract
1 egg
7 Oreo cookies, broken

Directions

In a bowl, whisk cream cheese, sugar, sour cream, and vanilla until smooth. Pour in eggs and beat until well combined. Fold in Oreo biscuits.

Lightly grease a 12-holed silicone egg bite tray with cooking spray and fill with Oreo mixture. Cover tray with foil. Pour 1 cup of water into your Instant Pot, fit in a trivet, and place egg bite tray on top.

Seal the lid, select Pressure Cook on High, and set the time to 20 minutes. After cooking, perform a natural pressure release for 10 minutes, then a quick pressure release to let out the remaining steam. Unlock the lid. Remove the tray, take off the foil, allow cooling for 10 minutes, and pop out cake bites. Serve immediately or chill for later use.

Cinnamon Plum Clafoutis

Total Time: 30 minutes | **Servings:** 4

Ingredients

2 tsp butter, softened
1 cup plums, chopped
1 cup whole milk
¼ cup half and half
¼ cup sugar
½ cup flour
2 large eggs
¼ tsp cinnamon
½ tsp vanilla extract
2 tbsp confectioners' sugar
1 cup water

Directions

Grease 4 ramekins with butter and divide the plums among them; set aside. Pour milk, half and half, sugar, flour, eggs, cinnamon, and vanilla in a bowl. Use a hand mixer to whisk the ingredients until the batter is smooth, 2 minutes.

Pour the mixture over the plums two-thirds way up. Pour water into the pot. Fit in a trivet and put the ramekins on top. Lay a square of foil on the ramekins but don't crimp. Seal the lid, select Pressure Cook on High, and set to 11 minutes.

When ready, do a quick pressure release and unlock the lid. Use tongs to remove the foil. Remove the ramekins onto a flat surface. Cool for 5 minutes, and then dust with the confectioners' sugar. Serve warm.

Mascarpone Cake with Berries

Total time: 65 minutes | **Servings:** 8

Ingredients

1 cup butter, soften
1 large egg
16 oz mascarpone cheese
2 cups flour
2 tsp baking soda
1 tsp salt
¾ cup sugar
¾ cup milk
3 cups fresh berries

Directions

In a bowl, mix the mascarpone cheese, flour, baking soda, and salt. In a separate bowl, beat the butter, sugar, and egg using an electric mixer until creamy. Add to the flour mixture, and stir in the milk and berries.

Pour into a greased baking pan and cover with foil. Pour 1 cup water in your Instant Pot and fit in a trivet with slings.

Place the pan on the trivet. Seal the lid, select Manual/Pressure Cook on High, and set time to 35 minutes.

When done cooking, perform natural pressure release for 10 minutes, then a quick pressure release to let out the remaining steam. Remove the aluminium foil and let cool for 10 minutes before slicing and serving.

Decadent Strawberry French Toast

Total Time: 40 minutes | **Servings:** 4

Ingredients

2 tbsp firm butter, sliced
3 eggs
¼ cup milk
1 tbsp sugar
1 tsp vanilla extract
1 tsp cinnamon powder
6 slices brioche, cubed
3 strawberries, sliced, divided
2 tbsp brown sugar, divided
¼ cup ricotta cheese
¼ cup chopped almonds
2 tbsp maple syrup

Directions

Put the eggs into a bowl and whisk with the milk, sugar, vanilla, and cinnamon; set aside. Grease a baking dish with cooking spray.

Spread half of the brioche cubes in a single layer on the dish. Lay half of the strawberry slices on the bread and dust with 1 tablespoon of brown sugar. Spoon and sprinkle the ricotta cheese on top of the strawberries.

Make another layer of bread, strawberries, sugar, and ricotta cheese. Pour the egg mixture all over the layered ingredients, ensuring to give the bread a good coat.

Pour 1 cup of water into the pot and fit a trivet. Fix the pan on top. Seal the lid, select Pressure Cook on High, and time to 20 minutes.

Once ready, perform a quick pressure release, and unlock the lid. Top the toast with the sliced butter, almonds, and maple syrup, and serve.

Baileys Hot Chocolate

Total Time: 20 minutes | Servings: 4

Ingredients

4 oz dark chocolate bar, chopped
2 cups whole milk
½ cup heavy cream
1 tbsp sugar
1 tbsp cocoa powder

4 tbsp Baileys
A pinch of salt
Mini marshmallows, to serve

Directions

Set your Instant Pot to Sauté and place in all the ingredients, except for the Baileys and marshmallows. Stir to combine. Bring to a boil for 10 minutes. Stir in Baileys and spoon into cups. Serve topped with some mini marshmallows.

Vanilla Liqueur Banana Bread

Total time: 70 minutes | Servings: 4

Ingredients

6 tbsp butter, melted
4 bananas, mashed
2 small eggs, beaten
1 tbsp vanilla-flavored liqueur

½ cup sugar
1 tsp baking powder
2 cups flour
1 cup water

Directions

Grease a cake pan with cooking spray and set aside. In a bowl, combine the butter, eggs, mashed bananas, and vanilla-flavored liqueur. Whisk in the sugar, baking powder, and flour until combined. Pour the mixture into the pan and cover with aluminium foil. Pour water into your Instant Pot and fit in a trivet. Place the pan on top.

Seal the lid, select Manual/Pressure Cook on High, and set time to 50 minutes. When done cooking, perform a natural pressure release for 5 minutes. Remove the bread from the pan and let cool. Cut into slices and serve.

Raspberry Crumble

Total Time: 40 minutes | Servings: 6

Ingredients

¼ cup cold butter, sliced
2 cups raspberries
2 tbsp arrowroot starch
1 tsp lemon juice
5 tbsp sugar

½ cup flour
¼ cup brown sugar
½ cup rolled oats
1 tsp cinnamon powder

Directions

In a small bowl, combine the arrowroot starch, 1 tbsp of water, lemon juice, and 3 tbsp of sugar. Mix in the raspberries, and toss well. Pour the mixture into a baking pan. In a separate bowl, mix the flour, brown sugar, oats, butter, cinnamon, and remaining sugar, and form crumble. Spread the crumble evenly on the raspberries.

Put a trivet in the pot. Cover the pan with foil and pour a cup of water into the pot. Put the pan on top. Seal the lid, select Pressure Cook on High, and set time to 20 minutes. When ready, do a quick release. Remove foil and serve.

Blueberry & Walnut Oatmeal Porridge

Total time: 25 minutes | Servings: 4

Ingredients

1 cup steel-cut oats
Salt to taste
½ tsp ground nutmeg

3 ½ cups water
1 cup blueberries
1 cup walnuts, chopped

Directions

Pour oats, nutmeg, and water into your Instant Pot and stir until well mixed. Seal the lid, select Manual/Pressure Cook on High, and set the cooking time to 10 minutes.

After cooking, perform a natural pressure release for 10 minutes. Unlock the lid, stir, and spoon oatmeal into serving bowls. Top with blueberries and walnuts and serve.

Wheat Flour Cinnamon Balls

Total Time: 40 minutes | Servings: 8

Ingredients

2 tbsp cold butter, cubed
¼ cup whole-wheat flour
½ cup all-purpose flour
½ tsp baking powder

3 tbsp sugar, divided
¼ tsp + ½ tbsp cinnamon
¼ tsp sea salt
1/3 cup whole milk

Directions

Mix the whole-wheat flour, all-purpose flour, baking powder, 1 tbsp of sugar, ¼ tsp of cinnamon, and salt in a medium bowl. Add the butter and use a pastry cutter to cut into butter, breaking it into little pieces until resembling cornmeal. Pour in the milk and mix until the dough forms into a ball.

Knead the dough on a flat surface. Divide the dough into 8 pieces and roll each piece into a ball. Put the balls in a greased baking pan with space in between each ball and oil the balls. Pour 1 cup of water into the inner pot.

Put in a trivet and place the pan on top. Seal the lid, select Pressure Cook on High, and set the time to 20 minutes. After cooking, perform a natural pressure release for 5 minutes.

In a mixing bowl, combine the remaining sugar and cinnamon. Toss the dough balls in the cinnamon and sugar mixture to serve.

Coconut Salted Caramel Cup

Total Time: 15 minutes | Servings: 1

Ingredients

25 soft caramels, unwrapped
¼ cup coconut milk

¼ cup mini marshmallows

Directions

Set your Instant Pot to Sauté and cook caramels, coconut milk, and marshmallows for 3-5 minutes until caramels and marshmallows melt, stirring often. Remove into a jar and leave to cool. Serve with strawberries or chocolate.

German-Style Apple Hand Pies

Total Time: 65 minutes | **Servings:** 8

Ingredients

1 (2-crust) box refrigerated pie crusts
2 apples, chopped
3 tbsp sugar
1 lemon, juiced
1 tsp vanilla extract
1 tsp cornstarch

Directions

In a mixing bowl, combine the apples, sugar, lemon juice, and vanilla. Allow the mixture to stand for 10 minutes, then drain and reserve 1 tbsp of the liquid. In another bowl, whisk the cornstarch into the reserved liquid and mix with the apple mixture. Put the piecrusts on a lightly floured surface and cut into 8 circles. Spoon a tbsp of apple mixture in the center of the circle. Brush the edges with some water and fold the dough over the filling.

Press the edges with a fork to seal. Cut 3 small slits on top of each pie and grease with cooking spray. Arrange the cakes in a single layer in a greased baking pan. Pour 1 cup of water into the inner pot. Fit in a trivet, and place the pan on top. Seal the lid, select Manual/Pressure Cook on High, and set the cooking time to 30 minutes. After cooking, perform a natural pressure release for 10 minutes, then a quick pressure release, and unlock the lid. Serve.

Simple Vanilla Cheesecake

Total Time: 60 minutes + chilling time | **Servings:** 6

Ingredients

1 ½ cups crushed graham crackers
4 tbsp butter, melted
2 tbsp sugar
16 oz cream cheese, softened
½ cup brown sugar
¼ cup sour cream
1 tbsp all-purpose flour
1 ½ tsp vanilla extract
2 eggs

Directions

Grease a springform pan with cooking spray, then line the pan with parchment paper, grease with cooking spray again, and line with aluminium foil.

In a bowl, mix the cracker crumbs, sugar, and butter. Spoon the mixture into the pan and press firmly with a spoon. In a deep bowl and with a hand mixer, beat the cream cheese and brown sugar.

Whisk in the sour cream until smooth and stir in the flour and vanilla. Crack in the eggs and beat but not to be overly smooth. Pour the mixture over the crumbs.

Pour 1 cup of water into the pot and place a trivet. Put the springform pan on top. Seal the lid, select Manual/Pressure Cook on High, and set the cooking time to 35 minutes.

Once done, allow a natural release for 10 minutes. Unlock the lid. Remove the pan from the trivet and allow the cheesecake to cool for 1 hour. Cover the cheesecake with foil and chill in the refrigerator for 4 hours.

Mixed Berry Cobbler

Total Time: 35 minutes | **Servings:** 4

Ingredients

2 bags frozen mixed berries, defrosted
3 tbsp arrowroot starch
1 cup sugar

Topping

1 tbsp melted butter
1 cup self-rising flour
¼ tsp cinnamon powder
5 tbsp powdered sugar
1 cup crème fraiche
1 tbsp whipping cream

Directions

Pour the mixed berries into your Instant Pot along with the arrowroot starch and sugar. Mix to combine. Select Sauté and cook for 3 minutes. In a small bowl, whisk the flour, cinnamon powder, and sugar. In a separate bowl, whisk crème fraiche with the melted butter. Pour the cream mixture over the dry ingredients and combine evenly.

Spread the dough over the berries. Brush the topping with the whipping cream. Seal the lid, select Pressure Cook on High, and set to 10 minutes. When ready, allow a natural release for 10 minutes; let cool before slicing. Serve warm.

Dulce de Leche with Apricots

Total Time: 40 minutes + cooling time | **Servings:** 6

Ingredients

2 cups condensed milk
4 apricots, cored and sliced

Directions

Pour 5 cups of water and fit in a trivet. Divide condensed milk into 6 medium canning jars and close with lids but not tight. Place the jars on the trivet. Seal the lid, set to Pressure Cook on High, and set to 25 minutes. After cooking, allow a natural release for 10 minutes; unlock the lid.

Allow jars and water in the pot to cool completely before lifting the jars out to avoid the jars from breaking. Open lids and use a fork to whisk caramel well until creamy. Serve with sliced apricots and reserve extras in the refrigerator.

Jasmine Rice Pudding with Blueberries

Total Time: 25 minutes | **Servings:** 4

Ingredients

1 cup jasmine rice
½ tsp nutmeg powder
1 tsp cinnamon + for topping
1 tbsp unsalted butter
1 cup coconut milk
¼ cup granulated sugar
A pinch of salt
½ cup blueberries for topping

Directions

In your Instant Pot, combine the rice, nutmeg, cinnamon, butter, coconut milk, salt, sugar, and 1 cup of water. Seal the lid, set to Pressure Cook on High, and set to 5 minutes.

After cooking, allow a natural release for 10 minutes. Stir and adjust taste with sugar. Spoon into bowls, top with blueberries, and sprinkle with more cinnamon. Serve warm or chilled.

Grandma's Stuffed Baked Apples

Total Time: 20 minutes | **Servings:** 6

Ingredients

4 tbsp butter
2 tbsp brown sugar
¼ cup toasted pecans, chopped
¼ cup sultanas

½ cup dates, chopped
1 tbsp cinnamon powder
6 red apples, whole and cored
4 tbsp chocolate sauce

Directions

In a bowl, mix brown sugar, pecans, sultanas, dates, cinnamon, and butter. Stuff apples with the mixture. Pour 1 cup of water into your Instant Pot and place stuffed apples in water. Seal the lid, select Pressure Cook on High and set to 3 minutes. When done, do a natural release for 5 minutes. Carefully remove apples onto plates and drizzle with chocolate sauce.

Japanese Chocolate Cheesecake

Total Time: 45 minutes + cooling time | **Servings:** 4

Ingredients

4 large eggs, separated into yolks and whites
½ cup cream cheese, softened   melted
½ cup white chocolate chips,

Directions

Line a 7-inch springform pan with parchment paper and set aside. Pour egg whites into a dry bowl, making sure not to contact water or oil. Cover with plastic wrap and place in the refrigerator.

In a bowl, whisk cream cheese and white chocolate chips until smooth. Beat in egg yolks until smooth. Remove egg whites from the refrigerator and beat on high speed using an electric mixer until stiff, glossy peak forms.

Fold into chocolate mixture one tablespoon at a time until evenly combined. Pour mixture into the cake pan.

Pour 1 cup of water into your Instant Pot, fit in a trivet with slings, and place the pan on top. Seal the lid, select Pressure Cook on High, and set the time to 17 minutes.

After cooking, perform a natural pressure release for 10 minutes. Unlock the lid. Carefully remove the pan and allow cooling for 3 hours. Release cake pan. Slice the cake and serve.

Ultimate Crème Brulee

Total Time: 50 minutes + cooling time | **Servings:** 4

Ingredients

Crust

¼ cup butter, melted
2 cups graham crackers

3 tbsp brown sugar
A pinch of salt

Filling

2 (8 oz) cream cheese, softened
½ cup granulated sugar
2 large eggs

2 tsp vanilla extract
½ cup sour cream
2 tbsp cornstarch

Crack-able caramel

4 tsp white sugar

Directions

Crush graham crackers in a plastic bag using a rolling pin and pour biscuits into a medium bowl. Mix in brown sugar, butter, and salt. Spoon mixture into 4 medium ramekins. Place in the refrigerator to harden the crust.

In a bowl, using an electric hand mixer, whisk cream cheese and sugar until smooth. Beat in eggs and vanilla until smooth. Fold in sour cream while adding cornstarch gradually until adequately blended.

Remove ramekins, pour in the filling, and cover with foil. Pour 1 cup of water into your Instant Pot, fit in a trivet, and place cups on top.

Seal the lid, select Pressure Cook on High, and set to 10 minutes. After cooking, allow a natural release for 10 minutes. Unlock the lid, carefully remove ramekins, and take off the foil.

Allow cooling for 10 minutes and then chill further for 2 hours. When ready to serve, take out crème Brulee cups and sprinkle 1 tsp of sugar on each dessert. Using a torch, caramelize the sugar until toffee brown in color.

MEASUREMENT CONVERSIONS

Weight Equivalents

US STANDARD	METRIC (APPROXIMATE)
½ OUNCE	15 GRAMS
1 OUNCE	30 GRAMS
2 OUNCES	60 GRAMS
4 OUNCES	115 GRAMS
8 OUNCES	225 GRAMS
12 OUNCES	340 GRAMS
16 OUNCES OR 1POUND	455 GRAMS

Oven Temperatures

FAHRENHEIT (F)	CELSIUS (APPROXIMATE)
250°F	120°C
300°F	150°C
325°F	165°C
350°F	180°C
375°F	190°C
400°F	200°C
425°F	220°C

Abbreviations

OZ	OUNCE (S)
LB	POUND (S)
TSP	TEASPOON (S)
TBSP	TABLESPOON (S)

INSTANT POT COOKING TIME CHARTS

MEAT AND POULTRY

FOOD	QUANTITY	PRESSURE LEVEL	COOKING TIME (FRESH)	VENTING METHOD
Beef, stew	–	High	25 mins	Natural Release
Beef, large chunks	per 450 g / 1 lb	High	25 to 30 mins	Natural Release
Beef stock or bone broth	–	High	4 hours	Natural Release
Chicken stock or bone broth	–	High	2 hours	Natural Release
Fish stock or bone broth	–	High	30 - 45 mins	Natural Release
Chicken breast (boneless)	per 450 g / 1 lb	High	5 to 8 mins	Natural Release
Chicken, whole	per 450 g / 1 lb	High	8 mins	Natural Release
Eggs, large, hard boiled	8-12	High	3 to 5 mins	Natural Release
Lamb, leg	per 450 g / 1 lb	High	15 mins	Natural Release
Pork, butt roast	per 450 g / 1 lb	High	15 mins	Natural Release
Pork, back ribs	per 450 g / 1 lb	High	15 to 20 mins	Natural Release
Fish, whole	1 to 1.5 lbs	Low	4 to 5 mins	Quick Release
Fish, fillet	1 lb	Low	1 to 2 mins	Quick Release
Lobster	2 tails	Low	2 mins	Quick Release
Mussels	1 lb	Low	1 to 2 mins	Quick Release
Seafood soup or stock	2 lbs	Low	7 to 8 mins	Quick Release
Shrimp / prawn	1 lb	Low	1 to 2 mins	Quick Release

BEANS, LEGUMES AND LENTILS

FOOD	QUANTITY	PRESSURE LEVEL	COOKING TIME DRY*	COOKING TIME SOAKED	VENTING METHOD
Black beans	2 cups +	High	20 mins	3 mins	Quick Release
Black-eyed peas	2 cups +	High	16 mins	4 mins	Quick Release
Chickpeas, kabuli or garbanzo beans	2 cups +	High	35 mins	5 mins	Quick Release
Cannellini beans (white kidney beans)	2 cups +	High	25 mins	3 mins	Natural Release
Kidney beans, red	2 cups +	High	20 mins	3 mins	Natural Release
Lentils, green or brown	2 cups +	High	8 mins	NA	Quick Release
Lentils, yellow, split	2 cups +	High	2 mins	NA	Quick Release
Lima beans	2 cups +	High	3 mins	1 min	Natural Release
Navy beans or Great Northern beans	2 cups +	High	15 mins	3 mins	Natural Release
Pigeon peas	2 cups +	High	10 mins	2 to 3 mins	Natural Release
Pinto beans	2 cups +	High	10 mins	2 to 3 mins	Natural Release
Soybeans	2 cups +	High	35 mins	17 mins	Quick Release

VEGETABLES

FOOD	QUANTITY	PRESSURE LEVEL	COOKING TIME (FRESH)	VENTING METHOD
Asparagus, whole or cut	Any amount	High	1 min	Quick Release
Beans, green, yellow or wax	Any amount	High	1 min	Quick Release
Broccoli florets	Any amount	Low	1 min	Quick Release
Brussels sprouts, whole	Any amount	High	1 min	Quick Release
Cabbage, cut into wedges	Any amount	High	1 min	Quick Release
Cabbage, halved	Any amount	High	3 mins	Quick Release
Cabbage, whole	Any amount	High	4 to 5 mins	Quick Release
Carrots, chunked	Any amount	High	1 to 2 mins	Quick Release
Carrots, whole	Any amount	High	3 mins	Quick Release
Cauliflower florets	Any amount	High	1 min	Quick Release
Corn on the cob	Any amount	High	1 min	Quick Release
Mixed vegetables	Any amount	High	1 min	Quick Release
Potatoes, cubed	Any amount	High	1 min	Quick Release
Potatoes, small, whole	Any amount	High	3 to 5 mins	Quick Release
Potatoes, large, whole	Any amount	High	5 to 8 mins	Quick Release
Squash, butternut, cubed	Any amount	High	1 to 2 mins	Quick Release
Squash, butternut, halved	Any amount	High	4 to 6 mins	Quick Release
Sweet potato, cubed	Any amount	High	1 min	Quick Release
Sweet potato, large, whole	Any amount	High	5 to 8 mins	Quick Release

RICE AND GRAINS

FOOD	QUANTITY	RICE : WATER RATIO	PRESSURE LEVEL	COOKING TIME	VENTING METHOD
Barley, pearl	2 cups +	1 : 2.5	High	10 mins	Natural Release
Congee, thick	2 cups +	1.4 : 1.5	High	15 to 20 mins	Natural Release
Millet	2 cups +	1 : 1.75	High	1 to 3 mins	Natural Release
Oats, quick cooking	2 cups +	1 : 2	High	1 to 3 mins	Natural Release
Oats, steel-cut	2 cups +	2 : 3	High	2 to 3 mins	Natural Release
Porridge	2 cups +	1.6 : 1.7	High	5 to 7 mins	Natural Release
Quinoa	2 cups +	1 : 1.25	High	1 min	Natural Release
Rice, basmati	2 cups +	1 : 1	Low	4 mins	Natural Release
Rice, brown	2 cups +	1 : 1	Low	20 mins	Natural Release
Rice, jasmine	2 cups +	1 : 1	Low	4 mins	Natural Release
Rice, white	2 cups +	1 : 1	Low	4 mins	Natural Release
Rice, wild	2 cups +	1 : 1	Low	20 mins	Natural Release

RECIPE INDEX

N

O

P

INDEX